PLATYPUS FLATS

In The Shadows of The Honey Trees

Autobiographically yours
Neville West

◆ FriesenPress

One Printers Way
Altona, MB R0G 0B0
Canada

www.friesenpress.com

Copyright © 2024 by Neville West
First Edition — 2024

All rights reserved.

No part of this publication may be reproduced in any form, or by any means, electronic or mechanical, including photocopying, recording, or any information browsing, storage, or retrieval system, without permission in writing from FriesenPress.

ISBN
978-1-03-919983-5 (Hardcover)
978-1-03-919982-8 (Paperback)
978-1-03-919984-2 (eBook)

1. FAM001010   FAMILY & RELATIONSHIPS, ABUSE, CHILD ABUSE

Distributed to the trade by The Ingram Book Company

TABLE OF CONTENTS

Foreword vii

Glossary xi

Prologue xv
The Lost Prince

Chapter 1 1
The Glorious Solitude

Chapter 2 11
The Barque of Millions of Years

Chapter 3 22
The Laws of Nature

Chapter 4 34
5000 Wild Acres

Chapter 5 88
The King of Blue Gum Flats

Chapter 6 96
The Black Horse Inn

Chapter 7 114
Further, Farther and Father

Chapter 8 122
There is no God of Boarding School

Chapter 9 157
The Flutterby

Chapter 10. . . . . *The White Dingo*	180
Chapter 11. . . . . *The Land of We*	188
Chapter 12. . . . . *Temple of the Dawn*	204
Chapter 13. . . . . *"Celestial"*	229
Chapter 14. . . . . *The Swan with Two Necks*	251
Chapter 15. . . . . *The Bunyip and the Beached Whale*	258
Chapter 16. . . . . *The Reckoning*	271
Chapter 17. . . . . *A Letter to The People of Australia*	288
Chapter 18. . . . . *Ad Aspera Virtus*	316
Chapter 19. . . . . *The Homunculus*	336
Epilogue	347

DEDICATION

To those vulnerable people of all ages whose freedoms and human rights have been abused; for those with no voice; for those who spoke but weren't believed; for those who died because they couldn't live with the inner conflict; for the families who felt the abandonment of estrangement by loved ones 'afflicted with abuse'...an evil curse ...a banshee forever screaming silently in the primal abyss of the soul. We all deserved better.

ACKNOWLEDGEMENTS

I could not have made this journey alone. I am eternally grateful to my loving wife Mariette for her endless support and great compassion and to lawyer Kim Breda, who became my comrade-in-arms in seeking my justice.

Cover art: 1855 water-coloured engraving by J.Gould

FOREWORD

Being human is having a story to tell. It is also human to generalize things we cannot know leading us to hold the mistaken belief that others' inner lives must somewhat resemble our own. It is impossible to know the landscape of another life. It is natural to fill the geographic gaps between someone else's facts with a story of our own inner confidence.

I offer you a glimpse into a single footprint in the sand on that cosmic human beach as witnessed by an old Sufi (who, for better or worse, was blessed with the curse of an episodic memory) ...that others might glimpse another world unveiled.

My life now lies like a dazzling carpet on the bottom of a deep, cool, crystalline stream, magnified in every woven detail by the fullness of time - the colours, the smells, the excitement of events, the joys and the sorrows - all float clearly yet distorted; warped enough by the rare combination of space and time to bring it into a focus not evident in the moment; a watery mirage; seductively near - yet always, elusively, just beyond my grasp in an untouchable dimension.

Wild words gallop forth, black horses on a snowy field, each letter an untamed hoofbeat guided by a *Fate*; a brush stroke on the canvas of a life; a note of a song unsung; a step forward in a dance without end. Words overspill the billabongs of my mind, run down my arm and dribble out my fingers.

Too many quick steps and I risk leaving the reader breathless. Too few and you may fall asleep. It requires impossibly exacting measures of excitement and dread, sympathy and sorrow, and surprise and awe to quicken the pulse of mere ink on paper.

The thunder of a thousand hooves is a stirring event. In the canyons of my mind the hoof beats of the war horse blur with those of the lamb. All have shaken the ground on which we stand in some way. The ghosts of battles great and small and wars won and lost, haunt our lives like casts of awkward echoes. Still, like lemmings, we bumble forward toward the inevitable ...our graves.

Words illustrate the texture of our lives but without tears to lubricate them we descend into the swamp where our souls fall victim to the swampsters leaving not a trace - ashes to ashes, dust to dust, mud to mud.

Some aboriginal people are mentioned here by their English honorifics. I intend no sacrilege. I mean to recognize them with the same respectful and affectionate consideration as they showed my people when they were strangers in a strange land. We *are* how we treat others. I believe we are never truly dead while our name still falls from someone's lips with love.

This is my story, my song ...my awkward corroboree. Compressing it between these covers is like baking a cake - the ingredients, each in their unique measure being almost unpalatable, are stirred together and allowed to ferment and then distilled to elevate the essence. For me it has been a surreal journey, for my healing in the telling and, hopefully, yours in the reading. After a lifetime narrating others' lives, untangling the threads of my own life was like sorting cobwebs. We all contain the melody of life, if we learn to listen!

N.W.

In The Shadows of The Honey Trees

Editor's note: I have balanced my English spellings between Canadian/U.S. of A. and Australian/British norms. Australia and Britain get their "*ou*"s, double "*ll*"s and "ph"s. Canada and the U.S.A. get their "*z's*" as in fantasize. It is not a one *size* fits all language anymore. I agree with the French on how to spell kilometres. They invented that measure. If miles were the unit in use at the time that is reflected in the text as 'true to time'. Any errors are my human responsibility not the perfect ravings of an AI bot and if found only prove my imperfect humanity.

Parts of this story deal with overcoming institutionalized abuses. If you find these passages 'triggering' please contact your local support networks for assistance.

GLOSSARY

Aguacate — small wild avocado

Alamo — Famous battle at a Texas fort

Apophis — *the epic serpent of the ancient Egyptian underworld*

Barque of Millions of Years — *Ancient Egyptian name for the sun*

Bridghid — *Germanic/Welsh goddess of the rills*

Bunyip — *dark never seen creature of Australian Aboriginal lore.*

Cerebus — three-headed dog that guards the gates to Hell

Chook — *Australian vernacular for chicken*

Conga — a line dance

Dreaming — *Australian Aboriginal concept of genesis*

Djinn	*malevolent genie*
Dryads	*ancient Greek spirits of the trees*
Eden	*the concept of paradise*
Epergne	*elaborate table server*
Fandango	*lively Spanish dance*
Fates	*three Sisters of Greek myth, whose last name is Fate, who spin and weave and cut the cloth of our life.*
Gringo	*foreigner in Spanish*
Hacienda	Spanish farmhouse
Herculean	*of Hercules, the impossible task performer*
Homunculus	*the inner human spirit*
Klong	*river channel*
Klotho	*eldest Greek Fate sister who determines how much pain and suffering are woven into each human life.*

In The Shadows of The Honey Trees

Lightning Man	*Australian aboriginal lightning spirit*
Mammon	*material wealth*
Minotaur	*the ferocious underground bull of ancient Cretan mythology*
Mula	*money in Spanish*
Nobis cum Deus	*the presence of God*
Nut	*ancient Egyptian goddess of the night.*
Osiris	*ancient Egyptian bat eared god of darkness*
Pachamama	*the Aztec equivalent of Mother Nature*
Potrimpo	*patron saint of serpents in Prussia*
Prometheus	*ancient Greek god of fire*
Quickshaw	*three-wheeled motorized rickshaw*
Ra	*ancient Egyptian Sun god who piloted the 'barque of millions of years'*

Sabrina	*the Welsh water nymph*
Sina	*ancient Egyptian Goddess of the Moon*
Sisyphean	*of Sisyphus who was condemned to eternally roll a heavy stone up hill in Hell*
Skewbald	*tri coloured horse*
Thor	*ancient Greek god of thunder*
"Transportation"	*a British criminal sentence of 'exile to Australia'*
mourning weeds	dark mourning attire

This list is not complete, and I encourage you to search out more information about the roles of ancient spirits. They are usually ancient spirits simply because they are the embodiment of timeless truths which cannot be denied. They are central, almost universal, elements in all the world's belief systems.

PROLOGUE

The Lost Prince

Far ago and long away in a place where wishing still worked a boy was born to a wealthy prince and his wife. When the old king died the wealthy prince inherited the kingdom which was so large that the boy on his horse couldn't reach the boundaries of it even if he started out at sunup and rode all day till sundown.

Now the new king was many things but among them was that he was very reserved. He rarely left the kingdom and if he interacted with people from other kingdoms, he kept it short and sweet. The family lived a life of plenty and whatever the young prince might reasonably wish for, the young king, in his power, or the queen, would see to it one way or another. Food flowed from the fields to the palace larders; fruit from the orchards; grapes from the vines; and pork and lamb and beef aplenty with turkey or goose or duck on feast days.

One day officials of a distant court ingratiated themselves to the new king and during the evening repast planted the idea in the king's head that his growing son might benefit greatly from their worldly companionship and that for a fair sum of gold they would take him into their care as if he were their own and educate him and show him the wonders of the world. The king was beguiled and delighted that they might provide his son strengths and opportunities he himself lacked and after consoling the queen (who begged that the boy was too young to be making his way in the world) the king paid the men, who smiled widely and promised again to take care of the lad as if he were their own.

No sooner were they out of sight of the kingdom than they came to a dark, gloomy forest and there the three men set upon the boy and tore from him his fine clothes and ransacked the bundle of goodies his mother the queen had sent him off with. They ate everything leaving him only the bones. When he objected, they beat him with rods until he dared not complain again for fear of his life. He wished with all his might but beyond his father's kingdom his wishes were for naught.

The men demanded that the boy become their servant and beat him cruelly with their cudgels or pulled his ears if he muttered a discouraging word. It came to be that the boy could say nothing for fear of oppressive retribution.

One day by a stream, where he was washing the shirts of the men into whose care he had been so trustingly given, a small, beautiful bird flew onto a branch by the lad and said: *"When next you see me follow."* And with that the little bird flew off. In his surprise the boy stopped washing the shirts and simply stared at the bush where the creature had been but one of the men set upon him for his sloth and thrashed him with twigs till his skin blistered and bled.

That night, as he slept on the straw in the stable where the other servants slept, he fell into a troubled dream. In it he was forced to cross a quaggy mire which sucked at his feet as if it were trying to eat him legs first. Just when he felt he could go no further there was a rustle in the bushes and the little bird he had seen by the stream that day reappeared in his dream. It then flew away looking back at the boy over its shoulder.

In The Shadows of The Honey Trees

The lad hastened to follow but the more he hastened the harder the bog sucked at his toes as only dream bogs can. When next he looked up the little bird was gone and before him stood a lone tree on a tiny island of grass in the middle of the sea of muck. Instead of bearing flowers this tree had leaves of silver and gold and from its branches hung little amber droplets. The boy plucked one and found that it was honey. The silver and gold leaves were each a word, so he plucked one after another. He found verbs and adjectives; nouns and adverbs; conjunctions and contractions. He began to order them on the ground under the tree until they ran together like the knots of a rug. Sentences began to form until they were strung out over the bog like well-trodden paragraphs and the boy ran back and forth to the tree until his path of words led him back to his bed in the stable just in time to be there when the men began calling for him to dress them in their fine clothes which his father's money had bought.

But every night the little bird would appear in the dreams of the lost prince and lead the boy through the difficult dreamscapes to the honey tree of words and from these words the boy learned to build his own castle, word upon word like stone upon stone until by morning it was finished, just when the cruel masters called him to dress them and to be beaten for their pleasure.

And thus, he escaped into his dreams every night for a thousand and one nights, learning to craft words so they became almost watertight and able to contain that slipperiest of all substances ...*truth*! This was his world, a possession the mean men could neither see nor take away. After a time, the men became tired of feeding the boy for he had grown so large that he now needed meals like all men and so one day they abandoned him in the darkest depth of a forest and took his fine black pony and sold it for a handsome sum.

The young man sat dazed. He couldn't believe all that had happened that shouldn't have happened and yet he could only believe that not being the prisoner of these men must be a good thing however dank the forest might seem. By comparison his new-found freedom and liberty shone within him like an amber flame in the darkness. As night was falling the little bird of his dreams popped out of the bushes and then hopped off through the forest beckoning the young man to follow. Soon they came to the tree of sweet words.

"What good can dream words be in this dark world?", said the youth.

"You can create a meal with your words just as you have used them to lay a path across the swamp of your dreams. Well-spun they are like silk to the soul," replied the little creature and then it was gone.

The lad began to pluck words from the tree and arrange them to create a sumptuous feast. First, he described the table and then all the good things he wished upon it ...all his favourite foods, fruit and vegetables all done to perfection ...and finally he described a very comfortable chair with a soft cushion before sitting down to the feast of his own making. He created friends, virtuous and loyal, to share the meal with and logs a plenty for the fires to keep everyone warm. When he was finished, he thanked everyone for coming, wiped his mouth on a fine linen handkerchief and threw it over his shoulder without a second thought about who might have to pick it up and wash it ...for such is the power of words.

He learned that he could use words like bricks (for they contain substance as well as texture) and so he created a shelter to keep himself safe from the wild beasts that roamed the forest at night. When they came at him with barbs sharpened, he placated their anger with clever words that led his adversaries to make other choices. He armed himself with a sharp quill and when he saw something wrong, he smote it with the sharp end and when he saw good, he caressed it with the soft part. The lad wandered on, lost in the forest of syllables; through canyons of constants; over valleys of vowels and contours of commas; past hills of verbs and dales of nouns along with many ruts of punctuation; until finally ...one day ...as he was resting under a shady tree, he suddenly realized that by the very power of words he had made wishing work again - he had found the way back to his kingdom and reclaimed his throne. And, while he would never forget the terrors and joys of his life and the lessons learned in the world, he lived contented ever after in a glorious garden of his own making, ensuring there were plenty of flowers for the bees to make honey and lots of places for the birds to perch to sing their enchanting songs.

CHAPTER 1

The Glorious Solitude

"If you want real peace in the world, start with the children."
—Mahatma Gandhi

1952

I was made of earth and wind and water.

Born into a land older than time itself, cut off from the rest of the planet by a dangerous six-month voyage through unknown perils, my ancestors were propelled to Australia by social forces which many did not choose but had thrust on them through what, in their day, passed for social justice.

Some were condemned to *"transportation"* as prisoners or orphans, others as refugees from the Irish potato famine that saw, it is whispered, as many as four million people starve to death when the crops failed repeatedly. For others many more had their entire world torn apart, their reality completely shredded, before being stuffed in dank holds of fragile wooden ships and sent in chains on a long journey halfway around the planet for as little as being accused of stealing a lemon. They were often removed against their will, comforting themselves all the seasick way by clinging to the thought that if they could just keep going one more day the peril would pass. Things can only get better when you are at the point where they simply cannot get worse. It was that hope that kept them afloat while lessers around them perished. It was a voyage beyond the heart of darkness, a place festooned with grief and anguish. In that half year-long seasick moment it must have seemed an abomination of desolation.

One in ten aboard those ships perished before they reached the mirage of coral shores on the far side of the blue planet. Some fell, some were pushed ...others shoved. I am a product of people from diverse backgrounds who took great dangers in hand and did the "best" they could with what history had given them to work with. It wasn't a case of what one had (which was often nothing, not even their freedom) but what one did with what one had. They mined their deep, unseeable depths for the ore of inner strength. They learned that the sharpness of a brave soul's glare could be sharper than a coward's sword.

They arrived at a land which had drifted ...a universe of its own creation and purpose ...almost unmolested by human hand for more than a hundred million years. It lay beyond the far horizons of the imagination of Europeans who stumbled upon it in 1770 when they were looking for something else. It was "the dark side of the moon" to Europe in 1770, beyond the edge of maps where cartographers feared to tread. It was the unknown, an alien landscape populated by equally unbelievable creatures which set the planetary theorists of the day abuzz. There were other people there already, but no one paid that much heed.

The local absurdities were so unimaginable to the rest of scientific *"fact"* that early-contact Europeans were thought to have gone mad on the long six-month sea voyage to *Terra Australis* when they reported their findings back to London. Shoddy negotiations with the indigenous tribes, who already, at times, engaged each other in savage boundary conflicts, led, understandably, to many more clashes with the invaders, who already were dealing with their own conflicts within their virtual prison state. Disease and malnutrition were common on both sides but devastating to the locals who carried no genetic immunity to the new diseases the strangers brought nor tolerance to their vice of alcohol. As the number of foreigners grew the more the locals were displaced into the territory of others, creating further friction. It is in the colonial playbook ...force the worst of any confrontation onto a neighbour.

From the first uneasy settlements around Sydney Cove my family filtered out into unknown reaches of the landscape from the bleak penal colony of Norfolk Island; to the Eureka Stockade rebellion; and to settling on a remote high plateau where they intermingled for more than a century, much like a tribe of stationary nomads.

I was born into this primordial abyss in the realm of reality so fathomless that if you held your breath, so as to not intrude, and if the deafening thrum of the cicadas and the chirping frogs and singing crickets fell silent, and ...if you listened with your eyes and looked with your ears ...on a clear bright night you could clearly see the songs of eternity being sung by the stars scattered thickly across the heavens.

There the Milky Way illuminates the velour night laid over *terra ab aeterno*. It is a mesmerizing, timeless cathedral into the *'dreamtime'*; into the starry stillness of a hundred-million-night years with stars so bright and clear it seemed they could be plucked with ease from the sky if I could but reach just a little further. With no electrical intrusions into the blackness the fathomlessness of deep space magnified my mind.

Platypus Flats

Alone under this celestial shrine I lay on a blanket in a grassy field, a small child looking up into that pure unpolluted space, while cradled in the all-loving arms of gravity's embrace.

Cushioned by the thick dry elephant grass that choked the field beside my home, a simple, solid, weatherboard house built by my ancestors from timber hewn from the surrounding hills, I experienced my relativity, my personal insignificant micro-part in a far greater whole.

On a high steppe of the New England Tablelands my birthright of *Weabonga* (Rest-Among-the-Hills) lay slap-dap in the middle of nowhere, auspiciously between *Rywung* (the Eclipse of the Sun) and *Niangla* (The Eclipse of the Moon), celestial syzygy, points of great significance demarking the historic boundaries of three tribes - the *Moonbi* to the north, to the east the gentle *Ingleba* and to the west, the *Kamilaroi*, the great people of the Red Chief. It is a place that still rings clear, a remembering that reverberates like the tintinnabulation of fine, far-off pealing bells ………….. each pulse drawing on the strengths of the pulse before …fading echo into echo …a solitude so deep and wide and glorious it has shadowed me all my life …a land steeped in the myths of giant man-eating dragons, against which all weapons proved powerless, and where spells, cast upon the earth on which we walked, held their secrets shielded from the world.

It was a place dreamed into being by the *Rainbow Serpent* and the *Crocodile* and the *Green Ants*. At the crack of the cosmic dawn, they had *"dreamed"* the land and made the world in which only extraordinary ingenuity made human habitation possible. These great spirits endowed the human inhabitants with the wonders of the didgeridoo; of the trance-inducing bullroarer; and perhaps most remarkable of all, the aerodynamic magic of the returning boomerang. These alone were enough to challenge "western" thought and outwit the cleverness of its celebrated inventors. There was a certain silent "invisible-to-the-naked-eye" magic that was needed to survive the *Never-Never*. Need always was the mother of invention.

There are no innocents in the colonialism that spawned me. The European invasion of foreign lands was a brutal one …everywhere. They brutalized their own class divides too, especially in Australia's penal colony infancy. Could anything less be expected when it came to the natives of this 'other' land? It is now a wall papered over with the annals of another era so unbelievable that when we look back, we must learn how to pick up the pieces, dust them off like artifacts, acknowledge them like elephants saluting the skeleton of all our fallen ancestors, then learn and move on together to a better tomorrow.

Disease, starvation and exposure were a common cause of death for all. The Europeans often had their teeth removed and had dentures fitted before departing home soil because delays in treating serious dental infections in such remote circumstances could kill. Even facing six months at the mercy of the often rum-soaked hands of a ship's doctor on the trip out was cause for concern, regardless of whether you were a convict under *"transportation"* or a first-class passenger sitting at the captain's table. A great x4 grandmother of mine gave birth to her first child on the high seas in 1787. She was likely little more than a child herself. In colonialism there were not a lot of medals of honour handed out on either side of the fence (another concept the invaders brought with them).

Cultures pass through many defining "eye of the needle" moments. The sins of those *'pasts'* should not be visited on the present. We can only be responsible for our own actions, and we all have a right to forget ...to change those things that came before us that can be changed, accept those things we cannot change and change the things we cannot accept. Only then can we all move on in our pursuit of our own fragile butterfly of happiness.

Ancestor *dreaming* had made all the things humans needed to survive here and a complex organizational social system of checks and balances was carefully woven into any incanting of the spell! Rituals were heartfelt.

Social membranes sometimes extended to armed forays into other tribes' territories in the hope of killing the men and taking their women to expand political influence over the territory and to populate the land thus ceded by force; or to seek to poach game which might have been pursued across rigid jurisdictional domains. In the name of "conquest" harsh things were done by all sides in history. Convicts and conflicts and brutal clashes between power struggles of all stripes the world over remain too common. No invading forces are granted any leeway. Culture grates against culture like glacial ice against granite and after, it can never be the same again.

Oral histories passed verbatim within all the local tribes, including my own. There was always some grain of truth reflected through the ages though the tellings might meander from hard facts. With time *truth* bends toward *right*.

Usually, interlopers were rarely tolerated on the territory of any tribe. Even granting permission to one from another tribe to cross one's kingdom was a great honour usually granted one king to another, or perhaps to a worthy warrior on a quest or as an emissary. Sharing land with strangers and their sheep brought conflict but also certain attractive advantages to the original Australian tribes including the availability to steel and copper and all metal's possibilities.

At a time when there was only one European woman for every six of the male invaders, the social pressure to marry women young saw my own great x3 grandmother marry a 38-year-old man well before her 14th birthday. There was much singing and dancing, of that I am assured. Elsewhere in the colony another great x3 grandmother lay in the wool bins at Parramatta Women's Prison giving birth to a son conceived during her fateful voyage from Ireland. An orphan of the Irish potato famine she was *"transported"* when Britain simply emptied the Irish orphanages into the new colony where they might be of use. At sixteen years of age, she was sent to the prison workhouse on her arrival as pregnancy precluded household servitude and she was alone and needed to eat. It was her only option and probably a better one than had awaited her in Ireland. It was another age.

The land of my birth was comprised of tens of thousands of rolling acres nestled on a large almost inaccessible steppe, a high plateau of pastures where kangaroos and wallabies have grazed since long before time began ...and where bunyips, real and imagined, lurked in murky water holes.

It enjoyed a rare aspect. The golden late winter sun attracted some of the rarest and most beautiful of all the world's birds whose daily morning choir roused the sun and called the screeching sapphire parrots into action while singing the nocturnal night shift to sleep. As winter wore into summer the birds became quiet in the noontime heat when all the world stood perfectly still ...waiting for the worst of the solar wave to pass ...save for the Laughing Kookaburras in their favourite tree at the bottom of the garden who seemed to favour this stifling silence to revel in their chortles.

And if the cicadas suddenly began their sonic song all other sound waves were completely drowned out, even the voice of someone standing beside you, and the birds all left to find less noisy prey. Tens of thousands of insects could then suddenly stop 'singing' at the same instant bending space as the penetrating wall of sound suddenly fell …tipping the mind into an aching silence.

At sundown, when the air began to cool, great flocks of hundreds of snowy Sulfur-crested Cockatoos screeched and wheeled in the darkening evening sky against a background of thunderheads shot through with bloody light. They jostled with brilliant Rosellas and patient King Parrots and pink and silver Galahs for prime perches in the acre of trees in the gardens that surrounded our homestead, a kaleidoscope of feathered finery.

The garden ended abruptly just beyond a gap in the citrus grove where a long concrete watering trough - the object of everyone's desire - served double duty as a barrier and a social place where the horses, cows and sheep could come to drink and as a watering hole and bathtub for thousands of avian divas.

Water spells life in a dry land. It was not only the white (and sometimes black) cockatoos but the comical Galahs and the brilliantly coloured Rosellas and Mountain Lorries who perched like bright animated blooms among the golden garlands of a tall avenue of Grevillea, which broke the cold easterlies when they flowed down off *"the tops"*.

Hundreds, nay thousands, of some of the planet's most spectacular feathered fancies flashed their neon glory in the last rays of the day, illuminated lamps of dripping color - all perched patiently waiting their space at a water trough that could 'sit' forty birds at a time …less if a horse barged in.

In The Shadows of The Honey Trees

Bee-Eaters, chastised by Willy Wagtails, flashed their rainbow brilliance; midnight blue Superb Fairy Wrens fluttered frantically between perches or hopped unperturbed into the kitchen to forage for crumbs under the table, while the Pied Currawongs and Magpies sat on the fence or atop the pepper tree and sang their sweet, delicious evening sonatas celebrating the end of another day in paradise. The Butcher Bird, tired from a day of butchering its neighbours, sang a particularly beguiling song completely at odds with its killer instincts.

It was a phantasmagorical sundown corroboree of feathered wildness, a time when all animosities were put aside, and the world gathered wingtip to wingtip to kiss the glistening Rainbow Serpent goodnight while bathing in the glory of a murmurating psychedelic cacophony of sound and color. Even the bees got in on the action, drinking en masse where water from all the splashing spilled down the sides of the concrete trough, before making a beeline back to their hive in a hollow of the pepper tree for the night. It could have been any god's garden.

When the light began to wane and cast the romantic gold-tinged landscape in a thousand shades of lavender another rousing chorus by the songbirds brought the brilliance of the day to a close with a practiced choreography of a final number of a magical opera performed daily for eternity, with never a performance missed by any member of the choir. After the last song was sung the feathered world bowed their heads and nestled down for the night beside their companions, never falling from their perches as they slept, further proof to my young mind of their part in some greater unseen conspiracy of nature. This ritual had been so forever.

Platypus Flats

Water, we were taught, is priceless, a responsibility and a privilege. It is something that must be greatly revered for all life depends on it. We were taught that one should never refuse to share water if another was without, whether it was our last glass or access to our streams by a needy neighbour's thirsty flocks of thousands. Nor could a price be placed on it. Slaking my thirst today from a plastic bottle in a bustling city on the opposite side of the planet is a far cry from the salacious delight of kissing a cold, babbling mountain brook, the veritable fountains of my youth.

In the cool shade by the billabongs of my far-ago childhood my father, a man of few words and a third generation native of this rare luxury of space, taught me to turn inward.

The world into which both he and his father before him were born was as remote as any place I have ever experienced in a lifetime of travelling forgotten corners of the globe. It was not a bleak landscape of existential dread, but a kingdom of tremendous majesty isolated by quirks of geography. This enchanted solitude I was bequeathed.

On a busy city bus stop where I now sip insipid water (which, by some quirk of commerce, has been hauled by a truck from far away), I slip with ease between the gilded sheets of memories, into this private cultivated *Eden*, its deep, clear pools reserved solely for my soul's respite. It is a rare memory. I can still hear the birds calling my name.

CHAPTER 2

The Barque of Millions of Years

*"Your beliefs become your thoughts,
Your thoughts become your words,
Your words become your actions,
Your actions become your habits,
Your habits become your values,
Your values become your destiny."*

—Mahatma Gandhi

Into a fuzzy marsupial wilderness, I was born a foreign feral. My first urgent cries rose just as *Ra* the Sun God reached his zenith. Angered by this disturbance, he rained down upon my new soul a raging heat so ferocious it baked the land and cracked the bottoms of the billabongs and creatures perished from thirst or starvation or worse, from both. Month after month *Ra* ruled the skies striking the land with his hot barbs.

Distressed, my young mother wrapped me in wet linen in my crib or carried me down to the cool springs at the nearby stream during the heat of the day to chortle away my hours cavorting in the limpid shallows with *Bridghid*, the Goddess of the Rills, and *Sabrina*, the water nymph, shielded from *Ra's* wrath by the kindly *dryads* inhabiting the river oaks sweeping overhead. There my cries of glee echoed the sweet early morning warblings of the songbirds and I flourished in naive bliss.

Swallowed each evening by *Nut*, the Goddess of the Night, *Ra* nonetheless blazed his reflection in the face of *Sina*, the Moon Goddess, and made himself present in a darkness lighted-almost-as-day.

On this anvil of the universe my soul was hammered fine and thin. Wrapped in my damp tent I dreamed the dreamtime dreams of all the children ever born under this starry dome and slept in a womb of deep galactic silence.

The eyes of the night creatures who peered out of the bush to wonder at this hairless cub had peered out so for eternity at all the children who preceded me here. I was the invader. This moon and these stars and these night creatures still whisper in my dreams.

For three generations my family had lived on this odd handkerchief-shaped ledge of pastureland on the western side of the Great Divide …a single ridge of mountains which stretches for more than three thousand kilometres and rises so sharply from the coastal plain that it is still only crossable at a handful of passes.

To the west it slopes down to the endless plains that sweep out to the distant, forbidding deserts. The hills themselves are old and worn round like the giant limbs of slumbering reptiles piled one upon the other in sunny repose. They come to an end where the thick cloud forests, which harboured some of the planet's oddest inhabitants, cling to the precipitous eastern escarpment that is covered by a tangle of subtropical forests more ancient than the dinosaurs. This world marked my eccentricities as a birthright.

The native creatures ventured forth every day at dusk, as they had since time immemorial, to forage and bask in the

In The Shadows of The Honey Trees

salubrious mauve light as it washed over the land and to watch *Ra* be devoured by *Tan* in a scene that daily bloodied the western sky, bring with it relief from the heat of *Ra's* rage.

Day after day the land shimmered and scorched, *Ra's* angry anvil. The horizon evaporated in a shimmering blur, merging the land with the sky, levitating heavy objects in the distance and making them float above the horizon of the eye. The ferocious heat was enough to make the head spin and to blister exposed skin ...and could spell death for the weak or feeble-minded.

Onto this quivering cosmic disc, the lightness of my celestial particles descended to inhabit my *homunculus* ...drifted here on destiny, alighting in the midday stillness on a long-forgotten afternoon on a long-forgotten island where nothing moves at noon for fear of *Ra's* wrath.

Draped in wet linen by the young mother who feared for my life in the stupefying heat, I lay naked as *Ra* raged day after day, the earth unable to give off the rays of the day before *Ra* rose renewed to continue the assault. Day after day the heat increased, pulsing toward an elusive, throbbing climax.

Then *Lightning Man* began his crazed corroboree across the arid land. Jagged javelins of light crackled and sparked against an increasingly angry sky as *Lightning Man* danced his brilliant, thunderous, unpredictable *fandango* ...

Thirsty eyes glanced skyward where the tantalizing smell of moisture hung heavy in the air ...so near and yet so far. Then, after perhaps hours of posturing and tens of thousands of lightning strikes, all this promise would recede, leaving the parched land aching in its thirst.

Each day tens of thousands of tons of water billowed into the heavens as *Ra* demanded the last drops as homage from the parched land below. Towering clouds darkened the day almost as night until late mid-afternoon when *Lightning Man's* first electrifying steps would signal his drummers to drum and thunder out with a terrifying force that shook the very soul.

Then, *Lightning Man* would take the second step in this jagged pantomime. Whirling veins of light hotter than the surface of the sun screamed, jagged across the sky, leaving a moment of sulfurous silence so deep it was as if you hovered breathless on the edge of a vacuum in the universe for a terrifying, trembling moment …then BLAM! …*Thor* would beat his drums; that vacuous moment would explode with atomic force; creatures quivered in fear the earth might suddenly open beneath their feet and swallow them. The earth and all upon it cringed.

Day after day the dance followed the same beat. Great clouds of moisture sucked from the surface rose angrily into the heavens. Heavy with water the skies slowly darkened until the first crackle of the day and *Lightning Man's* fingers would begin their dazzling concerto over and over again while the invisible wind touched everything sending windmills whirling wildly, pumping wells from which all the promise had already been sucked …empty now of all but despair.

Prometheus joined the fray and began to tag the countryside with grass fires. Pushed by the dry winds these fires formed into long continuous creeping lines miles long. They crackled and sparked, a long, slow serpent of flame stifling the air with a thick pillow of fine ash that choked the very oxygen from which all breath was drawn.

Ra became a burning orb of molten metal stifled each day by the pungent smoke of scorched earth. Day after day of searing heat crushed the swollen thunderheads against the blue celestial dome of sky as the rising heat exploded thousands of metres into the heavens in great columns of moisture, vainly trying to ransom *Ra's* wrath.

Day after day the crazed corroboree was performed …thunder smashed the sky like a porcelain vase shattered on a stone floor; shards of lightning set grasslands ablaze; and acrid smoke stifled the air and cursed the evening skies an angry crimson again and again. Day after day the skies turned red and bruised as *Ra* blushed furiously at every birth and again in the evening when his blood spilled across the horizon as he was consumed by *Tan*, rending the air an unearthly shade of slaughter that blurred the edge of solid matter and held the magic to turn tree stumps into kangaroos and, in the blinking of an eye, change them back to stumps again.

Week after week this merciless dance raged above while all below looked skyward to the tantalizing smell of water overhead. The corpses of the dead had no time to putrefy before being sucked dry of their last vestiges of moisture, left skin and bone, littering the land like mummified shipwrecks, a stinging reminder of how cruel the retribution of a vengeful god.

Then, when the expectation of the watery climax seemed inevitable, the racing pulse would once again retreat while every tree and creature stood listless, awaiting the quenching rain, which never came to christen new life. The air throbbed with threat and pulsed with promise. Horses stampeded in their pastures; cows gathered under trees for shelter; and every creature turned its back to the wind and bowed its head and prayed.

The croaking of the great green tree frog living by the seepage at the base of the elevated corrugated iron water tank in the garden always heralded the rain. Only he knew the true secrets carried on the wind. His voice, reverberating through ten thousand empty iron gallons perched on hardwood stilts, resonated deeply …a thunderous voice, one I imagined was fit for any god. It echoed, a dreamy didgeridoo cascade of vibrations announcing something we lesser creatures could not sense; this lime-green frog's magical voice, amplified by the empty vessel, was elevated to a fulsome prayer, a sure sign *'the time'* had come.

Finally, after weeks of anticipation (and if the *Frog God* had spoken) it came ...*The Great Joy*. It crept in like a breathless sigh, a zephyr which at first barely licked the face. But then it swelled with promise to become a rolling wave of hot, scented air which flowed over the arid land …wafting the clear, unmistakable musk of water kissing earth and of earth offering up hidden scents in the passion of a moment so longed for. It spilled across the hills and crept up the valleys; a flow of moist, fragrant air caressing the parched land; a reassuring aroma which travelled a hundred miles and excited every nose.

After the weeks of exasperating expectation and amid a by-now fury of wind, the heavens cried out and the earth answered. Thunder and lightning finally split the armada of heavy thunderheads that had crowded out the azure morning sky, and they surrendered their liquid promise in a gushing torrent.

The first heavy drops disappeared straight into the parched earth hardly leaving a trace. Every living creature turned its face skyward for its confirmation by the first wet drops and then the watery wave beat down in a fury. Outside, creatures great and small, began their gleeful dance before tiring of the joyous thrum, turning their backs to the storm and seeking shelter from the onslaught of their god. Hour after hour it pounded the corrugated iron roof over our heads making conversation impossible and driving the heat from the air like a magnet. Pots were needed here and there to catch errant drips. It always rains harder on a leaky roof.

The torrent of uncountable droplets united and roiled and boiled down the gullies. Babbling brooks transformed into raging, angry seas of water, thick with mud and debris, which carried away everything before it, cleansing the world of the remains of *Ra's* long wrath.

Lightning Man stepped on a tree and unceremoniously killed sixty cows sheltering there with a single blow; hailstones the size of a fist bludgeoned a thousand fresh-shorn sheep to death in a matter of minutes; smaller creatures, flooded from their burrows, along with their mortal foes, the serpents, called a truce and clambered together, sad and sodden, onto any common refuge, while the waters spilled over the banks of the rivers and the billabongs and spread across the western plains in an unbroken sheet of liquid mud that drowned a million acres and remained for weeks, gravity unable to find sufficient purchase to draw it quickly away. Instead, the *Rainbow Serpent* slithered slowly, snaking its way through a thousand kilometres of parched dry land under cloudless skies where not a drop of rain had fallen; wetting dry waterways; bringing life to the land around it; leaving in its wake a great green swath of vibrant wildflowers and verdant grasses as far as the eye could see. Such is water's promise.

And thus the welcome *Wet* sucked the heat from the world, filled the dry, cracked billabongs and scrubbed the air leaving it breathlessly fresh and, with the subsidence of the muddy waters, it left behind a world anew, awash in a thousand shades of green as sleeping seeds burst forth and rushed into flower to wither and perish as quickly as they had come before casting the seeds of next generation forward into the mud to await the promise of next *Wet*. Such was all life!

Only when the earth had really soaked for months would the strange Crucifix Frogs emerge after years hidden underground. Their fat bloated yellow skins sported a remarkable dark warty crucifix form in the center of their backs, so they came by their name honestly. They met and fed on the abundance of life at the surface, then mated and left their eggs in puddles of water they hoped would last just long enough for their tadpoles to mature before they burrowed deep into the wet earth to remain so perhaps for years before resurfacing again only when their world felt *'right'*.

Stilted emus hurried to find a suitable spot to lay their bright green eggs the size of a baby's head that would blend with the new grass but then slowly darken as they incubated in the sun, the father assuming responsibility for maintaining the eggs at an even 97.5 F for fifty days, the longest incubation of any bird, before the first pecks on the inside of the heavy by-now-dark-blue/green shells would begin and the awkward striped 'chicks' slowly pecked their way out, their odd whistling sounds echoed in encouragement by their father as they emerged, their mothers never known. It had been so since the days of the dinosaurs.

The father then led his small tribe of striped *leglings** off across the grasslands in search of insects. Their home became wherever dad sat down.

This was the *Never-Never*; a place which casts a captivating spell; where you are either so enraptured by its majesty that

---

*   *Calling something nine inches tall which just hatched out of an egg a dinosaur might have laid a 'chick' does not do the language justice in my humble opinion. The term 'colt' is used for baby cranes but that too seems inaccurate here).*

you *never, never* want to leave or it so terrifies you that you *never, never* want to go back. It was a sliver of the universe where an ancient magic presided, and incantations were cast. The gullies and the forests rung with the most beautiful bird calls - a kaleidoscope of liquid amber tones so sweet that on hearing this one forgets everything they know and wants nothing more than to hear it again over and over at the start and the end of every day. When it disturbs your slumber, you rush to the window not to close it out but in joy, to better listen. Such hymns are only sung at heaven's door.

The arrival of my Neanderthal genes had angered *Ra*. The air that buoyed up his *Barque of Millions of Years* had *"verily"* threatened to suffocate me. I had passed the first test on my *Herculean* journey through the maze of the *Minotaur*, though in hindsight it was the easy part.

Where *Potrimpo* had meandered his wet finger across this hard-baked land his serpent followers abound and to preserve herself and her children my young mother, alone in this wildness every day, had many ploys.

When a deadly snake (we knew no other kind) took up residence under our house Mum feigned absolution to *Potrimpo* and lay out milk for the serpents (their favourite food), but this was milk of a most poisonously ingenious device. To lure the scaley congregation the scent of milk laid bare might seem a strange totem but slyly mixed in the elixir my crafty young mother concealed *Montmartre gypsum* which, in milk, remains a soupy liquid but once separated from the milk by the serpent's digestion, meant a rigid, writhing death for the unsuspecting victim. It pained her to hurt another creature but defend her cubs she must. Living as we did by permanent water meant the dryer and hotter it became the more snakes would be attracted to the area.

Platypus Flats

Hens announcing they had laid an egg attracted not only snakes but other egg-eaters, the big two-metre-long goannas.

At sundown, when *Ra*, weary from travelling the sky, was again eaten as the evening meal by *Tan*, the furry marsupials crept wide-eyed from hidden crevasses to forage in the dusky light. At the moment the last blazing crest of the sun slipped beyond the earth's curve it was as if the world paused, magically breathless for one moment of enchantment, before everything became invisible in the gathering gloom as the earth kissed the light goodbye and the day was swallowed by the night.

I learned to love the failing light, those fleeting moments when day and night unite; when birds roost; and the creatures of the night, the messengers of *Osiris*, the God of the Underworld, take wing. This was when the great fruit bats, the personification of the bat-eared God of The Darkness, *Anubis*, would daily leave their shady forest treetop roosts and spread giant webbed wings, and, with babes clinging to their breasts, fly in undulating murmurations, an enormous silent cloud thousands strong, their numbers darkening the bloodied evening sky.

In chaotic order across this far-flung land they first circle the billabongs and then, in the fading light, they dive to the silvered surface to skim their fill of water, never a wingtip touching. They drop their head at a precise apex of the swoop, skimming the water's surface with their lower jaw to drink on the fly. It is such grace and majesty to watch. However, theirs is often a perilous flight for in many places the long-snouted freshwater crocodiles lay in wait to snatch them as they bowed their heads to drink. Thus, thousands will drink their fill before spending the night in search of fruit and nectar, seemingly without distress over the loss of a few from the colony to the ever-present-always-hungry crocs who know exactly what time dinner is served every day.

By dawn all were back comfortably hanging upside down in the trees growing on a point of land cut off by the river, their wings folded around their furry bodies with the nonchalance of parasols hanging high in some far-off city store, the alpha males squabbling over the sunny spots so they could sleep warm in the sun.

But uniting all these omnipresent forces and presiding over this global pantheon was *Pachamama*, the Earth Goddess, revered as the supreme power by the *Incas*, a primal deity recognized by the universal first cries of all the world's children …

… "*Maaaaaaaaaa!*"

CHAPTER 3

The Laws of Nature

"To call woman the weaker gender is a libel; it is man's injustice to woman. If by strength is meant moral power, then woman is immeasurably man's superior." (sic)

—Mahatma Gandhi

"M-u-u-u-u-u-m." The shrill falsetto of my young voice shattered the still listlessness of *Ra's* baking hour. My little brother and I had set out to investigate a *chook* clucking and thought we would be retrieving an egg. Somewhere along this joyous sprint through our Eden everything suddenly soured when evil raised its ugly head. Coming eye to eye with such a deadly foe chills the essence of one's being and, for an instant, panic sets in.

"Quick Mu-u-u-u-m! There's a sna-a-ake in the *chook* shed."

There was no need to await her answer. The troops fell into order. There was a clatter of swinging rifle butts as she flung the heavy kitchen door shut revealing an armory of several rifles of differing bores hanging on the reverse. She snatched up the snake gun, pulled a handful of .410 scatter shells from a neat cache on the wall and raced across the green expanse of grassy garden that separated the house from the *chook* run.

In The Shadows of The Honey Trees

"Where is he? Don't take your eyes off him," she called as she ran, apron flapping, flip flops clapping and her mop of wavy dark hair flailing wildly as she fled down the path and under the parching morning wash. (For some reason I never understood snakes were assigned 'he/him' pronouns).

She pushed her oddly-out-of-place-on-a-hunter (though-fashionable) cat's-eye glasses back onto the bridge of her nose in battle mode and, as she ran, she cocked two red shells into the twin chambers and stuffed the handful of spare shots into her apron pocket. She could have been defending *The Alamo*.

"Ok! I can see him. Get your little brother and climb up on that stump," she ordered without taking her eyes off the snake. We obeyed. Barefoot and snotty-nosed and wearing only ragged shorts my little brother, still not quite abreast of what the fuss was all about (and lost as to why our initial glee had so suddenly turned to dust) was pushed onto the stump while my mother, almost barefoot in her flip flops, stalked the deadly interloper around the bushes, always ready to appear threatening but at the same time creeping with the air of a hunter removing a deadly threat from her Eden. Such epic hunts were a regular ritual.

The great blue-black interloper had been after eggs. He sensed the enemy afoot, but he had trespassed on *Pachamama's* sacred ground, and the price of admission would be high. Carefully she inched forward, her ample bulk swaying gently like the grass to escape detection. The mesmerizing, glistening coils raised the delicate, deadly head; its eyes bright; its forked tongue vigorously working the air for any scent; the beady stare and reptilian brain trying to compute the alarm it tasted.

Mum's stealth was like that of a lioness fending for her cubs - a wild shot and the roiling coils could vanish through the smallest crack in a log or down a hidden hole in the parched and aching earth. A partial hit and it could unleash the serpent's ire and an angry, injured, deadly foe was just not an option.

"Mum Mum! just hit it with the gun and save the bullets," we encouraged nervously as she crept dangerously near. And then BLAM! and the hunt was over almost as soon as it had begun.

"Get a bucket," she called, not taking her eyes off the headless coils that writhed still in its death throes.

The decapitated body was deposited unceremoniously into the bucket and, using a stick, she pried the venomous head in with the rest of the corpse and then, with the loaded gun still resting in the crook of her arm (just in case we encountered another one), she led a silent funerary march - past the tractor shed, past the stables, beyond the haystack, further even than the pig pens where next year's bacon squealed impatiently at our approach, to the far corner of The Clover Paddock.

We halted at a slight oval mound some three feet wide by six feet long from which several cleanly defined spokes of bare earth radiated forth into the landscape, gradually tapering to invisible among the dry grasses. This was the mandala of the red 'road' ants, the spokes around the clay nest at the center of their universe worn hard by the daily tread of tens of millions of tiny feet, which had marched to and fro about their business here, at this very spot, perhaps for eternity tramping these clear trails ...perhaps since the very first *dreaming*. Invented time distorts in such a place.

Solemnly we looked on as Mum emptied the now still coils in the bucket onto the mound of hard earth. Instantly a great smell assailed our nostrils. From a thousand tiny doorways, the red ants in unison swarmed the intruder who had dared to break their rest, emitting a nauseous acrid odor of defiance so unpleasant as to cause me to take a quick step back.

In a terrifying moment the glistening coils suddenly sprang back to life causing us to pull close to Mum's skirts as a million pairs of carnivorous mandibles savaged the still fresh nerves of the great, red-bellied blue-black serpent, causing it to writhe again in death even as in life.

The carcass disappeared under the swarming *Lilliputian* assault. The ants' odor, sharp and acetous, intensified as more raced to the battle from deep within the nest. We watched, transfixed. An invisible army of tens of thousands had answered the call within seconds, the message to attack transmitted chemically in their odorous reaction, the order instantaneously transmitted one to another without need of word. After about ten minutes of this swarming the throes of the corpse finally, reassuringly, subsided. The great beast was now truly dead. Ten thousand angry ants seethed over its entire surface.

The next day we returned to a stark vision of the great creature's skeleton picked perfectly clean. The hollow metre-long remains were perfectly white, every scale, every trace of tissue had been removed and taken to the ants' fermentation chambers deep underground. It lay in its anatomic perfection, a warning to other creatures that this spot was sacred. It was a lesson learned. The albumen of life is fragile. I forever carried the knowledge that even the most dangerous foe on the planet could be easily dispatched with one quick, unexpected but well-calculated blow to the right department. I also noted the co-ordinated onslaught of a community's combined individual strengths was far greater than the sum of any individual part.

Over the years the ants grew fat on our offerings. Sadly,

some very majestic creatures crossed our path and were offered up to the red ants on their convenient funerary mound. Some summers as many as forty of the world's most venomous creatures made the long solemn walk in the bucket from our garden to be offered to the ungrateful ants, who were just as likely to swirl, biting, up my legs if I got too close. While individual bites weren't too toxic, being staked naked over a road ants' nest for a set period was a punishment meted out by the local aboriginal chiefs for certain crimes. I understand there were few repeat offenders.

And there too stood life's greatest lesson …from king of the planet to dead, to nothing-but-bones in less than twenty-four hours. It was a forever humbling reminder of the fleeting nature of greatness. And, true to the world of Voodoo's spiritual transfer beliefs, my young spirit absorbed each *Njim's* (snake's) displaced *loa* (spirit) cursing me with a lifelong unbridled curiosity …the yearning known as the 'thirst for knowledge'.

The *loa of Njim*, the serpent, knower-of-all-who-cannot-speak, borrowed deeply into my psyche and remained there, hidden, listening to the silence of this inner place …an enormous space so full of emptiness my imagination echoes. Silence speaks loudly.

Alone one day I stumbled upon a scene of such awe that, despite the obvious danger, I stood transfixed, unable to turn away …breathless should I crack a twig and break the spell. In that moment instinct trumped intelligence. It was a creature of such beauty it belied my eyes. Coiled gracefully on a sunny rock ledge about a metre below me on a steep hillside was the most enormous Red-bellied Black Snake I had ever seen, a creature so secure in its command of its kingdom it felt enough at ease to fall asleep fully exposed on its sunny throne.

It must have been almost two metres long and lay coiled in a relaxed confusion of electrifying coral red and shimmering opalescent blue-black scales the size of a fingernail that covered a body easily as thick as a large man's lower arm. Its head was the size of my palm.

I have seen several such mega Red-bellied Black Snakes and, although being very familiar with the species which is usually much smaller and skinnier, one this size struck fear in my heart. I stood truly mesmerized under its spell. I could never have imagined one so large. I was caught in the vacuum between my flight or fight response, an awkward voyeuristic abyss between awe and dread. Each second became an hour, each minute a timeless, silent eternity. I understand snakes continue to grow as they age as much as thirty years, so I truly had stumbled upon a king beast.

My mother, with a lifetime of living with this species in abundance, had some terrifying experiences with such mega serpents who seemed to go on the defensive rather than flee like their skinnier counterparts, fanning impressive hoods and rising up indignant at being disturbed. That some attained such great size led us to speculate that they may indeed be a separate species from their common, skinnier look-alikes. So much has already been forgotten which was never written.

Australia is home to one of the greatest concentrations of venomous snakes on the planet. What scaremongers overlook are the two non-poisonous species. It is rarely noted that bush boas don't really need venom since they can reach almost eight metres in length and can simply crush you to death.

The Olive Bush Python is rated second only in size on the planet to South America's famed giant Anaconda.

Thus, serpents carved a deep scar on my psyche. By age five I knew the word for *"snake"* in the language of every bird and animal and on hearing it knew to immediately marshal the forces. Gun for Mum if she happened to be down the hill and snake sticks - long supple sapling poles with heavy knobby ends that were leaned hither and yon around the farmyard - for quick defense from the deadly marauders.

I once watched as our cat battled defiantly with an Inland Taipan, the second deadliest creature on the planet. The praises of the mongoose may be sung but cats and even squirrels can mount deadly defenses against serpents. The snake rose to strike. The cat sat calmly defiant just inches from the poisonous fury.

When the strike came the cat was faster and unmoving, deflecting the venomous assault with a ready paw. The snake rose again to strike but the cat was faster, batting the strike off course again. Again and again the calm, unmoving cat defied the deadly foe that challenged it, never flinching and moving nothing except its quick right paw. The lesson learned was not to let the actions of others distract me from my tasks.

Eventually, exhausted after many repetitions of this act, the snake realized it had met its match and turned to flee but the cat was on it, crushing its vertebra just behind its head with its jaws and then, with a pride unspoken, he paraded his heavy victim home to show it off to a less-than-enthusiastic but nonetheless impressed audience.

Little did I know that I was witnessing a battle that dates to the beginnings of time. I had witnessed *Ra* in the form of a cat defend the souls of the dead from *Apophis*, the epic serpent of the ancient Egyptian underworld. It is why the

In The Shadows of The Honey Trees

Egyptians were often buried along with their mummified feline friends, such was the awed regard of the power cats held over humans' most-feared foe in this world ...or the next. But one day the cat met its match. He simply disappeared. We searched high and low but after several days began to fear the inevitable. A week after vanishing we found him immersed in a distant spring where the water was always extremely chilly. He was little more than skin and bone as he lay immersed in the cold shallows with just his head on the rocks above the water line. The tell-tale twin puncture wounds clear on his forepaw explained what had happened. He was on the brink of death. I gathered him up in my shirt and carried him home where he eventually started eating and recovered but the fact that his instinct propelled him to seek out the coldest water in miles when bitten, that he knew where that water was and that he had surrendered himself to its chilly embrace for days to slow the poison and survive, left my book learning confounded. Raw instinct saved his life ...something from within, which could not have been learned from any book, saved his life in the face of the most potent spell. The instinctive, unspoken knowledge of this creature when confronted with such a poisonous dilemma was not lost on me. It was another example of the unwritten, unseeable magic in the *Never-Never*.

All snakes are not created equal. But none are more equal than others when it came to the laughing kookaburras who jockeyed for positions along our clothes lines. These gregarious birds, the world's largest kingfisher, had no bones about scooping up any marauding snake, pecking it into submission and then swallowing it whole, slowly choking it down one still-wriggling inch at a time until they sat, too bloated to fly for days, happily digesting their poisonous meal. I never saw one removing the venomous head before consuming the still writhing reptile. They are a bird accorded great respect for having power over snakes ...part of the *Never-Never* hierarchy of respectful bush acknowledgement for awe-inspiring feats of heroic status. They were accorded their own stump in this complex culture.

Among the epic snake stories that sparkle in my crown was the survival of my maternal grandfather when bitten by a Death Adder while harvesting bananas on his banana plantation situated a hundred and fifty miles away down the mountains at the coast. A banana grows one stalk which bears one flower. From within this huge purple bloom the fertilized bananas curl upward creating a bunch of perhaps a hundred individual upward-curving fruit. The bunch is usually several feet from the ground and at maturity might weigh thirty-five kilograms.

Preferring well-drained soil, the bananas are usually grown on hillsides. To harvest the bunch, one takes a machete and slashes halfway through the trunk on the uphill side. This causes the banana plant to lean heavily downhill where the harvester can wrap one arm around the bunch and position it securely on his shoulder without having to lift the great weight. They then cut the stem holding the bunch before slashing the remaining base of the plant with the machete in their free hand, leaving it to rot on the ground, where it fertilizes the suckers that sprout from its base.

It just happened that an adder had chosen to sun itself in the convenient crook of the fruit on the plant my grandfather was cutting. When bitten he immediately dropped the bunch, extracted his snake bite kit from his pocket, applied a tourniquet, washed the wound with water from his canteen and hiked slowly and calmly back down the hill to the packing shed from where he was whisked to the local hospital. He lived to tell the tale.

On another occasion he was driving his Willys jeep along an overgrown path on the plantation when he noticed a Bangalow Palm had fallen over the track. He rode the front wheels over the trunk and only when he was directly over the trunk in his doorless tin-can-on-wheels did he realize the trunk of the "palm" was instead the body of a huge bush boa. It slithered quickly out of sight into the jungle, Grandpa never catching sight of the business end of the monster.

The banana packing shed was home to a couple of Australia's most beautiful snakes, the lovely Carpet Boas. Mottled scales of brilliant yellows and muted greens make them hard to miss but to the banana grower they were a welcome sight, dining on any rodents attracted to the usual mush of damaged and decaying fruit discarded as unsuitable for market. No banana shed was complete without one (or two).

But perhaps the most gruelling snake saga was one to which I was a witness. At the end of our fifty-six miles of largely dirt road Mum, home alone one day with us three little munchkins, was preparing lunch when she heard glass clinking in the pantry adjoining the kitchen. Going to investigate she didn't even pause to lay down the carving knife she was using to slice cold cuts from a roast leg of lamb.

When she opened the cupboard door where the preserves were lined in neat rows, she came face to face with a Taipan.

In the shock of the moment her inner cat struck first. The hand holding the butcher knife shot out and pinned the snake just behind the head to the back of the cupboard. But she could not gain sufficient purchase in the hard century-old wood to finish it off nor to secure it to the wall. She stood there for the longest three hours of her life while the angry snake thrashed and coiled its ample body around her arm sending bottles crashing to the floor in a frantic bid to escape.

I'm not sure who was more terrified, Mum or the snake, as she fretted over the outcome should it twist itself free of the knife point. We three tiny children offered excited encouragement from our perch atop the kitchen table where she had ordered us. We failed to realize the gravity of the life and death struggle we witnessed. We never doubted her power over the evil trespassers. That we had a ring-side seat to and event of great excitement was not lost on us. Today's world pales safe by comparison to our daily reality.

Looking back now Mum was an omnipotent presence who taught me how to walk and ride a horse, to swim and ride a bike, to escape into reading and writing, to play the piano and to sing like no one was listening but also that 'right' *was* 'might' and not to back down from the fight for 'right'. But above all the lesson gleaned in the pantry encounter that day was "never give up".

Dad finally arrived home a *ver-r-r-ry lo-o-ong* three hours later and, with a blast of the .410 that blew a hole right through the back of the pantry wall into the bathroom, won the day in spectacular fashion but that was enough excitement for *Pachamama* for one afternoon.

It is not by accident that the snake is a feature in almost every culture's cosmology. It *slitherrrrrs* at the center of the Christian Church and all its offspring families, the writhing inner wretch with whom all humans must wrestle in their internal primordial struggles where one path leads to the pious light and the other to unimaginable darkness. The Ancient Egyptians knew this wretch awaited them also in death so took their cats with them in their tombs.

In The Shadows of The Honey Trees

The serpent abounds at the center of Voodooism and springs forth as the Rainbow Serpent, the sacred spirit of the waterways, in the lore of indigenous cultures the world over. Snakes leave us caught between opposing forces - fear and fascination. Mesmerized by fear we are unable to turn away. Confronted by their immediate presence one becomes like supercooled water droplets, unsure whether one is a liquid, a solid or a gas. Should one flee, remain motionless or strike first? Thus confronted one has only a split second to make the call or your particles may dissipate back into the universe that spawned them far sooner than you imagined. Instinct then speaks with a clear strong voice that bypasses our rational mind.

The snake resides in the biblical *Tree of Knowledge*, speaking by its silence not its words. It knows all but does not speak. By acting first the serpent has no need to ask questions later. They are opportunists, waiting by the water where they know their prey must come to slake their thirst.

CHAPTER 4

5000 Wild Acres

"In a gentle way, you can shake the world."
—Mahatma Gandhi

Daily Dad saddled Rajah, his big skewbald horse, and rode out through a landscape made from eternity and sewn together by the timeless songs of a thousand birds of paradise …a world rarely pierced by human voice.

Lord of all he surveyed in this splendid exile, he lived his life almost as a monk committed to eternal wanderings in a world that time forgot, the oldest living landscape on the planet, following the footsteps of a song only he could hear.

Alone all day he dwelt in a wildness of his own creation. What sorrows or loves led him there I can never know but the sudden departure from his life of his beloved grandfather, coupled with the solitary example of his own father, and the complete lack of any other father figures in that splendid isolation, would make for a great likelihood that he developed what could be called a 'highly defended' personality.

At the end of fifty-six miles of rough, winding, dirt road it was either embrace the natural glory that surrounded him or go beyond the edge of madness …even if it meant embracing a glory that to most seems just a hair short of insanity itself.

He didn't want to know about his emotions, and it seemed that if he acknowledged them, he would likely lose his grip on life altogether. His transcendence was akin to a religious meditation but practiced as a necessity rather than as a devotion.

His back was against an invisible wall from a young age and anything beyond the boundaries of the property represented *"Change"* ...driving recklessly. He was trapped in a waking dream. There was no wriggle room to equivocate. He simply ossified.

It was easier for him to demonize the outside world than it was to try and understand it. His was a world that would scare the life out of most people and still, to his great credit, he turned and embraced it. It was an authentic, sometimes-gritty existence beyond the meddling of the outside world where he didn't just survive, he prospered.

His grandfather, the founder of this remote sheep and cattle property, had served as the mayor in the nearby town of Walcha, where he owned a carriage making and livery business, and later served as a local magistrate, but in the next seventy years the only law enforcement officer we ever saw was one who was hopelessly lost.

In my great grandparents' day if they found someone dead King Billy of the local aboriginal tribe would be called on to investigate. If someone was sick, they summoned Uncle Charlie the *"medicine man"* who no doubt knew the secrets of the death curse ... *the pointing of the bone* ...a psychological death sentence-by-proclamation, a phenomenon widely affirmed by early European observers and effected by an aboriginal shaman pointing a revered and sacred human bone at the maligned person. It was regularly witnessed that those thus cursed would sicken and die. That the invading

Europeans seemed impervious to the curse was known to have awed the indigenous population. It takes many magics to create a world from dust.

Dad eschewed what most of European cultural roots would consider "worldly pleasures". He was as content to sit on a log in the shade of a Honey Tree as on a feathered throne. He led an abstinent life in pursuit of an unuttered form of redemption - a quiet salvation of earthly spirituality - a journey of inner transformation where the simple was sufficient, the frugal was plenty and the bliss lay within. It was more akin to the thinking of our aboriginal neighbours than to that of a member of the invading tribe. The land became him, and he became the land. He respected it and all the crazy creatures he shared it with. He knew he was just passing through on the way to other pastures.

If there was work to be done Dad simply rolled up his sleeves and did it using an economy of energy and good cheer. It was the price of admission to the kingdom. He, and his brother and my grandfather, wandered the hills and valleys on their horses looking over the herds of thousands of sheep and cattle that grazed our pastures.

There Dad communicated with the half dozen dogs that followed at his horse's heels using the lost language of shepherds - a series of whistles. These were shrill orders to a dog that might be half a mile away on the other side of the valley telling the wily creature to go further up the hill, to the left or to the right, to gather sheep unseen from its vantage point. The whistles were often accompanied by a good deal of barking on both sides of the transaction. Sometimes they were accompanied by a string of curses which told the dog it had it wrong and to listen up, though I am pretty sure they figured out an angry, blasphemous *"JESUS CHRIST Toby!"* meant *'no not that, Toby!'.*

A good dog was worth its weight in gold. A bad one was hardly worth the bullet to put it out of its misery. How could it enjoy being stupid? Stupid dogs usually did themselves in quickly. One young blood foolishly chased a goat over the edge of a cliff. The goat, of course, landed safely on a ledge but the dog fell fifty feet to his death. The lesson learned? You can't fix stupid.

Others were just a bit too slow to figure out snakes were not something to be investigated. Even a good dog could fall victim to snake bite just by not paying attention in their haste. Work dogs could also become sly killers of sheep if not chained at night to their kennels by the hen house, (as a safeguard against foxes). Their genes could propel them from obedient work dogs to midnight killers and back to sitting smiling in their kennel again by morning if they weren't constrained.

I remember Dad's dismay and disappointment when one of his best dogs slipped his collar one night and was found the next morning sitting by its kennel with his chest soaked with blood. Dad at first thought he had cut his neck trying to slip the collar but later that day his victims, five adult sheep, were found dead, ripped about the throat, the unmistakable victims of a dog attack. After once surrendering to its primal urges and tasting the blood of the kill, a dog will continue to kill just for the sport at every opportunity - as many as a dozen animals each night ...or more. It seems like a canine curse. Dingoes and wolves are equally guilty of indulging in the thrill of the kill. For that problem there is only one effective form of behaviour modification ...lead! Bingo simply disappeared ...and his name was never again spoken ...a sign of respect. It was rumored he was part dingo. It wasn't his fault, but he had used up his share of oxygen. It was as cold and matter of fact as that.

Days for me began with school on the radio when we children in remote locales across rural Australia gathered daily at our kitchen tables to engage with a teacher *'on the air'*. Dressed in nothing more than baggy khaki shorts Mum oversaw our assignments as the teacher's voice crackled over the airwaves. We were usually done by lunch. Our completed lessons were stuffed into a large *"vanilla"* envelope (which gave learning a decided delicious flavour) and we were then dispatched to the mailbox (a four-gallon drum perched in the fork of a gum tree by the road a kilometre away from the house) to send them in on the afternoon mail, which was almost the only vehicle we ever saw use *"our road."* It was years before I realized they were called *'manilla'* envelopes but the early association with yummy things naturally extended the flavour to the joys of learning. (*"Our road"* is still mostly two-wheel tracks across hilly pastures).

Afternoons were idled away catching freshwater yabbies or collecting tadpoles, swimming in the creek, roaming the countryside alone, on foot or on our ponies, picking blackberries or perched in a fruit tree by a creek simply enjoying life's abundance. We bounced from one excitement to the next with Ma the chief instigator. We sometimes wandered for miles planting watermelon and squash vines on the sandbanks by the creek. Sheep didn't like to eat them, so no fence was needed. The world was my oyster!

Late in the day we children waited expectantly for the bright spot of Rajah to appear on the horizon. That was the signal to run barefoot (we were always barefoot) directly toward this beacon, mindless through the tall, snake-infested elephant grass, to meet Dad at the Top Gate and to ride home triumphant on this impossibly majestic seventeen-hand-high horse while six-foot four-inch Dad ambled alongside. Every day thus Dad wandered. It was a visceral umbilical bond with the land he was born to. Summer, winter, spring, rain, hail or fall he spent every day outside awash in his element.

During *The Wet* he and my uncles cut dashing figures in widely pleated oilskin capes which flared out over their horses' rumps, not only keeping the horse and saddle dry but also keeping the rider seated in a cozy bubble of air warmed by the animal.

Their heads were always shaded by the now famous, handmade, broad-brimmed rabbit-fur felt hats. (The hats don't change in the Australian bush, only the faces under them do). But Dad's had long since passed its "best before" date - the rim was sewn with silver wire to keep the whole thing afloat; holes were worn in the crown; and repairs were often needed. As this "work in progress" stretched over a number of years it began to sag woefully. He was like a nestling, refusing to abandon a sinking ship. And this great accumulation of years of sweat began to stink.

One day I did the world a favour and cheekily threw it in the rubbish fire when he wasn't looking. It was an action akin to shaving the head of a Rastafarian - I wilfully destroyed his only work of art, his crown, and offended his dignity, such was his thrift. But I did get his attention. Mum was secretly relieved. I could tell by her face and by how quick she was to find another *"almost new"* replacement in the closet. It was the "newness" of anything Dad didn't like. I don't think our father/son relationship ever recovered from this high point.

On rare days I accompanied Dad, my pony, Black Magic, dutifully following steps behind Rajah. These were long hot rides. The only break was when we paused by a stream to eat our sandwich lunch. As we approached the water the dogs rushed ahead, tongues lolling, to wade in chest deep to cool down while they drank their fill. Unlike the dogs Rajah and Magic waited patiently for us to dismount and bend to kiss the water ourselves before they waded in up to their knees, gulping great drafts of the cool liquid. Dad would fill a black billycan with water from the creek and build a careful bier of Honeywood twigs around and up its sides like scaffolding before igniting it with his smelly kerosene lighter. In silence we watched it blaze fiercely while the silky noses of our mounts were mirrored on the surface of the stream. Rajah and Magic drank thirstily, inhaling the moist air deeply through flared nostrils before they delighted in pawing the refreshing coolness onto their bellies.

My father was his usual silent self, as if the flaccid mid-day air was too vaporous to buoy up words. He was never one to consume more than his share of oxygen, preferring his remarkable solitude over empty phrases. The day smoldered even in the thick shade cast by the Honey Tree, where we sat savouring the heavy scent of the golden blossoms overhead. The water boiled quickly. He added tea leaves. I remember listening to the stillness of the heat. Not a leaf moved. Only a tiny dust devil a few feet high dared to break the spell of the sweaty silence by whirling across the hot dry earth, tossing shards of flaxen grass into the air with impish glee as Dad poured the tea into two enamelled mugs.

"If you sit quietly and watch eventually you become invisible and all the creatures great and small which disappeared when you blundered into their world will reveal themselves," he said with an awkwardness that always marked our talks. He stirred four teaspoons of sugar into his tea then sipped

In The Shadows of The Honey Trees

it. Too hot! In the pregnant silence that followed his words sank slowly into the bottomless pit of my young mind like coins tossed into a wishing well, glinting this way and that as they sank. To him silence was too golden to be broken needlessly. If you didn't have something worthwhile to say you simply shouldn't. It was his sage lesson in diplomacy ... think twice about everything before saying nothing.

"It is not something I can show you," he continued earnestly while looking at some far away point. "You have to look and see it for yourself."

Yes, I could see it, but I am not sure his thousand-yard stare ever allowed him to truly see the young boy who sat in a vacuum beside him hungry for acknowledgement that never came. It seemed we were each on a raft of our own making passing in the night. Perhaps we were too alike to really see each other.

This was *The Solitude*, a vast world full of emptiness, so rich and rare in every detail that no bent blade of grass nor trace in the dust was too insignificant for attention. Life depended on it. A twig oddly out of place in the landscape could be a deadly snake; a shoe left unattended outside might house a poisonous spider by morning; wet boots hung upside-down to dry atop bamboo shoots by the porch might be beyond your reach when you went to retrieve them. This sun-kissed world and all the beauty and the terror it contained had no sympathy for we human inhabitants who challenged it. It seemed like an extension of my skin, not always touchable but always there.

And learn each nuance of the land we children did ...so well that we regularly walked miles along bush trails on frosty moonlit nights doing the rounds of our rabbit traps without losing our bearings, collecting a bounty of rabbits that not only saved valuable pastures but kept our pocket change in a healthy state by selling them to *The Rabbit Man*, an unseen entity who drove our road at dawn twice a week collecting the rabbits trapped by us (and I assume other farmers) and left in roadside caches. It was a bit of a *Cargo Cult*. The rabbits would be gone, and a cash-stuffed envelope would be left in their place. It felt like a just reward for our effort.

At night we learned to hear with our eyes and see with our ears. Lit only by the eerie glow of the brilliant southern night, whose stars are as infinite as all the grains of sand from every beach on earth, the world loses its edges and space hallucinates. It encourages the mind to expand and to explore the hidden nooks in the cathedrals of imagination.

Finding the exact location at night of a steel-jawed trap buried in the dirt that morning does not allow for any margin of error lest one fall victim to their own cleverness. I learned to read the land as others might have read a bedtime story except my adventures were full of very real 3-D-fear-inspiring perils against which I always needed to be ready to prove myself wilier if I were to survive until bedtime.

I tread this moonlit mindscape still, looking back now through the golden mists of the late afternoon of a life lived in that rarest luxury of all ...space ...it assumes the geography of dreams; illuminated events joined only by the thin red dusty veins of cerebral animal tracks linking the waterholes of memory; the red web of a drunken spider laid across a mythical map of the mind and written in the unspoken language of instinct and belonging; a song of survival. Dangers surrounded us at every turn. We respected them but laughed in their faces and paid them little heed.

I walked right through the middle of something extraordinary, a living dream, innocently assuming everyone had a life such as mine. I know it now as a place unhinged from the rest of the world, floating free from the yokes of humanity. I romped through it at will and, in the canyons of my mind, I do so still. It became a precious timeless gem I can take out at will and enjoy at any time.

For the first five years of my life this land was my total cosmos. I was the product of a rare moment in time, a colonial peculiarity. Perhaps even more peculiar than the egg-laying mammalian neighbours who had lived here unmolested for more than a hundred million years. It was their world ...here it was I who was odd.

I rarely left this land and if I did it was to drive along meandering bush tracks to visit neighbours or my mother's family who lived up Red Hill, a sinuous dirt track that wove between the trunks of enormous trees and orange termite mounds taller than a man, crossing several causeways (which could be running 'bankers' requiring Dad to affix a potato sack over the grill of the car to prevent the water from stalling out the fan as we plunged through water window deep), while the greasy red mud track snaked ever upward to the high plateau, where winter could render a frozen waterhole equally as dry as when the summer sun sucked the bottoms of the billabongs until all that remained were the cracked, parched, thirsty lips of the earth.

It was here Grandmother would often catch platypuses, that oddest of all creatures, when fishing for trout in the river. Without hesitation she would bundle them up in her fishing apron and carry them up the hill to wherever grandfather was to have him carefully remove the hook from their rubbery bills before trundling them back to the bank and releasing them. No one told her they possessed poisonous spurs on their feet, and none ever assaulted her.

Most enigmatic of all our eccentric neighbours was my mother's little Pretty-faced Rock Wallaby, Cheeky, who Mum raised when she was orphaned. It was an achievement reflective of a century of my family raising orphaned joeys. Unlike the kangaroos, who would ultimately jump the garden fence and leave to join their wild friends, little Cheeky, (who was the size of a large terrier except for the extra-long, strong tail), dutifully followed at my mother's heels like her shadow wherever she went for almost a quarter of a century. In winter she languished before the open fire beside Spot, our little Fox Terrier, like two peas in an exotic pod of acceptance. Such feral love was at the center of my universe.

They were not the only faces I shared this wilderness with. There is not a horse whose silken nose I do not still feel nuzzling me; whose face I do not still see peering expectantly over the garden gate; not a dog among the many whose name does not immediately spring to my lips ...Tip, Ginger, Dusty, Rusty, Soot, Dutchy and Mick; the horses: Bess (who, with her four white stockings and high-stepping gait, seemed to float like an apparition before us as the summer sun zithered like lightning across her dark, gleaming flanks) and Blue and Jolly and Moke and Patsy and Rangy and Rajah and Rastus and, perhaps the most memorable of them all, Black Magic, humble in her silken coat *noire*, her dark shining beauty festooned with a single white star that shone brightly on her forehead.

These were the friendly faces that encircled me, the child. Many were third generation members of the family and the bond between the dames, the sisters and brothers of the station horses was remarkable to witness. Whenever one returned from a day's work the others raced wildly to welcome them home and once relieved of its saddle and

In The Shadows of The Honey Trees

duties the work horse would kick its heels in joy, fart loudly and gallop off in its new-found freedom to join its clan.

Not all such reunions were so joyful. One day Rajah, released from his toils, bucked and tossed as he galloped across the grassy flat in front of the house and then, by some horrible twist of fate, he stumbled and fell headlong to the ground. He had snapped a bone in his foreleg. My father was as aggrieved as I was ever to see him. Tears streaming down his face he returned to the house for a rifle, pressed it to his dear friend's head, pulled the trigger and ended a misery from which there was no hope of either of them ever recovering.

Then he placed a chain around the still warm creature's beautiful head, hitched it to the old tractor with metal wheels and dragged the body off to a far corner of the paddock where he built a funeral bier of dry Honeywood before setting it ablaze to commit his friend to the heavens rather than leave the carcass to the scavengers.

He retreated into his grief. As with all life we knew there were beginnings and ends. One simply had to get up, brush off your knees, and keep going.

My family's love of horses was legendary which made such tragedies more tragic. Horses are *people* too. I could ride before I could walk. Not some spry little pony but the family's biggest horse Thor, a massive twenty-hands-high Clydesdale with the demeanor of a kitten. He knew when he had been entrusted with a precious cargo and would follow my father around on his farmyard chores without trappings with we gleeful children balancing atop his broad back.

The strategy for catching Thor was easy even as youngsters. Being wary of his enormous iron-shod hooves we waited patiently beside him until he put his big head down to eat. He was more than familiar with having his head embraced by small hands and was always cooperative in taking the bit between bites.

Once we had the bridle on mounting such a monster took cunning. We waited till he put his head down again, swung one leg over his neck, clung to his mane and then, when he put his head up, wriggled backwards down his neck onto his broad shoulders before steering him home.

My great x3 maternal grandfather was said to have owned the finest pair of dappled grey carriage horses in Australia - high-stepping gaited Hackneys, the Rolls Royce of carriage breeds, European imports, a pair so beautiful a Sydney newspaper declared that an entire crowd of hundreds at a mid 1800's Bathurst Race Day fell into *"awed silence"* when his carriage *"entered the concourse"*. His father had been an officer of the famous Scott's Greys and had arranged their purchase back in England and had them shipped out on the long voyage to Australia. Horse blood runs in my veins with DNA reaching back to Berber roots. My mother's maternal grandfather had stables for a hundred horses and operated carriage rentals alongside his grand inn at Penrith, Australia's first tourist destination. Other ancestors operated similar businesses with horse and carriage rentals, a profitable side hustle that meshed well with lodgings.

Horses are sensitive creatures (not so all ponies), each an individual. They were part of the fabric of our family, tracing back a hundred years to when wild horse herds would be mustered into a box canyon stockade. The best horses would be selected, and the rest of the herd released back into the further reaches of the valleys where wild pigs, big-horned angora goats and wild cattle also roamed. The chosen wild equines underwent careful, respectful training and joined the stable.

My grandfather maintained that a thousand pounds of wild horse could be simply controlled by clipping its ears together painlessly with an oversized wooden clothes clip. Horses rely heavily on their hearing and can flick their ears independently back or forth, especially when nervous, to gather information. Arrested by this simple technique, grandfather claimed, left them focused on their human captor for information ...ears forward in 'learning' position, unable to lay them back in the fight-or-flight mode.

They were then coaxed into trusting friendship. Hunger eventually overrode fear and extended sweet hays and carrots slowly grew into trust until, perhaps patient weeks later, they allowed touching, then grooming after which the horse was yours. Such is the remarkable relationship that can develop between human and horse. They are not so different from us in many ways. No one likes to be hurt and everyone enjoys loving touch. They were then introduced to first halter, then bridle, then pack saddle, then coils of zinc wire on the pack saddle to equate the weight of a rider.

Once accustomed to these new events the animal could be led beside a regular mount during daily routines and rewarded with oats and apples like its counterparts until, after months of careful grooming, the wildness abated but the spirit remained noble. They became loyal much like a dog, always looking out for their rider.

So co-operative were these horses they would memorize the dance required of them as they passed through any of the many paddock gates, their fancy footwork, each an equine pirouette of sorts, unique for every gate, allowing the rider to keep hold of the gate with one hand as they passed through so it could be re-latched without dismounting ...a tiny illustration of their intelligence. The expectation was unspoken, the horse and rider one. There was work to be done if one wanted a good horse but one did it using an economy of energy. Their spirit never "broken" the animals became accustomed to returning the love they were showered with.

"You can catch more flies with honey than you can with vinegar," as Grandpa would say of horses. The wild brumbies slowly joined the family willingly, content to serve tirelessly and with devotion. My maternal grandfather's brother is now memorialized standing with his life-sized bronze horse in a riverside park in nearby Tamworth. He and his brother joined the New England 12th Light Horse, the Australian Cavalry, in WWI. They signed up, taking their own horses with them. Grandfather, on his beautiful buckskin mare, remained posed in a photograph on the living room wall, his emu feather cockade aflutter in the breeze. He had to withdraw later due to crippling arthritis but his brother, Charlie, was sent to the Middle East where one of the most heroic of all cavalry charges in history, *The Charge of Beersheba*, helped turn the tides of war as both sides scrambled to control the Suez Canal and its access to middle east oil. But the battle wasn't won on a personal plane. Eventually ordered to evacuate Egypt there was only passage for the men. Their horses had to be abandoned. Many, fearing their trusty steeds would be forced into brutal servitude under enemy ownership, instead took their friends aside behind the dunes and shot them. It was the kindest thing to do. Others turned their friends-in-arms loose and tried to chase them off into the dunes but when the ships loaded with men departed the remaining horses followed their masters, plunging into the sea and swimming after them until, exhausted in their love, they sank below the waves as the men who loved them could only watch from the rear decks in grief at the tragic loss of such loyal creatures. It was a demoralizing end. It is hard to say they "*won*". As one of the first generation of post-World War II babies, I inherited stories fresh from the indignities of war ...*lest we forget*.

The roundup of wild horses was no easy undertaking. A horse carrying a man is no match for a sprinting rider-free mustang with Arabian roots. Many fine station stallions broke out of their corrals when the scent of wild mares in heat unleashed their instincts. They often disappeared into these hills where their worthy offspring galloped wild and free.

There was one station roundup which took on the cloak of myth. It was carefully planned with numerous riders stationed at set intervals so that fresh horses could carry their riders at full gallop to the next stage of the relay with the hope that the final leg of the tag team could cow the tiring leaders of the wild brumbies before they reached the tree line, which marked the fringe of the gorge country where, if the wild horses escaped, it would be the last anyone would see of them for months.

The planned route took the horses through the tussock flats where the wiry grass grew as tall as the stirrups. The tough clumps of native grass would tire the brumbies as they bound up the muddy slope. Riders from the early legs brought up the rear to prevent retreats while the fastest horses were stationed for the final leg when the wild herd would be beginning to tire. The most noted riders wanted to be considered the most productive in the chase for that recognition meant they had the first choice of some champion wild horseflesh.

The herd had been watched carefully for weeks as it moved out from the tree line to graze, every morning nervously a little further, while under the watchful eye of the herd stallion who stood guard at an elevated vantage point watching his mares and their offspring graze and gambol. One warning sound would have him herding them sternly back to the safety of the gorges where a riderless horse could safely gallop under branches which would kill a rider.

The men gathered at the ready days in advance and, as the relay was staged, men moved quietly into position so as not to alert the wild herd. Then when the brumbies were at a point further from the treeline than was usual, two shots into the air signalled to everyone that the chase was on.

My great grandfather rode a huge horse. He was a tall man, and his horse was a fine-boned thoroughbred deemed too large for racing, but a tall creature filled with strength, speed and grace. He was among the final riders. His best friend and neighbour was stationed one leg back, at the head of the run that took the herd through the tussocks.

The earth trembled as the stampeding horses followed their stallion through the rolling valley, the riders in hot pursuit. They were turned this way and that, spilling like a wave of liquid energy around trees, leaping over unseen obstacles because the horse in front had leapt, always being herded toward the stockade built strong across the box ravine beyond the tussocks.

The herd raced wildly through the grasses, mud exploding from under their thundering hooves. They were fast and the riders had to urge their mounts into the wildest gallops. These were men who spent their whole lives in the saddle. They rode," never *shifting in their seats". [Apologies: A.B. Paterson.]*

But the chase was in vain. The bay stallion at the head of the herd raced his charges through the tussocks and cut a beeline for the forest edge. All efforts to cow them failed and the whole herd dodged around the outriders and vanished into the steep wooded terrain where the ground was full of wombat holes and pursuit was suicide. It was only then that my grandfather realized that his friend's horse was running riderless.

In the turmoil of the moment no one had noticed the missing rider fall. A frantic search began. The day was already fading as the dozen riders combed the tussocks which grew so thick as to obscure the ground. It was an area almost a mile long that stretched across the head of the valley. They crisscrossed the area until nightfall without finding a trace. It would be easy to miss a man pitched from the saddle into the tall wall of spiky vegetation.

When the frosty night air began to settle, they abandoned the call and returned home to the station defeated and demoralized. They sat around the open fireplace in the living room plotting the search to be resumed at first light. They returned to the flats the next day to repeat the process. There was still no trace. It was assumed then that the man must have been killed in the fall or at the very least be unconscious and mortally wounded or perhaps stunned, had wandered away from the search scene and collapsed elsewhere. After the second fruitless day of searching the effort was abandoned. Everyone had families and responsibilities to return to. A mourning mood set it and all hope of finding the man alive was lost.

My grandfather was determined to at least search until he found his friend's body and set out alone on the third day, leading an extra horse thinking he would be bringing home a corpse. Methodically he tried to imagine the path his friend might have raced from his relay station and rode it carefully retracing steps already taken a dozen times. Just before noon he saw a boot protruding from a thick clump of tussock. He leapt from his horse and tore the tough grasses aside. His friend's face was bruised and bloody. He feared the worst. Then an eyelid flickered. He brought water from his saddle and bandages which had been prepared by the women at the homestead.

His friend told a broken story of falling from his mount and lying for how long he knew not, lapsing in and out of consciousness. Grandfather checked him for broken bones but finding none managed to ease him into the saddle of the second horse. Strength, loyalty and determination won the day after all hope seemed lost. Such tales of valour are among the jewels in my crown.

My paternal grandfather had several magnificent horses in our stable. He lived in a rare luxury of space where he could indulge himself in such fancy and Grandma readily admitted that her only wish was to be reincarnated as one of his horses, such was the love with which they were showered.

My great grandmother rode side-saddle on her favourite mare, a broad brimmed hat fastened to her head with a scarf and her voluminous skirts tossing in the wind. She was captured so by her husband's camera, a new-fangled thing at the time which left an odd photographic legacy of frozen ancestors peering at me from the homestead walls. I never saw her thus but fifty years after her death one fateful Christmas day her side-saddle still sat hauntingly on its rail in the saddlery in silent expectation, as if its ghostly mistress might suddenly appear at any moment and call it into service. She and her horse must have covered many a hot, dusty mile together in the empty countryside travelling to visit her family, whose property adjoined ours at its furthest boundary, or ferrying food to the work crews.

In The Shadows of The Honey Trees

Mum was an excellent judge of horseflesh and rode Bess, a fine white-stockinged part Akhal-teke mare who, in summer, gleamed the most extraordinary shade of purple. Nary a horse was ever passed without Mum commenting on its strengths and weaknesses. My father, on the other hand, a man who spent his entire life in the saddle, never offered a single word of judgment on such matters.

There was also the company of the orphaned kangaroos (several, all called Joe) and Cheeky who entertained us by scaring the hell out of house guests who, on waking in the morning, might find a curious furry feral gazing blankly at them from close range, unaccustomed to finding strangers in the house where they were free to wander like our pet dogs.

To add to this peculiar menagerie my grandmother gave me a cow for my first birthday, perhaps an odd gift for one so young but one that kept on giving not only warm milk every morning but also a calf that fattened my bank account every year. It was an early lesson in the exponential factor.

Such long shadows cast by venerated ancestors could not but influence me, the forming child. Elsewhere on the planet, in the decades preceding my birth, the earth had wept with the sacrificial blood of more than fifty million people. It was a new age and a rare crown to inherit!

§

Each tree and landmark of these wild acres, however insignificant, was committed to memory. My life depended on reading every subtle sign. Was the trail of animal tracks splitting or converging? One would lead to water, the other to the dry expanses where death stalked the weak and feeble-minded.

More than Ol' Sherrin went over the edge or became lost and died in the tangle of the subtropical cloud forest that flowed over the eastern edge of this high escarpment like a green wave, following the flow of moisture which wreathed the inaccessible folds of the plateau rim. These were the canyons lost in time where a hundred million years of wildfires had been unable to penetrate and where rare families of plants, unchanged since long before dinosaurs roamed, still grace hidden groves.

When Ol' Sherrin disappeared King Billy, head of the Ingleba tribe, was consulted. He summoned the best trackers. The natural dangers coupled with booze had all proved too much for Ol' Sherrin, who was working as a station hand when he vanished into this great geophysical void on the far side of the planet, six months of treacherous sailing away from the rest of his kind and beyond the edge of any map.

At first the trackers just sat on the ground quiet and unmoving...for almost an hour. The station men were becoming impatient with the delay. What were they waiting for?

Who knows what messages they channelled but the trackers rose suddenly and without a word to each other or anyone else set off, at a nomad's lope, in what everyone thought was a most unlikely direction.

It took three days to find him, but the aboriginal trackers' instincts had been right. After disappearing, Ol' Sherrin was found naked, crazed and bloodied many miles away in a rocky crique at the far reaches of my family's boundaries, a place still named Sherrin's Creek.

By then the great Perentie, the gargantuan monitor lizards, were trailing him, tasting the air with their long, purple, forked tongues, awaiting the chance of an easy meal. They could taste blood on the breeze from miles away.

In The Shadows of The Honey Trees

Top of the food chain some of these huge carnivorous reptiles were more than two metres long and extremely strong and agile. Their spirit was revered by the local Aborigines, although they also deliciously hunted them, a classic case of "God is Good".

Natives and invaders alike embraced the healing properties of the rich goanna oil which the *"medicine men"* like Uncle Charlie used as a heal-all. (Among his other healing magic potions was tea tree oil and honey but I am sure someone else has usurped that knowledge by now.) Time, disease and addictions so undermined the tribe that by the time I arrived there was hardly an Aboriginal face to be seen within miles.

If startled, a goanna, a great earthbound dragon, uses its enormous claws and rushes up the nearest tree and there remains motionless. But waddling across the landscape they generally have nary a care in the world. They can outrun prey and, the better to survey their realms, can stand erect and walk upright, presenting a most extraordinary humanistic posture in this land almost devoid of humankind.

They meet during mating season, satisfy their libidinous urges, then lay their eggs in a hole excavated in a termite mound. The temperature there is a constant maintained by the termites which, in turn, become the baby goanna's first meal after they hatch, a life cycle so simple as to be unbelievable, yet unfathomably complex. The young never know their parents in the way even crocodiles do. They are eternal orphans, and it has been that way "forever", if that word has context here.

There were numerous smaller dragons but the giants, known as Perentie, can kill with a single bite. Their prey - animal or human - quickly bleeds to death after going into sudden septic shock. A powerful anticoagulant is excreted from the gums of these terrifying reptiles whose sharp claws several inches long are used to tear chunks from their prey if it is too big to swallow whole.

And no dog, including the wily dingo, is a match for the great reptile's whip-like tail, which can suddenly strike with enough force to break a dog's legs …not to mention the shock more than one unfortunate person has endured after being mistaken for a tree stump by a panicked sprinting goanna.

The feet and digits of a Perentie can be much larger than human hands. The aboriginal people regarded these huge creatures as a separate distinct species from today's many varieties of smaller goannas. I think it reasonably safe to assume the big Perentie were probably killed off by everyone when they were encountered because of the threat they posed. The myth of giant lizards devouring humans persists in the dreamtime stories of the local tribes so should be accorded due regard especially as there have been recent fossil discoveries in the Australian north confirming the once presence of Komodo dragon-size reptiles on the continent. Truth is always stranger than fiction.

A big Perentie killed Ol' Bill. He had taken to feeding the great dragon a slice of toast every morning as he sat in the sun outside his kerosene tin-shingled shepherds' shack. Human company was rare in this neck of the world, so it wasn't surprising a hermit shepherd like Ol' Bill, struck up a camaraderie with the immediate prehistoric neighbour. The great reptile quickly lost its fear of humans, especially as food was involved, and included Bill's shack into its lumbering daily routine.

One morning the goanna, perhaps drawn to the smell of Ol' Bill's unwashed toes, mistook them for the tasty tidbit they no doubt were and latched on. That is how the two were found - Ol' Bill dead, still in his chair, with the giant goanna still clamped down on his bloodied foot.

They said Ol' Bill bled to death, the secretions from the ugly brute's salivary glands preventing the wound from congealing and the rampant bacteria from its carrion repasts sending Ol' Bill into a likely-sudden delirium before he expired. Little was later said about the ultimate outcome for the goanna.

To just spook it up a notch all the reptiles in this Dante's menagerie sloughed the outer membrane covering their scales every year. It is breathtaking to find the life-sized translucent skin of a large snake, whose passing you feel thankful for having missed, wavering in the bushes like a perfectly cast ghost, while you cast sidelong glances just in case the owner of such a beautiful "gown" is still in the precinct.

Once a year the outer skin of snakes becomes loose, and the creature just slithers out with a glistening brand-new surface. Such an event is a rare, mesmerizing magic to behold. The new surfaces glisten with a gem-like orient, while leaving a crepe ghost in the undergrowth, perfect in every detail, wavering with a life of its own on every zephyr. It is part of the spell the *Never-Never* casts.

Or "terror" could lie quietly in a bamboo grove. It was there our friend and neighbour rode one day on his favourite horse. As they passed the grove they were ambushed by a wild boar. These feral creatures quickly revert from escaped short-nosed domestic pigs to being long-snouted sharp-tusked ferals in a matter of a few generations. The fierce attack caught horse and rider off guard. The boar charged and lunged forward tossing its heavy head in a great arc. The razor-sharp tusk disembowelled the horse, and it collapsed in shock to the ground. Our neighbour, who always carried a heavy gauge rifle in the scabbard on his saddle, leapt from the horse in its death throes, grabbed his rifle, then dodged the aggressive boar around the bamboo until he was able to take his one chance of striking the certain death blow now so necessary to inflict. The boar charged …he pulled the trigger …the gun roared. The terrifying beast then travelled another ten metres after it was hit by the .303 slug before it dropped dead almost at his feet. With his heart still in his mouth he then used another round to euthanize his terrified horse still struggling on the ground. It was a long walk home alone, saddle and bridle over one shoulder and the loaded .303 at the ready on the other. Just in case!

With such treachery afoot at every turn I learned from the earliest age to turn the flashlight of self-centered "living" off and to turn on the inner light of "being"…of being aware; attuned to every rustle in the undergrowth; of every bird call and its meaning - an unspoken world in which I knew my place without having to have it explained and without having to explain it to anyone - a true innocent state of "being"…a Kipling jungle boy of another stroke. That any other reality existed simply seemed remote. In "living" I looked out, in "being" I looked in. I was the enigma in this land.

For better or for worse, I was blessed with the curse of a graphic memory, remembering everything and anything in complete detail, an encyclopedia of seemingly utterly useless information that coagulates comfortably in the recesses of my mind.

I learned I could be reduced to insignificance by the thrumming of a million unseen insects, which could completely drown out human voice, or by a single bite of one of the world's most terrifying monsters. These truths were early lessons in humility. We laughed in the face of danger, having no knowledge of any other truth. With levity it all seemed so normal that any other reality was exotically remote ...of the stuff only read about in the musty books stacked in the family library.

Unbeknownst to me layer after intricate layer of feral spirituality was thus laid down in my soul and baked into place - the flagstones on my Appian Way along which my personal moments of crucifixion would come to pass.

I still cultivate this rare geography of mind ...my Promised Land ...planting cherry trees, apricots and more cherries, apples and figs, mandarins and limes and, far down the mountain by the topaz sea where the gullies grow thick with Bangalow Palms and feathery Tree Ferns, I plant papaws, pineapples, mangos and bananas. It is by a sandy sea full of fish and with golden beaches framed by deep warm dunes where my spirit shelters from the wind.

There the bamboo groves reach forever skyward amid the guava trees along the riverbanks and hammocks are slung in deepest shade to afford the greatest relief from the searing sub-tropical sun. It is peopled with the spirits who have made my life a joy, a place devoid of parking tickets and all the other baggage of the modern world ...a perfect hidden Eden.

It is a place gloriously pregnant with space, inhabited by platypus and echidna, great grey kangaroo, black wallaroo, wallaby, sugar glider, muddle-headed wombat and a thousand birds of paradise, whose songs still echo now in my aging ears.

Heir to such a cornucopia of animated madness there is little need to make demands of my imagination in the telling of this tale for the toads of truth are far stranger than the lies of fiction (and can reach the size of a small dog). Anything that eats toads, even their tadpoles, dies. Even goannas. Toads (an unfortunate imported alien), rule.

As I sat with my father in the cool shade of the spreading boughs of the Honey Tree by that far-ago billabong watching our horses drink it was as if I became invisible even to him. While he talked to me, I never felt he never really saw me. He always seemed to see past me, focused on some far-off point. In time my life would reveal itself as bloody and tortured as the struggle of any other soul seeking to define itself. But I always had this legacy, the luxury of space, a rare hidden place, as my retreat. The art of life, Dad taught me, was learning to see what the eye does not see and to hear what the ear cannot hear. It was my Kingdom, my Power and my Glory, for ever and ever ...a world without end.

I carry no papered title, but it remains the realm to which I will always belong. When I matured and stepped out on the world stage from behind the folds of these timeless mountains, I simply continued to act like I "owned the place", wherever I went.

The horses withdrew with dipping muzzles and moved to the bank to graze. My father sat silent and motionless, a halo of wispy cigarette smoke shrouded his sweat-soaked hat as an army of a million bees buzzed overhead, collecting the nectar which would fill the many hives that stood like a forlorn white cemetery of gravestones atop a grassy knoll, close to both the forest of Honey Trees and the cool clear water of the creek where the thirsty workers could drink. This made for happy bees and more honey. The hives were carefully sited to catch the full morning sun to rouse the troops to early action. In return for this careful husbandry more than a million bees produced hundreds of gallons of their magical elixir every year, the final product extracted by spinning the waxen combs in a hand cranked centrifuge before it was funnelled into four-gallon tins to be shipped to market.

After several silent minutes lost in this constant overhead thrum, the first brave creatures began to emerge and go about their business, the inhabitants of a world of misbegotten aliens.

The ferocious red and black bull ants, which can jump several feet in a single leap to defend their nests with poisonous jaws; the deadly serpents great and small; the lizards and dragons of immense diversity; and all the while possums and koalas snored away the heat of the day in high treetop perches, each in its universe ...for the noon hour belonged to those that slithered and slid.

This was no small village but a vast unwieldy metropolis of nature where a man could ride all day in any one direction and fail to reach the boundary of his property by nightfall. And if he couldn't read the land, he might not make it back...

With plagues, war and starvation staring them in the face in Europe my ancestors fled across the oceans in the holds of fragile wooden ships at the height of European colonialism. They traded their known terrors for unknown ones. Many were not volunteers.

It was a migration akin to one nation emptying the populations of its jails and orphanages, the spawn of years of wars and famines, into another unsuspecting country and committing them to years of exiled indentured servitude there. They lost their families, their culture and some their lives. For most there was no going back. There were two days about which they could do nothing ...yesterday and tomorrow. They had to seize each day and wring as much life out of it as possible.

Many had committed blatant minor offenses just to get a government-subsidized seven-year ticket to a new world. They had little to lose. Such seemed a small price to pay for the faint hope of possible redemption in a land where winter was rumoured to be little more than a rumour to those conditioned to ice and snow underfoot. Under those conditions if you ask for work and it is refused then you must ask for alms. If alms are refused humans are driven to take what they need be it food or shelter. Others were considered unsavoury 'influencers' that the status quo wanted gone from the neighbourhood. On their arrival in Australia most were assigned to work clearing farms and, in the jungles, felling the giant tropical trees that clung to the coastal escarpment of this new world. The weather was mild and bush food plentiful. Most of them probably couldn't believe their good fortune to have a tent for a home in such a placid clime.

But in many cases, including that of one of my great x3 grandfathers, by the time they earned their 'ticket of leave' (anyone 'at large' had to hold one to prove they were no longer an indentured convict) they were married with children.

The enslavement for the most treacherous "villains" (those sentenced for rape or murder) was shackled work gangs ruled by ruthless overseers, often criminals themselves, who didn't hesitate to whip a chained man till he bled to death if they felt so inclined. Life and death were treated that casually. It was said that in homage to the witness of such atrocity the earth would never again let grass grow on such a spot. This is not just a myth. Blood, once dried in the earth, is waterproof, denying grass its needed moisture for many years to come.

The road that ascended the range to my homeland was carved from the solid rock by a gang of such men. The task at hand was dangerous and difficult enough that they were promised their freedom for volunteering for and completing such a daunting task on schedule.

When my convict ancestor's first wife was struck by lightning on the veranda of their Stringybark home one Christmas morning while ironing the family's "Sunday best" with the only iron thing around, he did the only proper thing and married her sister. She too met an untimely fate a few years later giving birth and so, with a gambler's determination and a dire shortage of women, he went for three times lucky, and wed the third sister.

Who better I suppose to mother your motherless children than their late mother's sisters. This ancestor rests forever on the still-peaceful banks of the river at Coolongolook where his funerary procession was halted by floodwaters, and he was quickly off-loaded and buried under a tree before the stifling heat could cause his body to putrefy. As a nineteen-year-old he had been *'transported'* for stealing a lemon. His London court records state that he was an Irishman who wore a silver ring with a blue stone on one finger and had his initials tattooed on the inside of his wrist.

But for fare-paying free settlers the invading forces declared the country *terra nullius*. It was considered, in the best self-serving colonial sensibility, "empty".

With endless available lumber felled to clear pastures, cheap convict labour (whose shackles were found stuffed in an old tree stump on the family property a century later) and endless acres the original hardwood homestead on my family's five thousand wild acres sprawled within an acre of rambling gardens.

My great grandparents, with considerable means, loaded the best the "civilized" world of the day had to offer onto bullock drays and dragged it off into the wilderness where

Platypus Flats

they laid it out like a 3-D cultural picnic on the luxurious tableau of the timeless "untamed" land.

An avenue of Kurrajong trees was planted along the long drive to the creek crossing that led to the main road, their waxy leaves ensuring cool passage under the brutal summer sun while doubling as emergency fodder during crippling droughts, when they could be denuded of their soft chewy leaves to feed starving livestock. But even the hardy slow-growing Kurrajongs could succumb to unforgiving drought and the ravenous appetite of the horses, whose assaults left toothy gaps along the young lush colonnade.

A pair of enormous Canary Island date palms were planted to deeply shaded the reception area, where horses could be tethered and visiting carriages (and later cars) parked in their shelter. The palms blocked the afternoon sun and the great sweeping fronds deeply shaded the air which kept the verandas cool. There was another pair on the other side of the house and two Washingtonia palms, which towered to unfathomable heights, at each side on the opposite axis of the building, enabling travellers to locate this human oasis from a hilltop kilometres away.

It was customary in the early days of the colony for wandering itinerants to arrive in the late afternoon seeking station chores in return for food and shelter. Sometimes mounted on ill-fed horses these "swagmen" were *"The Sundowners"*, men who wandered the landscape, escaping what demons we knew not, blown hither and yon by the winds of whim or fortune, crisscrossing this vast island nation in the endless eddies of seasonal station work. They were born largely of the colonial age when many had a past they would sooner forget, then later they were refugees of World War 1 and then the Great Depression. One such wander, asking for employment when times were tough for all, volunteered to work in exchange for two pumpkins drying on the roof of the pig shed when told finances did not permit any hirings. Those were desperate times. My grandfather gave him the pumpkins and the pigs went without that night. The Second World War seemed to have killed off such need to wander or perhaps it merely killed the wanderers. Post war infrastructure projects sucked itinerant wanderers into more stable employment but did little to address their ghosts of war.

Given the penal history of the early colony of the country one had no idea who they were sheltering. We were taught not to probe a stranger's past but to treat all with respectful consideration regardless. You cannot know a person strictly by appearances. We all have our *bunyips* to bury. People had a right to the privacy of their misfortunes and were to be taken at face value and offered what charity one could afford. There was always wood to be chopped, manure to be hauled and, at shearing time, the workforce could swell by more than a dozen and require well-manned kitchens.

Most of these seasonal people were familiar faces for, unlike some stations, our work gangs were pampered with copious feasts at morning and afternoon 'smokos' and full-course hot roast lamb 'sit down' lunches.

"You never know what they eat when they leave here," my grandmother would say as I helped her organize the seating at a long table on the veranda. "And you can't expect a man to do a decent day's work on an empty stomach," she would add as she poured a second gallon teapot of brew in preparation for the lunch crowd. It was simply hospitality we could afford to extend and another case of catching more flies with honey.

Platypus Flats

The side veranda looked out over a grassy knoll created so as to be inaccessible to all but the most mischievous lambs. In the manufactured shade of a metal pergola my grandmother indulged her fern collection and here, protected from frosts, in an airy arbour of graceful tree ferns, flourished bougainvillea and fuchsia washed over by the intoxicating scents of jasmine and gardenia. It also provided excellent roosting spots for the peacocks that graced the place with their glittering regal presence. By the Kurrajong tree, a pair of enormous Grass Trees raised giant spear-like flower stems metres high in competition with the crimson Gymea Lilies which sent flower spikes as thick as a man's forearm five metres into the air before erupting in a spray of crimson blooms the size of serving platters. Even the plants were eccentric.

The peacocks weren't all for show. They served as astute watchdogs and the females could also incubate enormous numbers of chicken and duck eggs. As standard outback incubators they could mother three dozen chicken eggs or two dozen duck eggs, many more than a hen or duck could manage alone. And the screeching midnight mating calls of the males were also a reassuring herald of the approach of the always-longed-for *Wet*.

More than one peahen provided comic relief when her family of ducklings tumbled into the creek and paddled off leaving their frantic landlocked mother rushing up and down the bank in alarm. There could be no mistake, my Mum was a poultry woman at heart and her gaggle of fifty geese, her rafter of turkeys and her ostentation of peacocks contributed greatly to our table compared to the scrawny pickings any native birds could have provided (the neighbours' pet emu might have been an exception).

In The Shadows of The Honey Trees

After parking horse or vehicle in the shade of the palms, guests entered under an arbour of fragrant roses, red on one side and white on the other, rambled through with sweet smelling honeysuckle and jasmine. The trellis framed a tall cast iron-lace gate which featured a pair of gilded rams-head capitals at the upper corners, a reminder to all who entered that the hospitality they were about to enjoy was courtesy of our vast herds of these imposing animals which produced the world's finest fleece.

The garden, fuelled with an assortment of aged manures, was tended by my grandmother, or others under her direction. It was every bit an oasis of subtle consideration in an ocean of nature filled with callous disregard for the human condition. One stepped through the garden gate from a gritty world where animals gnawed every green thing into a manicured land laid out with rolled lawns for carpets, bushes for furniture and ceilings of vine-draped trellises sheltering under a canopy of palms. Stepping into the deep shade of the wide verandas after the achingly brilliant sun outside you might blindly pass by the luscious but forbidden fruit of the potted peppers and the row of bronze hooks sporting bridles and stock whips and hats and oilskins, before your eyes adjusted to the lack of light.

My mother hated gardening but did it because she "disliked a house without a garden even more." To make the chore more pleasurable we usually only tended the garden in the late evening light when the cool air encouraged the sacred fragrances of exotic moon flowers and gardenia and jasmine and roses to permeate the dusk …a just reward for services rendered.

On either side of the main veranda entrance grew two carefully clipped tea bushes, gifts from a Darjeeling tea family who had unsuccessfully tried their hand at fine wool production on a neighbouring property before abandoning it, along with their magnificent home, which far exceeded the opulence of any built in that part of the world before or since. No one bothered to pluck and dry the fresh tea tips, instead ordering a fifty-pound box of this essence to fuel the thirst of a hard-working clan.

On entering the broad verandas fringed with *chinoiserie* lattice and festooned with passionfruit, wisteria and the extraordinary flowering *cuppa del oro*, one usually took their audience with my grandmother looking out over the shady courtyard to the tennis court beyond. The wide verandas functioned as outdoor rooms and shielded the low-slung homestead from the worst of the summer heat. They were furnished with a variety of cane chairs and chaises, day beds and long wooden couches whose slats were painted a rainbow of colors, a long wooden table and a series of large potted "Edith" flowers - rare, large-leafed orchids that bloomed sporadically to a rhythm no one had yet figured out. Inside, several spacious bedrooms, each complete with a fireplace, opened onto a central dimly lit corridor illuminated by frosted cranberry glass lamps and the rainbow glow from the stained-glass door that led to the veranda. It was a home designed to shield one from the outside world and not invite it in.

Waxed hand-hewn hardwood floors shone, pleasantly cool to our almost always bare feet. On one veranda or another the family gathered in quiet moments, Mum knitting a new sweater for some lucky person while my aunt and Gran tatted, crocheted endless laces or embroidered gowns and cushion covers or fashioned delicate lace fans trimmed with peacock plumes. In his down time Grandpa taught the cats to perform tricks much to our amusement. Idle hands were the devil's work.

Grandfather often bent over his latest saddlery repairs as he sat in his comfortable cane-bottomed chair wreathed in tobacco smoke from a roll-your-own stub that seemed permanently balanced (lit or otherwise) on his lower lip.

My favourite chore was helping him to shoe the horses, swinging on the handle of the huge bellows in the blacksmith shop pumping the flame till the black nuggets of "coke" glowed crimson. He patiently measured and trimmed each horses' hoof then cut an iron bar the correct length. I heated it till glowing in the fire while he trimmed the old shoe away and levelled the hoof. It intrigued me how the horses all stood so calmly while he fussed over the fitting, never flinching as he lifted their feet or when hot shoes were quenched with a sizzle in a bucket of water by their head or burned into the keratin of their hoof with a cloud of smoke to ensure a perfect fit. Finally shaped and carefully fitted the new footwear was then carefully nailed into place. It was back-breaking work, standing with a horse's hoof clamped between his knees, resting only briefly before moving onto the next hoof. It had to be done about every two months for all the working horses, four feet each.

The chore finished I'd run home pell-mell down the hill while grandpa followed with a wide hand-made wheelbarrow full of wood from the woodpile by the stables for the fires. The lesson learned? ...Never push wood uphill.

The hallway of the house bisected the central living room and led on to a huge kitchen some thirty feet long on the side of the winter sun where audiences were granted in the winter months. Beyond that, in the garden, was another cooking chamber, an open-air lean-to under an iron roof wreathed in grapevines known as "the summer kitchen", maintained to keep the cooking fires from heating the house to unbearable temperatures in summer. It was attached to the house by a floor to ceiling insect-proof wire-screened eat-out whose floor was tiled with patterned ceramics in colonial post office colours. It was *al fresco* dining at its finest with meals eaten here having the air of a picnic - minus the biting sun, mosquitoes, ants, flies and pesky parrots.

The bedroom doors were supplemented with knee-length curtains so maximum air circulation could be achieved while retaining elements of privacy. If you really needed more private space, you could go outside and drink deeply of this copious commodity in any direction you choose.

When my father received a new pony for his fifth birthday his mother, Violet, was ill in bed with the flu. Grandpa took him to the stables where the surprise was waiting. He then told Dad he better ride home and show his mother the new mount. Excited, Dad rode the spritely animal down to the house, through the rose arbour, across the veranda, down the hall and wheeled right into her bedroom to show his pony off without even bothering to dismount.

Following Aboriginal custom we slept under cozy possum fur rugs (or down quilts) while the soft fur of tanned kangaroo skins kept cold floors snug against the nippy nights during the chill dry winters.

The huge main kitchen with twelve-foot ceilings terminated in a massive red brick fireplace, which in winter heated the entire room, the energy from the simmering red-gum logs exploding back into the cavernous room amplified by a heavy metal disc (a cracked saw blade from the original lumber cutting) mounted in the back of the fireplace.

In The Shadows of The Honey Trees

Here the family gathered on winter afternoons to be entertained by the flames along with competition for every chair from my grandmother's clowder of twenty-one well-fed cats. You had to pick up a cat if you wanted to sit down here but they kept the chairs warm in winter. My grandmother's extraordinary talents as a pastry chef, skills gleaned from her stepmother, a former housekeeper to the Bishop of Australia, would be served up with tea to the delight of all while the winter sun glimmered through the coloured glass in the French doors that led to the *"dairy"* while in the further corner of the adjacent sunroom an enormous potted *Flor de Maio* cactus, perhaps a century old, bloomed an exotic fuchsia every May. It was as close to royal treatment as anyone might expect anywhere, let alone in a place so remote from *"civilization"*.

Dusted with snowy patterns and elaborate delicately-etched sugar traceries, my grandmother's triple-decker raspberry and Chantilly cream layer cakes (baked with her secret ingredient - duck eggs) were transformational.

Mere cake was elevated to awe. Creations of cream and sugar with peaks of icing decorated with gold and silver sugar balls competed with raspberry and apricot shortbread birds nest cookies dusted with castor sugar snowflakes and gave cause to my frequent Epicurean indulgences as Gran daily churned such wonders from her wood-fired ovens, feeding workers as well as guests and extended family appetites. My five-year-old eyes still grow wide just remembering. It was hard to decide what to eat first.

It was Gran who ruled our unpolished kingdom. It was her magic touch that turned squealing pigs into tasty hams and bacon. She had a spell for every culinary transformation and had a recipe for every part of the cow except the *moo*.

She also knew the routine and rotation of the flocks; which were getting old; which cut the heaviest fleece last year and when a flock needed to be *'dosed'* to keep the intestinal worms at bay.

In the early days of shepherding shearing the sheep of their fleece was accomplished by hand shears before the wool was rolled into neat fluffy balls and stacked in bins of assorted grades before being compressed into huge bales to await shipment to England for sale.

The animal was then "dipped" - plunged into an open earthen well filled with some toxic substance - to kill the ticks which could plague the animals to death if left untreated.

Originally all this took place in the shade of the spreading boughs of the Honey Trees with an air of a working picnic, the only sound being the click of the hand-powered shears as the sinewy hands of the shearers worked tirelessly to remove the fleece in a single warm pillow of cream fuzz, while birds warbled in branches overhead and the heady scent of spring perfumed the air.

The earliest flocks were walked seventy miles down the mountain to be shorn at the coast as this was deemed easier than trying to ship the clip down the treacherous, almost vertical face of the range.

This incredible steep incline, wrapped in a tangle of jungle vines and soaring tropical hardwoods, was once traversed by a train of one hundred mules and their Andean muleteers, all imported from Chile by the government of the day with the express purpose of transporting the highland crops of potatoes and wool to the coast, where subtropical heat made such a bounty impossible. By my day the modern motor car made traversing the road up the mountain possible, though sometimes only in the reverse gear on the steeper pinches.

But by the time of my arrival razor-sharp shearing blades were powered by a noisy, stinky, diesel motor. Add to that the yapping of the dogs as they moved the sheep from one pen to another, leaping onto the animals' backs and yipping in the ears of the leaders to cajole the unco-operative critters through the next gate; the scream of the emery wheel where my uncle honed the blades as fast as the three shearers blunted them; plus the shouting of the men over the din and you had a perfect, harmonious chaos. Within the course of three weeks every sheep on the property would be mustered to the shearing shed, stripped of its fleece, treated for ticks and intestinal parasites, marked with our brand of a dotted diamond in a color denoting its flock, and returned to its pasture. All this action stopped and started to my great grandfather's silver pocket watch which looked over the whole operation from a rusty nail in the shearing shed wall. Bought as a commemorative piece to celebrate Australia's Federation it still keeps meticulous time in the back of my sock drawer.

High above the turmoil of the shearing shed nature waved her wand and blessed the scene with something so remarkable as to defy the imagination.

Hiding in plain sight above the *"board"*, where the shearers stood in line bending and twisting with sometimes uncooperative animals and where roustabouts gathered the lanolin-scented fleece as it fell away from the shears (balling up in such a way it could then be unfurled in a large unbroken web on the sorting table), hung another enigma. Above all this was a long glass skylight, one corner chipped by a long-forgotten stone thrown by a cheeky boy, long before he became my father. Suspended from the rafters under this skylight were a series of rusting four-gallon kerosene tin buckets. These strange vessels held a most macabre secret ...the skeletal remains of the only wave of war to ever blight this kingdom ...the war against the rabbits.

   These were the toxic remains of rabbits poisoned with arsenic, the first volley of chemicals unleashed on the wall of rabbits that swept across the nation in the early 20th century eating everything to the ground. The hollow eye sockets of the skulls looked blankly out from something so toxic not even bacteria dared inhabit it. To prevent a domino effect on the predator populations scavenging dead rabbits, all the toxic carcasses were collected daily and hoisted to the place least likely to be ever disturbed to ensure that nothing could be inadvertently poisoned by consuming the bones. Still, the rabbits won. Despite our best trapping and hunting efforts as children and the hearty appetites of Grandma's cats, when we left to attend to our education Dad had to hire permanent help to keep the rabbit numbers in check. That is when Bunny, an elderly gentleman, and his almost-blind wife, who we children called Mixie, appeared and proceeded to live there for years, camped-out in the wilderness at the back of the property in a large canvas tent. They spent their days hunting rabbits which they shipped to a market somewhere. We often wondered who bought all those rabbits,

   The strange aerial rabbit crypt was the site of perhaps the rarest of all the disturbing enigmas to haunt that realm. Every year, above the ruckus of the shearing process, a small unremarkable grey bird would fly in through the chip in the skylight and do something quite beyond belief. It would make its nest in this noisy *catacomb macabre*. This bird could have chosen any quiet crevice in the surrounding wild acres, but it came here every year to raise her brood among the din.

In The Shadows of The Honey Trees

My father could not remember a year when the little grey bird had not slipped through the skylight he had broken as a child and, amid the din and the chaos, laid her bright blue eggs and raised her chicks in this toxic crypt, committing an act of defiance as remarkable as any. The bird was either very long-lived or the nesting territory was handed down from generation to generation, neither fact unknown in the avian world. That the bird would always be accommodated was a condition of the sale of the property when eventually all we children went on to pursue other lives and the property bearing *Torrens Title* was sold for the first time in history. Like the cockatoos and the parrots and the little grey bird, my soul always wings its way back to *Platypus Flats*. Home is a place of mind.

Our trips to visit neighbours usually revolved around "church" which was held some nine kilometres away about once a month in a tiny wooden structure, where again birds flew in through chipped glass windows to nest in the rafters of this solitary little house of God, a weather-beaten landmark of gold-rush evangelism once conveniently situated between the township's two pubs during its frenzied gold rush heyday a century past.

Now it stood alone, the pubs, having a different spiritual foundation, had crumbled after the gold petered out and everyone drifted away seeking *Mammon* elsewhere, abandoning their temples of liquid spirituality to the wrath of the elements. Of them only the forlorn stone chimneys remained, silent, solitary sentinels of better times. But the little hardwood church defied all odds. I doubt its wooden walls had ever been painted and it now stood silvered and baked hard by a century of sun, defying the gods that challenged it.

Those who stayed in the village had deep roots to the gold which had put Weabonga and my family on the map a century earlier. Some of the surrounding properties have still never been sold, the names of neighbours unchanged in more than a hundred and thirty years, many with close connections to the now defunct mines.

Dust storms sometimes swept in from the great red western deserts depositing their rich fine bounty on every surface or it simply arrived as muddy rain as the moisture from the east coalesced around the airborne particles of dust from the west before falling, leaving many a washday effort splattered with disfiguring red muddy spots.

The tiny six pew church was polished by community effort before each service, so the congregation didn't leave with a layer of red dust blessing the posterior of their Sunday best. It provided one of the few opportunities for us children to meet other children and to learn how to be part of a greater whole, however small.

The rare *Primavera* trees outside the chapel tried vainly to shade the little congregation and the exotic fragrance of their blooms wafted over the worshipers like the blessing as mother hammered out the Psalms on an organ of dubious pedigree in the corner and the colourful *Eclectus* parrots peered solemnly in from the branches by the windows, where they munched quietly on the nutty seeds, their favourite food. As the Reverend warbled on from the pulpit, much in the form of the black and white magpies which warbled outside in the trees, the two warblings merged and my young mind fluttered away with the birds to perch in unseen daydreams. Yes, the Lord works in mysterious ways. I assumed that just as Santa Claus looked out for seven-year-old me that there must be a *Lord God Bird* overseeing my feathered friends, its passing evident by the wind of its invisible wings.

Planted in the wilderness by the extraordinary efforts of those early war-and-disease-wearied refugees the religious roots of this small decaying hamlet clung tenaciously to the dry earth as a bonsaied tree defies an inhospitable cliff face.

The church yard also served as a holding pen for our ponies when we were deemed old enough to ride the nine kilometres to the one-teacher school. The Church of England ponies and the Catholic ponies in their respective churchyards never met and represented the community's sharp religious divide.

If I remember anything about "after church" visits with neighbours, it was that their houses smelled funny and lacked the warmth and familiarity of fresh baking. Many relied on kerosene lanterns and the shacks of some of the local hermits, to whom Mum would occasionally send me to deliver a pound of butter or a dozen eggs, were little more than an airy slab lean-to with cool, oiled earthen floors.

I remember being dispatched once to the home of Old Edith in the village with a note from my grandmother while Mum chatted with the other women in the shade on the church steps. There were only about five dwellings left in the village, now spread in varying disarray, their connecting streets reverting to pasture. It was with trepidation that I crossed a burr-filled field and entered in at the unfamiliar gate, a creeping feeling on the nape of my neck that felt a lot like *"trespassing"*.

When there was no answer to my knock on the open door of the tiny cottage (all doors in this climate were always open) I decided to look in the garden. It was a completely overgrown ramble of bushes and vines; petals showered down like pink snow from a climbing rose that arched wildly through the treetops, lending an air of enchantment to the rampant floral struggle. I was lost in this jungle of the imagination when startled by a croaky voice from the depths of the shadows.

The raven of my flight-or-flight instinct flapped raucously on my shoulder, its hard wings slapping the side of my head as I turned in terror. As my eyes adjusted to the dark shadows, I beheld an ancient crone dressed as if in shade itself who overflowed an equally ancient cane chair which struggled to contain her mass. It seemed as if she may have sat unmoving here in the shadows of this strange, enchanted garden all her many obvious years for she seemed rooted among the volume of variegated vegetation.

Her skin was mottled with age and, with a few black flies buzzing in lazy circles above her head, if she had not spoken, I might have taken her for dead. We had driven past this tiny house a thousand times but I had never seen her before, not once, not even from afar…not tending the garden, not sweeping the stoop. Never! Nothing could have prepared my young mind for this moment of confrontation. It was as if I had stepped into an unknown universe and found myself without the guarantee of gravity.

She sat in what I can only describe as a "humpy", the term used for the makeshift dwellings erected by the nomadic natives when in temporary hunting encampments. This makeshift hovel was almost completely obscured by the vegetation which seemed to be its only visible means of support. On the earthen floor a slow fire smoldered on the bare dirt under an ancient three-legged iron pot from which strange smells emanated, a spell that haunts my memory still though at the time was unknown to my senses …the tang of boiled turnip! It was a smell never to be forgotten, a miasma which has haunted the caverns of my aural senses for the rest of my life.

The woman herself held little resemblance to any known human form my young mind had ever encountered and I stammered, shaking as I proffered the small beige envelope in my hand, half afraid of being thrown into the stew that bubbled at the feet of this apparition so at one with her isolation in a garden of deep shadows. I supposed she had no idea who I was either.

The woman's wrinkled face unfolded into a semblance of a smile as she took the neat envelope I proffered, all the while peering at me through gold wire-rimmed spectacles. As she lifted the delicate seal and extracted the neatly folded note within her face broke into a wide beam of unruly teeth. I obviously had been explained by the words in the envelope. She smiled a deep satisfying smile. My fear abated like a tide suddenly rushing out. That a tiny slip of paper and what was scrawled on it could render such a sudden transformation seemed miraculous to me. I saw clearly the power of the written word. In that moment I felt my grandmother reaching through the hills, past the last telephone post to this apparition in the cane chair, her old friend from their younger days, now a world so completely "off the grid" as to represent the last vestiges of humanity living in such enchanted isolation from the worries and woes that blight the outside world.

Old Edith croaked her thanks and asked if I'd like a biscuit. At that point the nervous raven of instinct on my shoulder smelled the questionable smell of the boiled turnip again and took flight. My fears followed, and I stammered a polite: "No, thank you!" as I bolted through the undergrowth for the gate so I could return to the familiar world by the shortest route possible. For one terrifying moment the latch on the ancient wooden gate stuck in the haste of my retreat and when I did manage to free the rusty hasp, I bolted without bothering to close it properly behind me ...the ultimate of bad country manners. The raven on my shoulder didn't stop flapping until I arrived back to the familiar scent of Mum's Moonflower perfume and the other "knowns" at the church steps.

We really did live beyond the end of the line. The government telephone access ended some distance away from our home and we maintained several miles of private telephone line, twin zinc wires snaking across the hills, which we children were tasked with clearing of any fallen sticks. This meant eliciting the co-operation of our ponies whose rumps we often had to stand tiptoe on to remove offending twigs. These caused static on the line, sometimes rendering conversation impossible.

We also generated our own electricity using a big diesel generator to pump up a huge bank of batteries once a week. For reasons I could never comprehend, these motors also interfered with the telephone and radio reception and seemed, to my young mind, a violation of the laws of nature. But many local households maintained kerosene lamps as a primary light source, including kerosene driven refrigeration. I never quite grasped how, by putting a flame under something, you could make ice?

A government power grid finally made an appearance in the mid 60s but by then I had left for boarding school. Again, we had to supply and maintain a mile or so of private access line to the main government installation. As fate would have it a television signal was found about half a mile away from the homestead which meant holidays at home were now dominated by Dad watching the slowly creeping days-long cricket matches he loved ...the equivalent, in my then (and now) worldly opinion, of watching paint dry (sorry cricket but that bug never bit me).

To my cricket-mad family I was considered an inferior species, but I could never grasp the complexity of the character-building cricket is supposed to bestow. Whenever I played it felt a lot like farming but less fun. I arrived at the conclusion that I preferred to watch ink dry.

The cricket commentators droned on through the listless summer heat like blow flies, discussing the invisible possibilities, filling the gaps in a game known for its slow, crawling pace ..." if only Ian had been fielding in *silly mid-off* as he was five minutes ago, he would have had that ball..." There was also some mention of a *'gully'* and sometimes someone got a *'duck'*, usually too much applaus*e*. It was as warriors who might relive their momentous battles to draw out the glory of a moment for a few more minutes before the next ball was bowled hard and fast with enough force to rip half your face off, as happened to my father, who until that point (and even after), had loved the game all his life. After that episode I made a point of being good, instead, at tennis.

The commentary left me listless, and I wandered off to a room adjoining the kitchen. Behind the colorful stained glass French doors, was the dairy where milk was separated from the cream which was then churned into butter and where the wheys and curds were clotted and cheesed while grandmother whipped anything remaining into the finest Chantilly cream with which to delight the family's taste buds.

This cool room, in turn opened onto a low flight of stairs that led to the herb garden which was shaded by a large mulberry tree and several rare, delicious varieties of trellised table grapes that completely shaded the whole adjoining courtyard, cooling the meat house in that pre-refrigeration era. In summer the rambling vines shaded the roof and wetted burlap curtains could be swept around the exterior of this building to cool the interior space. The hotter it was outside the cooler it was inside. It created a solar refrigeration unit the size of a small garage - large enough to process a whole cow, sheep or pig.

Having the water to use for the very effective evaporative cooling was a luxury afforded by a small earthen reservoir further up the hill, whose contents were collected from the roofs of the blacksmith shop and carriage house before being gravity fed to the garden via underground pipes. To my young mind the invisibility of this process rated alongside magic. Inside the meat house large oak barrels held beef sides being brined and processed into corned beef. Half a sheep or a pig might be hanging there. Death was definitely permanent, of that my young mind was left with no misunderstandings. Hams were treated in a special distant smokehouse to keep the risk of fire a safe distance from the homestead.

On the veranda shaded by the passionfruit vine, big canvas water bags fitted with porcelain spigots at the top corner were used to cool drinking water by evaporation. They could be easily moved about to where they were required by workers and could be hung from the crash bar on the front of the jeep when working remote from the homestead. We drank that or scalding Billy tea. Water was our champagne. In a land where fresh water was not always available no alcoholic inspiration was needed.

Wide verandas were active living spaces which almost doubled the floor space of the house and when we took our breakfast there in summer cheeky parrots would fly in and steal food right off the table. You haven't lived if you haven't had your salad tossed by a beautiful bird searching for sunflower seeds. I remember having to repeatedly pull them out of my cereal by their tail feathers. They were as voracious as flying rats and would dive right back in the moment I let go.

The central living room was an enormous cavern with walls and high ceilings clad with ornate embossed tin panels with equally decorative mouldings all painted my grandmother's favourite color ...ashes of lilac ...and furnished with Queen Anne mohair-upholstered settees a century old. A jade green and violet stained-glass door to a further veranda was the room's primary source of light, a deeply shaded respite from the heat. Outside, vines of every persuasion draped the broad verandas. It was a place which had stood strangely still for more than a hundred years, its garden of earthly delights blooming as if synchronized to some invisible force which cared not about the humans who had brought them here. Brilliant blue wrens nested in the vines just inches from the table where we usually ate and darted about looking for crumbs the moment the humans vacated.

The living room was screened in almost total darkness, an eternal twilight, by the low roofed verandas, which stretched another twenty feet beyond the perimeter of the house. These verandas were where guests were entertained after strenuous games of tennis. Our family might slog the ball around dressed in nothing but baggy khaki shorts but if guests were being entertained everyone wore Wimbledon whites. That the worlds of Old Edith and my grandmother could be separated by mere kilometres I could never reconcile.

The breakfast room stood to one side of the living room, a place where breakfast was never served. Instead, its long white cedar table served as a party buffet when holiday entertaining or, on those few occasions every year when sufficient numbers could be roused, for serving treats for guests enjoying themselves in the adjacent ballroom.

The ballroom was little used but large and spacious with a horsehair-sprung floor. Music came from an ancient upright ship's piano on a low stage in one corner (the top and bottom octaves had been removed to conserve space aboard a sailing ship). It was empty other than for a billiard table in the further corner and mainly served as a place where we, as small children, could race our tricycles on rainy days.

All these trappings of the invading culture had to be carted here by bullock dray, wagons lacking the necessary maneuverability to navigate between giant trees too massive for removal in those early days of the invasion. Vision and engineering and a great deal of 'just getting things done' with unquestioning determination was demanded here and left little time for social interactions. Anyone looking after thousands of animals spread over far-flung acres is busy most of the time just checking everything is okay. It takes management. It takes time in the saddle to ride the hills and creeks to ensure there are no serious problems.

My life here consisted of random moments as if nothing ever existed before that second and nothing was to change after. It was, in the true indigenous sense, *dreaming*. The past, the present and the future were simply one. In this remote enigmatic vacuum my person prospered.

In the dim center of the elaborate living room was an exotic Persian carpet of rich kingfisher blues and rooster reds whose swirling designs were sprinkled here and there with an icy tracery of shiny white silk threads. In the middle of it stood a wooden music table with impossibly delicate cabriola legs that clawed at the rug with taloned feet. It was simply decorated with a large pale pink frosted glass centerpiece of a leaping fish all lit from above by a retractable white porcelain lamp shade fringed with a long-patterned veil of colored glass beads.

My whole universe revolved around this serene, frozen altar which stood there as the center of this chaotic wilderness, a glass shrine to loveliness caught like a jewelled insect in the cultural web of an invisible intergalactic spider. Lying here on the cold polished wood floor on hot days I felt most comfortable in my skin. It was a world apart from the earthen floored humpy where I had delivered the secret smile in the beige envelope to Old Edith.

The Victorian mohair furnishings showed no signs of wear even after a century of use. Everything was of exceptional quality, or it simply was not purchased and brought here by lumbering bullock dray in the first place. It was the family economics that you bought only the best and only things you had fallen in love with. There was simply nowhere to dispose of anything, so nothing was ever thrown away, not even the burned-out A model Ford which remained under the willow tree behind the blacksmith shop where it had been torched by angry arsonists sixty years earlier. As we children put the gearbox through its paces and pretend-drove the rusting hulk into eternity we had no inkling of the tragedy it represented, and no one bothered to explain and perhaps spoil our fun. It was a silent lesson that, with time, even a tragedy could be turned into a valuable resource.

The homestead sat with commanding views down the valley, an edifice to a culture that had squeezed itself comfortably into strange boots. It was surrounded by The Horse Paddock, the exclusive domain of the horses. Cattle and sheep were relegated to further fields. The Bullock Paddock harked back to an earlier age when a team of twenty trained bullocks either made you or broke you in this pastoral business.

The floor to ceiling library stood to one side of the tall red brick open fire in the living room while several works of art and historic ancestor photographs graced the opposing walls. Here my x2 great-grandmother mourned tragically forever beneath a flutter of black funerary feathers that would do an ostrich proud, clad in elaborate Victorian 'mourning *weeds*' in an odd photographic celebration of her new (but to be short-lived) dowager status, following the sudden death of her husband at age thirty-six. That she was the grandmother of both my grandparents was never explained.

Outside in the shady lower garden was the meat house where various creature corpses were dissected into delicacies. Anything exceeding its allocated space in that universe might suddenly find itself plucked from its perch and dispatched unceremoniously with the blow of an axe one morning and find itself gracing the table by sundown. But such transformations took magic.

Carcasses of kangaroos, sheep, pigs, chickens, ducks, geese, turkeys and even occasionally peacocks, could be found there hanging deliciously dead, sacred sacrifices of the best our heart could grow.

It was important to know your place in the food chain: Pigs were slaughtered in the late fall after having been fattened on the dropped fruit from the orchards but in time for hams to be cured by Christmas; cows only met their fate when a frost was expected to chill the fresh kill; sheep were sacrificed weekly; kangaroos met their fate whenever the station dogs looked hungry; but duck and everything else that waddled or squawked could be summarily executed without a moment's notice. The sheep, pigs and cows were, somewhat more religiously, sacrificed only on Sundays, a timeless ritual that was the only nod to the Christian God in our isolated kingdom. Then again it might have just been a force of habit. When Mum cooked kangaroo-tail soup in a big pot on the garden stove, slowly simmered over hardwood coals for hours, it filled this valley of enigmas with a wafting ambrosia that would tempt the tastebuds of the most ardent vegan.

The slaughter yard was always verdant, fertilized by the regular letting of blood, the iron rich life force, which weekly seeped like a sensuous scarlet boa through the tall, lush grass of its own making, the striking visual fertilizing my young imagination. It was an embedded rite. Every Sunday for a hundred years this yard had been flooded with the crimson blood of sacrifice.

If you wanted to get to the tasty parts there was work involved …killing, skinning, plucking, gutting. It could be sweaty work. The tasty parts we then roasted in our ovens, fuelled by the dried hardwoods of long dead ancient Honey Trees. Death! It has a place in life, a purpose, although it took a lifetime to recognize that this was the takeaway from this remote but complex childhood.

CHAPTER 5

The King of Blue Gum Flats

"A man is but the product of his thoughts. What he thinks he becomes."

—Mahatma Gandhi

1852

Early colonial preachers in Australia simply announced services at a set time under a designated tree and people of every religious stroke within a ten mile ride by horse or buggy gathered, not just for the encouragement to keep going or for the sermonizing, but to enjoy the company of other far-flung neighbours in the before-and-after chatter which more generally represented grassy picnic teas in the shadows of exotic trees while whiling away the heat of the afternoon, a rare opportunity to socialize.

The preachers (who could be anyone who could read needing a vocation) were entitled to a limited stipend based on the collection from the bums on the logs.

I must pay tribute to one stalwart evangelist *Reverend Alfred Glinney* on account of whose notes I was granted a rare third-party account on the workings of my x3 great-grandfather's kingdom.

Among other notes I came across was an inventory of his property *"Gosford Park"*. It seems my grandsire enjoyed the labours of "three convicts employed felling timber" and some "twenty acres under vegetables" cared for by a Chinese gardener. To keep all this crisp vegetable matter from being consumed at night by hungry kangaroos and wallabies he engaged a veritable army of "27 dogs". Keeping that pack fed must have necessitated the services of a hunter as well but of that there was no mention. I assume the many members of his tribe took care of this just as we did in my childhood at a different location a century later. With fourteen children from two wives and dozens of grandchildren who married into every other local family he was simply known as *The King of Blue Gum Flats*. By the time of his death at 103 years old he had ninety-two grandchildren. His sister headed a similarly sized tribe having born seventeen children of her own.

Rev. Glinney made extensive notes on matters after he crossed swords with the king (a.k.a. *William Walmsley*) over the necessity for a school building for which he wished the king to volunteer the building materials.

With his tribe of grandchildren in need of "learning" the king obliged although he himself was illiterate and believed that too much book learning "dulled the mind". Given his propensity to prosper his position might be worthy of some consideration. On the flip side of that coin, without the written records of the Reverend, I would never have enjoyed such a window into the past. He was there when I was not.

The king's tribe controlled the only road between Australia's two major cities of the time, Sydney and Newcastle. It remains there still, a wondrous curving sinew hewed from the canyon walls by a team of convict labourers under the rumoured-ruthless whip of one *Solomon Wiseman* from whom the king obtained ownership of the road and the grand sandstone inn that overlooks the orange cliffs on the further shore at the convenient attraction of the government ferry across the river.

Hospitality was my family's middle name. Huge verandas were built here also to accommodate the view of the landscape for the guests who could also partake in a round of riverside golf on the king's private golf course, the first of its ilk in the country. All this remains there still, almost unchanged but for the absence of horses as transportation. The rooms are still there, small, upstairs and with all sharing the same small bathroom down the hall. Rooms were, after all, simply for resting and that doesn't require much space.

A century earlier a fleet of small row boats awaited dalient lovers, who could find complete privacy just around the next bend in the river. It was also the necessary thirty miles from the city, which gave it the licence to play host to city *"travellers"* and serve alcohol on weekends when city hotels were closed by law. It was, in the reality of its relative isolation, a law unto itself …a kingdom by the standard of any day. I can now go and sit where he sat and, for the penalty of some small cost, order up a feast and fine drinks and act, for the moment, as he did …and wear the crown as if I own the place, thanks to the long ago sweat of his brow.

Further down the river toward Gosford, where the king lived in a modest home built on a low knoll, he constructed a racetrack that circled the house so his ninety-two grandchildren and their friends could gather on weekends to race their horses while he looked down from the cool confines of the sweeping verandas. It was yet another brainchild of an illiterate man who possessed uncanny vision, grace and a strong familial hand in how to dish out "authentic" hospitality. The racetrack has now been relocated but they still race the horses at *Gosford Park* every week, probably still competing for the solid silver cup he commissioned for the main event each year. Build it and they will come!

The other branch of that maternal line was much more narrow. *Elizabeth Beatson* was the youngest of two daughters of the proprietors of *The Emu Plains Inn*. It was a large double-story building purpose-built on leased land, because the first title to the land was held by a man sent to Australia as a convict and who had served his fourteen-year sentence for murder. The land was inherited jointly by his seven children and their consensus to sell was impossible to obtain but the location was optimal, so the Beatsons leased the place, now a museum, for seventy years.

The owner of the house next door was the young entrepreneurial quarry owner, my x2 great-grandfather, *Andrew Turnbull*, who came to Australia as a young man and tried his hand at many turns during the gold rush era. When everyone was clamoring for the best agricultural land in the country, he opted for a big bend in the Nepean River, a body of water a hundred metres wide in places. He was mocked, for the land was stony, completely unsuitable for crops and would flood twice a year. But he wasn't planning to grow crops. He bought a barge and began shovelling gravel and floating it thirty miles down the river to provide the city of Sydney's foundations …for its buildings, its roads, its railways, its water systems and its sewers.

He dug enough gravel to construct the Warragamba dam which still today provides the city's water; and whenever it flooded the river filled his gravel pit back up and he would start shovelling again. The government of the day finally recognized that perhaps one man held too much power and nationalized the company, appointing him managing director for life. Until he was unable, he rose every morning and rode his fine horse the many kilometres to the gravel pits and back to oversee all matters, as much for the joy of the ride through the morning and evening chorus of birdsong as out of a sense of duty. The regatta events for the 2000 Sydney Olympics were held on the Macquarie Lakes, his former gravel pits. His message? A golden opportunity isn't golden if you can't recognize it.

He and *Elizabeth* married and had two sons and four daughters. Both boys died of misadventure by the time they were twenty years old and of the sisters *Agnes*, my great-grandmother, married *Edward Walmsley*, one of those ninety-two grandchildren of *'the king'*. The sisters were all master dress designers, a passion passed down in the family to my mother. *Agnus'* wedding was well-publicized with reports that the family gathered wattle blooms and ferns from the bush to decorate the entry and the fence outside the low stone Emu Plains Anglican church. The dresses in attendance were lavishly described in the local newspaper, recorded almost stitch by stitch, the writer noting: "Many of the gowns were from the hands of the Walmsley sisters."

These stately elderly aunts would once a year arrive in the *Never-Never* by train to spend a few weeks with us. Their beautiful dresses and fantastic hats I took as reassurance I was related to the Queen of England, who looked down on me from the wall of our little one-room school, for no one else I knew wore such beautiful gowns. From their pampered position in life they bore no attitude of elitism. They lived in a world of silk and cashmere crepe trimmed with swan down and ostrich plumes but as my great-aunts I knew them as very warm down-to-earth, matter-of-fact genuine old people who proclaimed, with a chuckle, their vocation to be one of simply *"turning rags into riches."*

In The Shadows of The Honey Trees

"*It is not about what one has but what one does with what one has,*"...their well-enunciated voices echo still.

They took pleasure in long ocean voyages together on freighters, visiting friends operating refugee camps in northern China. They bought bolts of exotic silks in China and Japan before climbing aboard another freighter spending the next month at sea busily designing and creating with their latest discoveries. That would have them arriving in India where more fabric of every type was loaded aboard (no baggage limits on a freighter). Then the designs would fly from their fingers until arriving in Europe where they gathered ideas of the latest fashion trends before pressing on in whatever direction they chose, bolts of cloth stockpiled alongside the growing racks of gowns. They loved what they did and never considered it *"work"*. They would eventually arrive home to Sydney with a stock of hundreds of chic dresses in tow. The society fashionistas on the day mobbed them at the docks all wanting a piece of the action.

I remember a story told of their mother *Elizabeth* hosting a special dinner. All the guests were seated at the long table where her husband *Andrew* loved to entertain his business associates.

In the center of the table stood a tall, tiered silver *epergne* festooned with flowers and chilled dessert grapes from the garden piled high on its silver servers, all held aloft by silver cherubs.

The dining room was lit by candles, *Elizabeth* refusing installation of those *"horrifying"* electric lights in the dining room. No one in her social circle was going to be given *"that close an examination"* of her wrinkles! Wrinkles mattered even then.

The party had enjoyed several rounds of good cheer in the garden and at the table before the main course entered carried by a young maid. The girl was a perhaps-slightly-nervous twenty-something-year-old who arrived from the kitchen carrying a canopied platter on which rested the main course - a roast turkey surrounded with baked trimmings. As she approached the table, she caught her toe on the rug and went flying with her prize, the silver cloche a-clatter amplifying the disaster.

Grandmother, without drawing a breath (it was said) reassured the maid as she gathered her up along with the bird and the fallen vegetables: *"Don't worry dear,"* she announced perhaps too loudly: *"Let's take this back to the kitchen and dress the other turkey."*

There was no other turkey but a few minutes later grandmother reappeared composed with what appeared to be the *'other turkey'*, neatly arranged on the platter. It was a lesson in poise and appearance and how to be quick on one's feet should one stumble. Such gems of wisdom in how to pivot in a crisis illuminate my crown.

On moonlit winter nights the community from miles around travelled in their best formal wear to dance the night away in a wonderful limestone cavern hidden amongst the folds of The Blue Mountains which rose almost immediately behind their Emu Plains home. Known as *The Devil's Coach House* this spectacular geological wonder was carved from the limestone landscape by the underground meanderings of the aptly named *River Styx*. It had, over the course of four hundred million years, created this labyrinth of awe-inspiring caverns which glistened when illuminated by reflected candlelight.

In The Shadows of The Honey Trees

Lofty limestone jewels glittered above the gathered crowd as drinks were shipped, pastries served, and the violins led the way to the dance floor as one by one elegant couples stepped into the circle of light and swayed through the evening in this rare chamber of acoustic loveliness. The polished limestone floor saw a thousand slippered feet dance the enchanted night away, the dancers' shadows flirting among the glittering stalagmites and stalactites, nature's gothic arches, buried in the bowels of the mountain.

Between the numbers as musicians massaged chilled fingers the dancers stepped out into the cool mountain air and drank in the spectacular moonlit landscape that towered above them. Later, weary from their exertions, everyone would pile sleepily into their carriages and snuggle down under possum skin rugs for the long, chill, magical, moonlit ride home. The horses, which had stood waiting patiently for hours, knew the way home and made haste for their stable without need of direction or encouragement.

CHAPTER 6

The Black Horse Inn

*"The best way to find yourself is to lose yourself
in the service of others."*

—Mahatma Gandhi

My family's entertainment gene carried far - far from *Platypus Flats* ...back across the oceans to the *Black Horse Inn* at Hockwold-cum-Wilton in Essex, England, where they can be traced serving ale and refreshments from the early 1700s until the middle of the 19th century; to the *Emu Plains Inn* outside Sydney, which early colonial family ran for seventy years and which several family ghosts still haunt; to the grand sandstone Inn at *Wiseman's Ferry Inn*, north of Sydney; to the *Penrith Inn*, (later turned into a boys boarding school) which served as a community center and hosted lavish entertainments; to several inns operated by a x3 great-grandmother, a slip of a girl, who married the first of four husbands before her fourteenth birthday and operated several inns in Singleton and Sydney (including the still operational *Bird in the Hand Inn*); to my own bed and breakfast, *Casa Mora*, which my talented wife and I opened, operated for ten years and then retired from without knowing a whisper of my ancestors' similar business proclivities ...the trail of good hospitality flows like a stream. We were all obviously experienced enough to know that travellers are happily relieved to find fresh, clean, comfortable, home-style accommodations and good food when enduring the rigors of the road, regardless of cost. I know I do. It helps the illusion that travelling well is by design rather than fate, which is more often the case.

The first rule of hospitality is 'never be seen working'. Everything must seem effortless ...*facile* as the French would say ...or the whole idea doesn't float. It also helps to know how to feed a sudden crowd: Lunch for a dozen in thirty minutes? ...curried egg and cucumber sandwiches; breakfast for twenty? ...fruit salad and yogurt made the previous evening and marinated overnight then served in martini glasses for *pizazz* with a dollop of yogurt and a strawberry on top; dinner for fifty? ...Hurriedly slaughter and spit-roast a lamb at the bottom of the garden (it also keeps the guests entertained outside).

At *Platypus Flats* we didn't often entertain overnight guests, but the hospitality was thickly applied when needed. During infrequent dances the billiard table was moved outside to the veranda so the ballroom could accommodate the action. At either end of the ballroom giant fireplaces, capable of accommodating six-foot-long logs, made sure no one caught a chill between the numbers.

My grandmother played classical violin, losing herself in tunes she had practiced since childhood in the middle of the wilderness, without the need for sheet music. Grandfather played it too but when he picked it up it turned into a foot stomping fiddle, quite a different beast, a nod perhaps to his Irish heritage.

Players volunteered themselves and their instruments and I remember my mother hammering out honkytonk numbers on the slightly-off-key piano to the delight of dancers while babes rode in the crook of the arms of young parents; grandmothers danced proudly with grandsons; fathers twirled daughters gracefully; mothers cherished being held in the arms of their sons no matter their age; and awkward teens vied with each other for the limited cohort of partners for the next refrain.

As one they swirled and swayed the night away, stepping lightly and gracefully, joining together in a singular stream of unpretentious elegance, a spiral of grace and joy that echoed into the frosty night air as it silently settled over the landscape like a white cloak of icy diamond shards making lamplight sparkle like the flash of patent leather shoes as the dancers twirled as one to time-honoured tunes in the kind light cast by gas lamps. Couples trotted and spun as single graceful four-legged creatures; cozy; cheek-to-cheek; each aware of the other's toes ... before they twirled apart, discovering their own separate center of gravity, before once more joyfully flowing together again. When circular rotations were called for, a cog of males moved one direction, the women turned the other, each swaying and stepping to the beat till the next partner was decided by chance. Rarely again have I ever experienced such a societal *"oneness"* of the collective human spirit, the whole far exceeding the sum of the parts, amplified by the fact there was hardly another living soul within a radius of thirty kilometres. It was unquestionably a *nobis cum Deus* moment. No one could have been happier in that instant than we, wrapped in that memorable moment, all of one mob.

Feet stomped familiar rhythms until the bouncing floor fairly gave wings to the dancers' feet. *Old Jim*, having consumed sufficient liquid courage from his brown paper bag, took up his ancient squeeze-box concertina and began to play, falling into such a trance that he had to be shaken out of it when it was time to break for 'supper' (a pot luck repast around 11 p.m.) when the favourite recipes of all the district women were served for all to feast, with gallons of fresh brewed tea to wash it all down.

Then the music would begin again, graceful circles formed once more and dancers moved one partner to the right or left after each set of intricate steps, which had no doubt been passed down through centuries, mothers to sons and fathers to daughters. Side by side partners executed the prescribed curtsies and twirls, hand to hand, toe to toe, heel to heel, moving as a single endless joyful entity, the clap of leathered soles on hardwood thrumming in the cold night air like human cicadas, starting and stomping to magical cues. It was a pattern hammered out in small community halls and ballrooms and woolsheds all across the country, a cultural intersection, a jumble of humanity that had been tossed together and fermented in this wide strange land, a fateful cultural side dish of a history half a planet away.

Our *"dusky"* neighbours readily embraced the odd corroboree of the invaders. Music is always common ground. Everyone was welcomed. Diseases have since decimated their numbers and booze and difficult-to-obtain substances have dulled our cultures all. I regret I never knew the rhythm of their steps even though their traditional corroboree ground was less than a few hundred metres away from the original homestead of my ancestors. The European invasion all but obliterated the social structures that had developed here over eons of isolation and the human cost alone of the invaders' diseases on the original people now leaves us ashen.

Platypus Flats

The local corroboree ground was abandoned after an unfortunate historical incident which left everyone shaken. In the early days of settlement removal of tree stumps from pastures was affected using the new fangle powder called dynamite courtesy of one Dr. Nobel, whose odd legacy still funds great minds today. The supply of this potent substance had to be secured somewhere dry and away from human habitation. No one could remember who might have chosen to secrete it in an old hollow log by the corroboree ground but there it was forgotten until someone preparing for a corroboree decided the log would be a good foil for the light of the fire and lit the blaze beside it. The evening's entertainment of singing and dancing and musical performances was in full swing, the didgeridoo players hitting their top notes, when, by all oral accounts, without any warning, the cache of dynamite stored in the log reached a critical scientific turning point causing the whole log to erupt in an ear-splitting explosion which shook the earth and sent people, splinters and smoking cinders flying in all directions.

People fled into the darkness and while there were no reports of serious injury the local tribe decided to abandon that site as it was obviously now inhabited by less than friendly spirits. It turned out, however, to be perfectly suited for cricket matches, the river fielding in *"silly mid-off"*.

In the *Never-Never* know that, while *Crocodile* and *Green Ant* are still dreaming beautiful places into being, the spirits can also show their displeasure. What can never change is that yesterday is today is tomorrow. One didn't need to divide it into past, present and future. It simply *"is"*, a continuum, undivided by invented tense.

Now, a century after that ill-fated explosion, the dancers sashayed and swayed as another fire scene unfolded at the bottom of the garden, where a slow charcoal blaze provided the heat to roast a whole lamb that turned slowly on a spit, surrounded by those with brown paper bags containing personal libations, all attracted to the throbbing mass of coals and the wafting aromas of charred flesh, like human moths drawn to a cosmic flame. The music undulated over them, an incantation on the frosty air as they warmed themselves at the womb of the fire.

In that wilderness it was everyone's responsibility to be entertaining which might account for my many eccentricities. I too could play piano and loved to sing without caring to notice if anyone was listening, for there wasn't usually anyone within earshot ...or *coo-eee* distance, as we called it, an ancient communication pronounced with a whip-like crescendo to fling out the sudden scale of human voice as far as possible across the valley where it echoed from stony outcrops atop the hills.

Well into the small hours the throng would thrum. As the evening ended about 2 a.m. my aunt with the fiery red hair would cross the floor in a beautiful dress of her own manufacture and take her seat at the piano. I can still hear the notes rising crisp in the air as everyone responded to the familiar farewell and began to sing:

"*Show me the way to go home, I'm tired and I want to go to bed, I had a little drink about an hour ago and it went right to my head....*"

Someone would start a single slow, rhythmic Conga which would wend its way out into the chill air of the veranda and back in the further door to the warmth of the now low-simmering fires.

There were several more verses, growing increasingly ribald, until finally my aunt would rise, curtsy gracefully, thank everyone for coming and wish everyone goodnight. All good things must come to an end. Everyone present knew, as they milled about saying farewells and finding their coats, that something special had passed here in the blinking of an eye.

When the sun finally rose, guests too tired to return home the night before or who lived too far away could be found bunked on the extra veranda beds, which were permanent fixtures in case it was just too hot to sleep inside during the summer. The overflow would find shelter in the shearers' quarters, or the wool shed, which were empty this time of year.

Breakfast would be a drawn-out affair as sleep was rubbed from eyes and everyone availed themselves of the enamelled wash basins in the sunlit courtyard to freshen up, washing their faces in the gushing stream of water from the high faucets before emptying the water collected in the enamelled wash-bowls onto the grape vines growing against the wall below. The women took turns flipping eggs and crisping bacon or remnants hacked from the remains of the prior night's grand repast as the line of stragglers snaked through the kitchen. The gaiety of the previous night languished like the lovelorn and we children delighted at waking to find the house still in party mode.

Those who had brought or ridden horses attended to them while other guests lingered late in the garden playing tennis or enjoying the remaining roast lamb and chilled cucumber sandwiches on fresh-baked bread for lunch. After eating, the riders raced their horses over cross country trials, fording streams, clearing gullies and leaping logs while under a clock to pass the time in a pursuit with which all were familiar.

These events were usually fun but not all recountings are. I once accepted an offer to ride someone's leggy dappled grey Arab pony. She was a beautiful creature with dark points. I had never ridden her before nor was I familiar with her quirks. Ponies are notoriously naughty and as I swung into the saddle, she (never trust a pony) snatched the bit in her teeth with a toss of her pretty head, and I was atop a pounding mass of animal over which I had not the slightest control. As she bounced across the gully effortlessly, I saw an enormous pile of loosely coiled barbed fencing wire ahead.

There was no way the pony had any chance of clearing this especially running up the slope, but she made a beeline for the mess at full speed, and I had to prepare for the seemingly evident failing leap and the following tangled-pony-on-top-of-me demise. At the last moment she pivoted ninety degrees to the right, almost sending me headlong into mangle. Only my hand wrapped in her mane saved me and I somehow recovered my seat and took the change of direction to turn the pony tightly, her nose was almost touching her tail before she relented and stopped. I dismounted and casually retrieved my hat.

As I mounted again the pony repeated its taking-the-bit trick and galloped full speed at a tall, barbed wire fence about twenty metres away. I knew nothing of this horse's capabilities so again prepared for a seemingly impossible uphill jump. At the last moment the pony abruptly propped, coming to a sudden stop at the fence line, its front feet solidly together. I shot over her withers and, in a frantic effort to save myself, reflexively flung my arms around her neck. When all the moving parts finally came to a stop both our noses were just inches from the ground on the other side of the fence from the rest of the beast, my hands knotted tightly under her chin. This was not like my family's polite horses who warned us of dangers, not plunged us into them. I remounted on a very tight rein and rode calmly back to the alarmed crowd of onlookers, shaken but managing to keep the horse under control. I was never so glad to dismount.

Horse games over, people began to finish their afternoon tea and take their leave. The lesson that good manners and kindness cost nothing but are the fabric that binds the human web was not lost on me.

My grandmother possessed such grace that if anyone complimented one of her pieces of artistic loveliness she was just as likely to force it on them saying:" No *dear, please have it. You like it so much more than I do.*" Perhaps she saw it was one less disaster awaiting a wayward cat. Finally the last guests departed, some days after arriving.

These moments of rapture could only be truly appreciated after the fact when our old dusty norms and the ubiquitous outback flies settled back in and, in hindsight, one realized that in those moments we were swept up in an epiphany where the self and all its worldly baggage were carried away and the pure essence of being human shone, a magical lightness of being, as if we had, for a moment, passed through some cosmic portal that closed again after the last guest departed and life settled back into its routine of enigmas.

§

My uncle and a work crew were building a new fence. They erected a long line of sturdy red gum posts ready to string the wires the next day. When they returned early the next morning to thread the zinc wires while the dew still glinted on the long grass they found, to their utter astonishment, peering through the thin veil of early morning mist, a koala perched mutely stop almost every post in the fence line.

These sage creatures seemed silently enthused by the miraculous appearance in their ancient world of a new invention ...flat topped "trees". It must have been a socially levelling experience for them, but the impact of this vision reverberated through generations of my family. One can only imagine the thoughts of these enigmatic creatures on the sudden appearance of such an innovation after an eternity of solitude perched in the slippery forks of gums. You can't make this stuff up!

It leaves me to wonder if secretly they still don't, in the dead of night, all steal over to the *flat trees* to meditate after eating their fill of moon-kissed gum tips. No one can know all the secrets of the night. That they came to investigate and try something new on for size prompts more questions than can possibly be answered by *"book learning"* for they are generally considered solitary creatures. Such daily enigmas left us struggling to interpret our own reality with any imported rationale. Such events only rendered us all the more solitary.

It takes a keen eye to spot koalas high in the branches of the gums. They are revered by all. By Aboriginal decree one must be facing death from starvation before killing such a powerful totem. They are regarded as the *Wise Old Men of the Woods* but there was the subtle message in some native lore that anyone who failed to share would become a grumpy old koala.

Up close and personal they are heavyweights and defy the obvious cuddle factor with enormous claws used to scale their craggy kingdom where they live, largely dependent for moisture on their dewy gum tip diet. There were many when my dad was a boy, but an epidemic of some kind swept through the area and few survived. Sadly, it has now been years since I saw one in the wild though some remain in far flung corners of my family's former land. It is a case of everyone thinking there are lots of them 'someplace else' when habitat is destroyed, usually by greed. They are fickle eaters and one can only hope ignorance of their needs does not mean that we didn't know what we had till it's gone.

§

In my sojourns by the billabong with my father I learned to slip into conversations with myself and these spirits that surrounded me. That all did not live such a life was beyond the boundary of my innocence. My "village" comprised my immediate family - grandparents, parents, uncles/aunts, two brothers and several younger cousins - and those living on neighbouring equally remote properties linked by the red dirt tracks through the wilderness whose dust clung to everything and everyone like a second skin. That any other world existed was incomprehensible to my young brain.

I learned to cherish the laughter of kookaburras and the pleasure of meals of unforgettable delicacy, of loved embraces and kind strangers and the warm fuzzy marsupial faces that daily confronted me. I hear their voices still, ringing as clear as an early morning cow bell pealing in crystal alpine air.

This was no bleak landscape of existential dread but an unbroken solitude where words seemed redundant. This was not the pain of aloneness but an overabundance of absolute, endless, majestic isolation. It's winds caressing my hair; it's sun warm on my skin; it's rain wet on my face; these are the sacred murmurings my soul yearns to hear whispering in its ear.

In The Shadows of The Honey Trees

The ingredients of my life are my song. The rhythm of the cadence of words intoxicates my brain into taking voyages buoyed up by the remnants of memory ...a little of this ...a touch of that ...coloured with incantations as old as the earth itself ...all slightly distorted by space and time and here baked together like a cake, the various ingredients now inseparable with the whole definitely greater than the sum of the parts.

Days on the station always began with Dad rising early and starting the fire in the wood burning cooking stove in the kitchen before taking his big zinc pail to the milk shed where our well-trained cows waited to give up their warm white bounty of milk. The cats joined him and sat by, patiently waiting for him to squirt milk directly into their open mouths from the cow's teat. He was among his friends.

After feeding the horses and letting the chickens and turkeys and the peafowl out (the latter two were apt to prefer to roost in the hayshed rafters) he would return in time for breakfast which ranged from rolled oats and toast with home-made conserves to bacon or lamb chops with eggs.

At the end of the day any leftover milk was offered as a treat to the horses who stood at the back garden gate promptly at 5 p.m. every day without fail, ensuring that no one forgot this ritual.

In the summer evenings we often had family picnic dinners by the swimming hole in the nearby creek, with a sumptuous feast of cold cuts, salads and cake. If we lollygagged here by the stream long into languid evenings, we would encounter kangaroos and wallabies coming down from their hillside encampments to drink at the cool springs before setting off to forage in the cool of the evening air.

Some were pets, which had returned to the wild. Kangaroos are almost identical but any of our pets would acknowledge us and, smelling familiar treats, would approach cautiously looking for a carrot or a stalk of celery. Handing a carrot to a trusting wild creature as extraordinary as a kangaroo has a kind of *Dian Fossey* moment about it but my family thought it *"de rigor"* for a century. Once during a brutal drought Mum looked out the kitchen window to see a mother roo with a yearling and another joey in her pouch browsing in the shady part of the homestead garden, the only patch of green grass for miles. Our old pet felt enough at home, even after an absence of years, to know where to find the greenest grass. The station dogs, which would normally bark wildly at the end of their chains at the approach of any stranger, human or animal, would recognize these wild pets as having privilege and not offer a single challenge when they approached.

Being an avid reader I devoured my family's library. *Ion Indress* was the primary resource which addressed many of the issues of the colonial day - especially the saga of the crocodile hunters and the associated myths these great reptiles inspired. They were almost hunted to extinction by colonial demand but have since rebounded with such vengeance they are now held responsible for the disappearance of thousands of cattle from far flung acres every year. Indress' words explored such frontier fears.

As well as the crocodile hunters there were the tales of the wilderness wanderings on camel of people drunk on the raw beauty of that moment when, after foregoing all of society's creature comforts, one is left completely and utterly dependant on one's own resources - alone with the majesty of the wilderness, for richer or poorer, for better or worse, in sickness and in health …until death. These tales, and others, led me to explore the world through words …usually slanted colonial era literature with a good dose of classics …tales you hope your grandchildren might one day read and enjoy the same lessons: *Rudyard Kipling, May Gibbs* and later *Voltaire, Castaneda, Marquez, Allende* and *Ovid* who all gave me voice through their cerebral wanderings.

When I complained of boredom Mum quickly showed me how to read the dictionary …it was an easy, immediate fix. Open it at any page, read until you have read enough, then close it and open it afresh at another page next time. I found the limitlessness of the combination of twenty-six letters fascinating.

With an aunt in Sydney who was a pioneer of modern library lending I was fed a steady stream of intellectually stimulating books. The words of *T. Lobsang Rampa*, among many others, appeared miraculously via a brown paper packaging tied up with string delivered into the wilderness by the *Mail God* who appeared twice a week. It was akin to finding the can opener to your mind under a Honey Tree at the end of a long dirt track. You just had to know which tree to look under and, more importantly, you had to look. As Albert Einstein mused, the mind, like a parachute, only functions when open.

The *Mail God* was the only regular movement on our narrow dirt road, two rutted wheel tracks that were our only link to the outside world. The *Mail God* trafficked in dust, a great red cloud of it billowed out from all four wheels, the belching of the old, rusted blue '*station dragon*' driven by an unseen entity. It wasn't just mail and our returned lessons that were left there but fresh bread from a baker in a village some twenty-five kilometres away and the daily newspaper, where I would eventually cut my journalistic teeth. It was a visceral connection but significant that word of the greater world was invited into that remote place. Sometimes we

Platypus Flats

would find a wooden case of bananas deposited in the shade under the five-gallon drum that served as our mailbox ...or a case of mandarins or oranges, gifts from distant unknown-to-me family delivered by the *Mail God* who was personified by the dusty blue *"station dragon"* that would coast silently down the hill toward our mailbox. I never saw the *Mail God* up close, not once in fifty years. When the dust settled the leavings under the mail tree were received with the joy of finding *manna* from heaven. We had often eaten half a loaf of the still oven warm bread by the time our little legs reached home with our cache.

It was rough travelling over dozens of miles of dusty track to the nearest service centre, but generations of bush living had bred a canny sense of creative resolution. Dad famously grew beefsteak tomatoes and beans and any variety of melons and squash and maintained a large orchard. Mum encouraged strawberries and rhubarb and garlic and kept the egg crates filled. She was definitely a poultry woman and we had every kind of domesticated fowl. Grape vines shaded the courtyard in summer and admitted the sun in winter and kept our pallets tempted in the late summer when the various varieties of grapes took turns ripening.

Once every month or so a trader would roll down the drive in a small truck outfitted with a mobile store on the rear bed. He was a small Hindu gentleman who wore a neat vest with a satin back and he would flip up the doors that held everything in place on the shelves while he bumped and rattled over the landscape, pulling into station after station to offer up his wares. He was a welcome relief to the dearth of human interactions out here and I'm not sure Mum didn't buy more than she needed just to keep encouraging the visits. He carried the basics, flour, sugar, essence of this and pinches of that and brushes and other kitchen small goods, things which might require a lot of leg work to find all in one place in the city.

He also carried an assortment of root vegetables wrapped in wet newspaper and canned fruit and vegetables and even, on occasion, small pieces of furniture or carpets that he may have taken in trade. One never knew the plight of others who inhabited the *Never-Never*. People played their cards close to their chest. Some came to escape their past while others, like my family, had simply been there for so long that any other option seemed lacklustre. While some properties were huge by the standards of a crowded world the tempest of drought and misadventure could soon leave a family "dirt poor" ...meaning they may own lots of dirt, but it had bled them of all their cash.

This kind Hindu gentleman was assisted by a young lad about fourteen-years-old, who he said he had taken on as a helper when his parents had perished in a fire somewhere along his route. Such arrangements for orphaned children were not unheard of when far flung communities were faced with such dilemmas. Historically there certainly were not any official forms of welfare. My maternal x2 great- grandparents adopted a young, orphaned neighbour to add to the twelve children already at their table. What was one more? It was the right thing to do, and I doubt any paperwork was completed.

Trips to town were only done in times of great need or when taking stock or goods to market. My great-grandfather went to town once a year to deliver the wool from his flocks to the docks in Sydney, where it was loaded onto ships and ferried to the Belgian and Manchester wool markets. His shopping list of essentials was generous as his shepherds would draw from this station store against their salaries. I can only assume they helped themselves to fresh lamb as needed.

But the advent of the railway line changed that and made the three-hundred-mile wagon trek to Sydney unnecessary, and the advent of unlimited zinc wire soon made the lot of shepherds obsolete as fences were erected crisscrossing the land and the sheep and cattle could then largely be left to their own devices. Then the dingoes were fenced out to the eastern escarpment when the government erected a six feet tall netting fence many hundreds of kilometres along the relatively flat forested rim of the plateau.

My great-grandfather, the founder of *Platypus Flats*, was a brave and determined young man, one of the new breed of sons of first generation invaders of that subtropical wonderland, Australia, a land of harsh but lavish environs, who saw his opportunity when *The Australian Land Company* divested itself of its early colonial land monopoly in the late 1800s. I was always aware that I enjoyed the life I did because of decisions he made decades before my arrival. At the crossing of the Sagittarian stars that signalled my future I survived to thrive in this land of bush critters in a valley so vast that the beating wings of a million migrating butterflies made small demands on its confines.

Once a year, driven by unfathomable forces, they fluttered by wingtip to wingtip; a great crescendo of migrating silence; pulsing and undulating on breathless zephyrs; murmurating effortlessly like a giant sheet of embroidered cream silk tossing in the thin diaphanous blue of the sky. They were buoyed up by the notes of the rare sonatas my mother hammered out on the old upright piano below, oblivious to the ghostly enigma floating silently overhead.

In The Shadows of The Honey Trees

Mum was the embodiment of the earth goddess *Pachamama* and mothered every creature in its hour of need. Her bush medicine skills were never wrong whether it was us or some hapless animal which needed her knowledge and compassion. She taught me to love all life and those around me. She warmed sodden ducklings (rescued from flood waters) in a basket in the wood-fired oven; she accommodated orphaned baby kangaroos in sewn-up sweater pouches hung by the stone fireplaces; and presided over the birth of everything from calves and foals to hatchlings; and for twenty-five years she was shadowed by the charismatic furry silhouette of Cheeky. Of anyone I have ever known she loved all life the best. (I am inclined to agree with the Hindus belief that the gate to heaven is manned by every creature we met in our life, and they get to decide if we are worthy of entry or not!)

CHAPTER 7

Further, Farther and Father

"*Strength does not come from physical capacity. It comes from an indomitable will.*"

—Mahatma Gandhi

'*Father!*' …Even the very word hints at something distant, somewhere perhaps a bit '*farther*,' just beyond '*further*'. Every young boy looks to his father but mine was a creature of isolation. Day after day Bon mounted his big, beautiful tri-coloured horse Rajah and rode off into the *Never-Never* where he ambled along in the shade of the forests of Honey Trees that blessed our land.

He had been born to this vacuous wilderness where there was little need for the human word. In this splendid luxury of space he communed with the vastness in silence, addressing only his horse or his dogs.

He lacked fathering skills. In retrospect, knowing what I now know, this was hereditary. His grandfather's father had died young leaving his grandfather Eagle fatherless at age four. Eagle in turn found his footing and went on to financial success in this new frontier but with the tragic loss of one son, estrangement from his stepson and a brutal interpersonal conflict with the last remaining son, and his wife, must have left a vacuum in Dad's young life. In 1892, the year Eagle founded *Platypus Flats*, he married Janet, the granddaughter of early pioneers and, on her paternal side, the granddaughter of the terrified sixteen-year-old orphan of the Irish potato famine, who had arrived pregnant and alone. It is my duty and my honour to carry forward the flag borne by such brave, determined people. It was a period of great change. With galactic gravity my ancestors planted the seeds that created my universe and all that revolved around it.

A severe recession hindered the establishment of the station in those early years. As luck would have it Eagle's new father-in-law owned the "steam donkey" sawmill and the family rode out that recession cutting and sawing the giant stringybark trees and constructing the rambling homestead, the adjoining carriage houses, the shearers' hut, the nearby stables, the blacksmith shop and the slightly distant shearing shed that could, at a pinch, accommodate six hundred sheep under cover *(footnote)*. For its age this was industrial strength wool production, the property grazing thousands of the world's finest wool-producing Merino sheep. A hundred and fifteen years later the shed is still in use.

Eagle and Janet started out constructing a simple two room hut with a lean-to kitchen and bathroom, complete with galvanized iron bathtub. This is where they lived for the first two years while building the homestead. When the homestead was eventually completed the hut was used to accommodate the station hands or, in my time, the occasional professional hunters who flew in from Germany to hunt the big-horned wild angora goats which roamed the steep backcountry. When these buildings were demolished a

Platypus Flats

century later it was discovered that every nail used had been forged by hand.**

With the push toward Federation of the new Australian nation it seemed that things were finally on the up and up. When the homestead completed, Eagle travelled to Sydney and bought a commemorative silver pocket watch which, for the next century, ticked off the seconds, the minutes and the hours dictating the station's stops and starts. It is still as accurate as it was a century ago. He then went to the Homebush stock markets and purchased ten thousand quality Merino sheep and set about walking this sea of bleating *Ovis aries* a long three hundred miles home.

It took almost three months following the stock routes (public grazing lanes) that crisscross the nation. Every day the herd of forty thousand sharp hooves churned up the dust destroying as much pasture as they ate. By selling off selections from the flock to other stations he passed, when he pushed the last five thousand weary stragglers through the home gate three months later, he had effectively stocked the property for the cost of the time spent droving. Given Australia's brutally unpredictable weather, it had been a stunning gamble with sweat equity the stake.

In the wool business there is only one paycheck a year. The clip was pressed into tightly packed bales weighing three hundred pounds and shipped via bullock wagon to the rail head, then to Sydney, for shipment to the UK for sale. In the early 1900s the longshore workers union in Sydney called a strike and refused to load the wool onto the ships. Eagle

---

** *(Sheep cannot be shorn if the wool is wet and a thousand sheep is only about three of four day's work for a modern three stand shed)*

took it upon himself to strike-break and loaded the wool himself with the assistance of his three sons.

The unions retaliated by torching his magnificent new shearing shed and his early model Ford before his youngest son, Raymond, was shot in a tragedy of epic proportions.

Fifteen-year-old Ray failed to return to the homestead one evening not long after the arson incidents. A frantic search into the night failed to find him and it was mid-morning before the cawing of a pair of crows in the middle of a field some distance from the homestead attracted the attention of the searchers. Ray was found unconscious with a bullet wound to the head but no sign of his own gun. The crows had already pecked out his eyes.

He was rushed the fifty-six miles to the nearest hospital by buggy, the recently burned-out wreckage of the new A model Ford of no use in the emergency.

It was a frantic trip that seemed to take forever with Janet, tears streaming down her face, cradling the limp body of her almost lifeless youngest son in her arms as the horses gave their best. The two older boys raced ahead down the mountain on the "mailman's track", a steep, rough but much shorter bridle path, while the buggy navigated the difficult cut down the face of the mountain that had been hewn out of the difficult descent by hand by the convicts. The boys were ready with replacement horses at the roadside at another family property located almost halfway to the hospital when the exhausted group arrived. They quickly switched the animals in the harnesses and led the weary relay team away to the stable as the parents rushed off. The boys followed on fresh mounts of their own after tending to the exhausted animals.

At the hospital Raymond was pronounced dead and sent to the morgue while the family retreated, shattered, to mourn in the shuttered accommodations above the starched white linens of the darkened dining rooms at the nearby Royal Hotel. Still reeling from the worst, nothing could have prepared them for the shocking events of the next morning.

They were racked with fresh grief when they learned that Raymond had been found sloughed against the inside of the mortuary door. He had obviously not been dead, had regained consciousness and had blindly searched for an exit from his tomb. This time he was truly dead, and his terrible fate became a family *bunyip*, carefully buried in the swamp of exasperation and grief to never to be mentioned again until a chance encounter between two unrelated women almost half a century later.

My mother was attending a church picnic where she was wearing her name tag when she was approached by a tall woman of approximately the same age ...seventy-five! She introduced herself as 'Letty' and asked if Mum was "a Weabonga West". Mum replied that her late husband was. Letty explained that her father had been my paternal grandfather's estranged stepbrother and then the two women sat down and began a conversation that would forever change our lives.

Letty had met my mother before. Fifty years earlier they had been in the maternity ward of the local hospital together and had been the only two women who gave birth that day ...both having baby boys. One of those babies was me. When my grandparents arrived to welcome me, Letty had immediately realized who they were, but she did not know the details of the bad blood in the family so held her tongue and did not reveal herself. It was she who told my mother of the saga of Raymond's death.

In The Shadows of The Honey Trees

Mum, quite excited, phoned me to tell me the news. I listened on the other side of the globe transfixed as this muddy family *bunyip* emerged from the swamp of ages. But I had an addition to the tale that neither of them could have foreseen. I had been friends with this other great-grandson of Janet when I was about seventeen. It only flashed through the fog of half a century when Mum revealed that Letty's son had died in a car crash when he was only eighteen. I knew we shared the same birthday but never imagined we were born in the same ward to the same extended family. What were the odds of stumbling onto that knowledge that half a century of silence later? A little late for our friendship but it felt again like a wind from invisible wings had again pushed me hither.

Janet's eldest boy Arthur, after marrying the daughter of the family on the adjoining ten thousand acres and building a new home to the original homestead plan at *Platypus Flats*, had a falling out of great magnitude with his stepfather, Eagle. Arthur left, tearing his house down board by board and taking it with him loaded on bullock drays. Arthur's name would never be spoken again for almost seventy-five years. The first clue to his existence came when I was about fourteen and was rummaging through the family library one rainy day and found a notation in an old bible stating: *"Arthur H. has received a thousand pounds and has no further claim on the estate."*

I remember walking into the cozy family afternoon tea party gathered around the roaring fire in the cavernous kitchen and asking: *"Who's Arthur H. and why did he get a thousand pounds and why did he have a claim against the estate in the first place?"* It went over like a lead balloon. There was a quick explanation that he was grandfather's half-brother and then the subject abruptly changed direction leaving me with my first experience of familial whiplash as the *bunyip* of Arthur's estrangement half a century earlier was herded back into the swamp for another thirty-five years.

Letty didn't know the whole story but after Arthur had struck out on his own, a violent hailstorm had pummelled a thousand of his newly shown ewes and their lambs to death. It was at this point Arthur had returned to *Platypus Flats* with Letty as a child, cap-in-hand, to elicit aid. Janet had given her a kitten, so the meeting had resonated with young Letty. Arthur received a thousand pounds and *"had no further claim against the estate"* to help him on his way after the disaster ...and more than half a century of silence settled again like a shroud over the matter until that fateful day at the church picnic.

It all must have been a tragic loss for Eagle and Janet. Their only remaining son, my grandfather Bob, who had taken up the lonely duties of shepherd at age twelve, then chose to marry Violet, his first half-cousin. That too must have gone over like a lead balloon.

To pile tragedy upon tragedy, Janet then died of the Spanish Flu one Christmas morning. For Eagle it was a final failure. It became an untenable situation for him, a *damnatio memoriae.* With continued animosity (and blame for failing Janet during her bout of the flu) from Violet and Bob, who had built their own replica of the homestead a few hundred yards further down the rise, Eagle found the solitude of such 'close' estrangement unbearable.

One bright morning when the birds of paradise were singing their melodious chorus and the air was still redolent with dew, he hitched his beautiful pair of grey horses to the best carriage; loaded it with his prized camera collection and a suitcase containing all his possessions; set the sprawling timber homestead ablaze; and vanished down the long drive forever into the wilderness with the maid and her four-year-old son in tow. Eagle's name, along with Arthur's, was simply never spoken of again and all statues to them both were melted down.

The glorious galactic solitude Eagle had created out of dust collapsed around him like an imploding star. That of which he had dared to dream when his sun had once shone young now set, crushed and battered in a blaze of defeat. He was consumed by the wilderness and was never seen nor heard from again until eighty years later when I discovered a photograph of him in the council chambers in the small New England town of Walcha, where he had served some years as mayor before establishing *Platypus Flats*.

Bon, at that stage an only child, must have felt abandoned by this loss of his grandfather due to some little-understood war between Eagle and Bob and Violet. Having no experience on which to base a normal father-son relationship he bumbled on in self-imposed alone-ness in a realm of extraordinary "alones". He was never one to make a meal of his various vicissitudes and took life on the chin. It was that or go mad. There simply was nothing to be gained by talking about it. He did as his father had done and retreated into the canyons of his mind and remained there for the rest of his life, in a rich, promised land where disbelief was not an option.

He became as one with the great two-metre-long monitor lizards, the water dragons, the koalas and the songbirds that overflowed the valleys with the most beautiful of choir. Caught in a *dreamtime*, that fold between past and future that is always present, he found it easier to plod on in his isolation as it was laid out for him rather than upset the applecart of life. He simply let his future unfurl at the whim of the winds.

CHAPTER 8

There is no God of Boarding School

"Object to violence because when it appears to do good, the good is only temporary. The evil it does is permanent."

—Mahatma Gandhi

1964

From the warm cocoon of such splendid isolation I stepped out on the most difficult path of my life, my own voyage of a million years. At the tender age of barely four thousand sleeps I was tipped unceremoniously into the hollow, vicious jaws of a boarding school.

My initial enthusiasm for a secondary school education was quickly blunted by brutal physical, psychological and moral abuse at the hands of brutal elder prefects who operated completely without adult oversight. That a democratic government department charged with 'education' could so seriously neglect the care of so many children held on an isolated campus and that the secret society ruled by abuse could go unnoticed for decades is beyond my comprehension. It was a place of infamy.

Severed from all that was safe and familiar there was nowhere to turn when the walls, the roof and the windows of every social construct I had grown up with ...was suddenly

In The Shadows of The Honey Trees

stripped away until I stood naked. Then I was brutally assaulted with every form of abuse imaginable.

I was a willful child and did not respond well to the systemic abuse hurled at me from all quarters - older students, ruthless prefects and unforgiving teachers alike. The sunlight in my life turned dark. I was drawn into a black hole, a point where time is stopped and from which there can be no escape.

My body was whipped with supple canes by teachers and more treacherous knotted electric light chords fashioned into cat-o-nine tails by cruel prefects who ruled our dormitories. I was rendered mute. No words can describe what happened without inflicting moral injury on you, dear reader ...the physical and sexual abuse; the humiliations; the brutal retaliatory assaults if every demand wasn't met; the cruel coercive control of every aspect of my own and others' lives. It was a sick buffet of debauchery with physical and sexual abuse served as main course. Days turned into nights turned into weeks turned into months turned into years! It became my personal *1001 Nights* where I had to talk fast and never miss an opportunity to elude my tormentors. Unlike the heroine in that saga I had no one to share it with. I was completely alone. I felt ashamed. It was an awful feeling. The feral rage of injustice kept me alive.

Perhaps I carried my pain too proudly. But why not? I wasn't going to let them break me. Human spirits need any available ounce of encouragement at any age. I had none. I had to be the adult in my life.

Home became a faraway mirage of all that is lovely, yet distant; beyond the far horizon; magnified even, in the balmy light of nostalgia. I didn't realize that this was a permanent condition, but it has remained a solid cornerstone of my far-flung life, which was less a rational choice and more a motivational fearless curiosity about what must come next …that things must get better somewhere else. We should all live fearlessly until we are dead. I learned that when you fell, for whatever reason, you picked yourself up, dusted yourself off and kept going.

I squeamed silently in fear in my bed at night that I would be the one singled out by an abuser. It was almost a relief when I only had to witness someone else treated cruelly. When I did suffer direct abuse, my mind vacated to the center of the carpet in the living room at *Platypus Flats*. Beneath the pink frosted glass fish, directly under the table on which it stood, was a thumb print of sacred kookaburra-blue at the very center of the exotic carpet. It was a sign, a small rectangular pool of sky reflected in water seemingly at odds with the convolutions of the rest of the design …it was geometry in chaos. *"I am here"* it stated loudly, a skylight in the floor or, perhaps a well from which I bent in supplication to drink for my psychological survival.

This small rectangle was encircled by a fence of red madder set in an oblique field of faded-lichen greens and golds. In turn this was surrounded by a bleached field of red madder that opened into a cascade of fish scale forms, each a different muted hue, unfolding on and on into an intricate lotus form, fringed in silver silken threads. This dreamy garden exploded in a confusion of multiplying eights, each framed by an elegant cartouche of screeching rooster reds edged by an escarpment of sculpted midnight-blue mohair mountains that glowed with the fierce velour of a cloudless desert night, or perhaps the *moire* of water rippling in a channel. The pattern became increasingly tumultuous with wild coils of vines, intertwining at the boundaries, each bearing enormous ornately woven blooms of muted hues set against a riot of

In The Shadows of The Honey Trees

faded blood reds that merged with Kurrajong greens while more fleshy tones buoyed up copious flora at its edge.

Rivers of sacred blue meandered between the fields of every color with the regularity of ancient irrigation ditches dug into the earth a thousand years ago to channel life to a desert, making it bloom. There were the great purple stamens that extended from the central cartouche with the same sexual urgency that the Grass Trees and the Gymea Lilies exhibited outside under the Kurrajong. It was magical thinking - a parallel universe into which I could fall and become invisible. By focusing on the intimate detail I found I could make time stand still.

The pattern of golds and greens and madder wound themselves sinuously around the perimeter, curling across a field of deepest blue. The rich velour of the deeper-than-deepest midnight blue sparkled in the light ...the mohair standing remarkably straight and bright despite a century of wear. Floral imaginings of illuminating richness curled across the midnight field, creating the illusion of a view of a glorious rectangular garden from the perspective of someone riding a magic carpet high above on a moonlit summer night.

At the corners of the carpet the cool blue waters, channelled so carefully around this floral dream, burst forth in the rushing coils of falling silken water so expressive I could feel the coolness of the spray upon my face.

Then came another midnight blue fence, perhaps an inch wide, which wound its way around the field before exploding into a final border of more rude reds and an intoxicating wave of blooms that edged the whole phantasmagorical riot of magical illusionment.

Two final perimeters of blue, first the kingfisher blue and finally, a last wall of midnight mohair, ended in a wild white weft of tufted cotton that splashed across the cool dark hardwood floor like a crashing ocean wave rushing over a polished ebony beach.

If the abuse hadn't stopped by the time I had worked my way through the intricate maze of knotted fleece to the edge of this *"other"* universe I could always go back to the blue thumbprint at the center and begin my journey again.

When I finally climbed sobbing back into bed my tears watered these gardens, into which I learned to escape, and refreshed the ponds of kookaburra blue and those thin rills of silver silk that brought to my bleak landscape a tinkling vein of hope in a world otherwise devoid of joy. The chemical resonance of those events settled out in the sediment on my hippocampus where, while the physical abuses healed, the evisceration of my soul forever remains stained, always just a hair breadth away, framed between the pair of large Chinese urns which stood as silent witnesses on either side of the hearth at the end of that beautiful escape carpet, the demure figures peering out forever silent from their pink palace courtyards, expressions of shock frozen on their faces, witnessing everything from their far pavilions but, like me, rendered eternally mute in the profusion of flowering vines and flying birds that soared across the white porcelain ground above their heads. The sad memories remain trapped between the gilded dragons on the shoulders of these beautiful urns and the silent double foo dogs on their necks.

I clung to '*Hope, that feathered thing, that perches in the soul, and sings the tune without the words, and never stops - at all.*'

This was my singular truth. Someone called Emily Dickinson had written it. I found it in a book in the school library. I had no inkling who she was or where she may have lived but her words printed in black ink on fading paper bridged a chasm so deep and wide I couldn't see the other side. I found strength in her words as time dragged on and a sense of helplessness pervaded my world. She must have known about the *Lord God Bird* to write something like that. It gave me a ray of hope to cling to.

Those words buoyed me up when *Miseria* came to dwell, followed closely by her hand-servants *Inadequacy*, *Hopelessness* and, ultimately, *Denial*. There can be no forgetting. The face of evil cannot be unseen.

I stumbled on in ignorance. It was a bottomless zoo of lusts; a cruel harem of petty evils, the sum of which was loneliness and the fear of 'when-everything-is-lost'. I walked a road of intimate sadness; of humiliations; beatings; whippings with knotted electrical cords; physical and sexual assaults and coercive control of every aspect of my and others lives all the while under threat of unknown further abuse. It was a land populated by me alone; a place we all sometimes pass in life only it didn't pass as sadness is supposed to pass. I was not alone. It did not help that there were many other victims. It cannot be forgotten as much as one might wish to forget. The memory just doesn't fade.

There was nothing I, the child, could do about it. It remains, a chemical brand on my feathered soul, a desolate footprint that can never be erased, crushed like a dove under the boot of oppression. My hatred of these cruel captors was my hidden treasure. It sustained me on my long, dark journey. I had to live with a depraved level of cruelty akin to being forced to dig one's own grave, with the added barbarism of not knowing if I was to be buried alive or dead. As it turned out I was to be buried alive, forever tainted by memories akin to the reeking miasma of an invisible slovenly drunk, beside whom I must sit for the rest of my days.

Platypus Flats

Apologies may drop like pearls from the lips of those now representing those responsible for my childhood neglect, yet they evaporate, forgotten, like drunken slobber, before they reach the dry, cracked surface of my soul.

At night I wandered in my dreams, stepping in puddles of luminosity that followed me wherever I trod. Within that whirling gyre all manner of madness existed; ghosts, spirits and visitations; restless pursuits and frantic searches for unknown things lost; and everything else that my brain could conjure in sleep to ease my waking terrors. It was a time of confusion clouded with fear and desire and awakening passion. How easily the sky-blue robin eggs of my fragile dreams could have been crushed ...the frail porcelain of undreamt promises dashed to the floor by evil forces greater than I. But sometimes wishing still worked. The seemingly fragile human spirit is like mud and when fired under extremes becomes an object of admirable resilience. *Ad aspera virtus! (In adversity strength!)*. The Latin motto mocked me. I was powered by an internal monologue, quiet yet subversive. It ordered words like bricks in a road, leading to new horizons and to unknown shores of the mind, washed by the pulsing universal tides of my vivid imagination.

When I saw my parents, no words would come. I opened my mouth, but the sounds remained unspoken, caught in my throat like the unwritten words in a pen. I felt betrayed by my own voice. I tried to speak but emitted only an aching howl. My rivened soul infected my jaws; the words throbbed in the back of my throat like erupting molars; I could speak only tears of desperation which I wanted my parents to understand. How could I make the invisible visible when the words were but twisted embryonic forms that squirmed insidiously in my gut like poisonous tapeworms I could not expel? My parents' own tears at my distress came from a different lake than mine. We all only have so many tears in us and then we eventually run dry. I went back to my prison. I saw no other options and I don't think they did either from their naive position. I was lost. I had only myself. I had to be strong. I had to be brave. I had come to an abrupt and unexpected corner in life and had hurried off the sunny way and down a steep slippery embankment into the treachery of a dank, septic swamp from which there was no escape. The only thing I knew with certainty was that life could never go back to the way it was. I went forward through this dark place I couldn't know.

There was no use dissecting what happened yesterday. I had to be hyper-alert to avoid as many negative interactions as possible today. I awoke each day fearing the path I had to tread. At age eleven years I had unwittingly stepped from one solitude into another …an unfathomable opposite parallel universe invisible to outside observers who, ignorant of my reality, no doubt envied the educational *"opportunity"* I had been afforded. I was instead delivered to a remote country campus peopled by a barbarous secret society with the initiates subjected to every form of abuse imaginable. There was not a single receptive adult face in sight. It became my personal hidden bunyip. All the people I had known before receded from my view almost completely. I was '*lost*' in every sense of the word.

Every time after a weekend at home when my father's car made that final turn into the long deceptive avenue of Grevillea trees that lead to the three-hundred-acre campus I felt betrayed again and again. It was the gate to my *Hell*. My heart surged tumultuously, torn between fond hoping and vain longing for something I seemed powerless to affect.

Cerberus barked invisibly at the back of my soul every time the car turned in at those fateful iron gates. One head barked to announce my arrival, one barked to prevent me leaving and the other head secretly savaged my soul in a place no one else could see.

I escaped to the library. Being surrounded by a wall of words felt safe. The librarian was the only sane person in the place. She was also the English Master. I excelled. There were shelves and shelves of books, row upon row of faded lies …stories told the way some writer wanted it to be written …words of the dead telling tales. It's how *"writtens"* morph into mythical *"truths"* to be recited and passed on unquestioned by the following flock.

I had only to put my finger on an image hidden in the pages …a planter in an exotic courtyard; a parrot on a pirate's shoulder; a horse in the turbulence of battle …and I would be transported there …to long away climes and far ago places, into another world with the innocence of a child discovering the new universe of a worm squirming on the bottom of a puddle. I'd sit there with my finger on the page as if of intently reading but my mind was far, far away; beyond the wall of books; over the furthest horizon; yonder; in a place past the edges of my imagining as if I had been sucked up by a transformative vortex of words into worlds I could not possibly know.

I cradled this elusive madness which I had no need to explain. There were none of today's electronic distractions for directions. It was a dark abomination of aloneness akin to the dank ship's holds which had transported my ancestors from afar. The only window into the wider world was a small black and white television set we were permitted to watch for an hour a week (the headmaster selecting from one of only two available channels) and after we spent an hour in the classroom writing letters home, establishing the form my parental relationship would follow for the rest of my life.

When I made it through a whole day without being brutally whipped by someone with authority over me it was a good day. But there was always someone, teacher or senior, ready to squish any joy I might have allowed myself with the same glee that mean kids get from squishing hapless bugs. They enjoyed producing terror. Being able to make myself invisible in the wilderness sense, was my only escape but it didn't always work. They could beat me, but they couldn't make me cry.

My abusers had to go above and beyond their last brutal assault in order to gratify themselves. It was all about violent domination, power and control fuelled by nicotine addiction …sociopaths with antisocial personality disorders for which there is no cure. They knew right from wrong. They just didn't care. Laws and morality meant nothing to them. They weren't insane, just clinically indifferent to any suffering they inflicted on others. Under such oppression I was peeled like an onion of every layer of my innocence in a most depraved and brutal manner.

I learned the sweet taste of revenge. If I was whipped with a cane by a teacher he would one day - not today or tomorrow but maybe in a week or so when his casual brutality had been forgotten - he might bounce out the door after class to head off in pursuit of whatever joy his freedom permitted and find not one but two flat tires on the passenger side of his car (where they might not be noticed until it was too late and he had driven down the street and the tires were ruined). One could be replaced with the spare, but two flats really stuffed up his plans for the rest of the day. Or perhaps

I would let the same tire down time after time so it would seem like a failing of the tire when really it was the failing of the teacher. As I left each scene, I would walk backwards brushing any evidence of my humanity away with a switch of eucalyptus leaves, leaving no footprint nor trace of my scent as my father had taught me when setting a trap in the wilderness. Still, they never seemed to learn. If I found a pair of socks with some brutal prefect's name on them hanging in the drying room, I'd discretely flush one down the toilet leaving the other lonely sock to let the air out of his tires when he discovered his loss. These were small futile guerilla tactics, but they were salve for the bitterness that disturbed the *Ioa* of the serpent which slithered out of my sleeping soul and joined the dingo, the *God of Cunning,* that lurked in the darkness just beyond the beaded fringes of my sleep. Revenge is but a shadow of justice.

In my bed I would stifle my sobs as I listened with an earplug to my transistor radio ...to the ruminations of the only soothing voice in that complete isolation ...the rambling monotony of the preacher-voiced Garner Ted Armstrong ...crackling alone across the late-night air waves in search of savaged souls...

Accompanied only by his voice I wandered alone in that emotional wilderness where death stalks the weak and feeble-minded. Like the *Lord God Bird*, Garner Ted was invisible, but his droning was a beacon on the late-night country AM radio waves washing across my desolate spiritual landscape like a monsoon of words sweeping away the detritus of my situation by luring me into a vacuous void beyond my dormitory existence. I can't say how his words affected the development of my character, but it was the kindly far-off droning like a human cicada that blunted the brutality of my reality of being forged on the anvil of a wrathful god. Like a star Garner Ted shone, a twinkle of friendly light that throbbed distantly in the darkness with a willow-the-wisp of human warmth and compassion. It kept me putting one foot in front of the other believing that this too would pass, and fear could dissolve into resolve and determination ...determination not just to do what I *could* do but what I *must* do ...survive ...if I were to emerge a moral mortal. Sometimes I tried talking to Garner Ted's angels in the sky but what they heard only made them cry. The violence and coercive control crept into every nook and cranny of my life for the next four years. The secret society of abuse obliterated my understanding of everything which had come before. My being was crushed; my body beaten. I can still taste the fear of a terrified child clinging to the feeble belief that 'they wouldn't dare kill me.' Such innocence! Invisible scars haunt the veteran survivors of abuse. It is a heavy burden, made especially so because it is invisible and often borne alone in silence.

When I tired of the droning of Garner Ted I retreated into sleep, back into the gullies of my dreams; to the forests that rang with the most amazingly beautiful sounds, a kaleidoscope of liquid amber tones, that on hearing it one forgets everything as one's senses are sauteed with traces of metallic peacock blues and the ruddy, roasted ambers - sounds which still warm my soul - floating just above the murky depths of the despair that had inserted itself into my persona and so polluted the cathedral of my mind.

Beethoven was deaf yet hIs notes still command us to listen. Helen Keller was deaf and blind but somehow, she showed us how to see. I was only me. I held on to dignity. Eventually sleep overcame fear and I was again trudging through the swamps of my dreams. I watched as an elephant climbed a tree, then impossibly walked out along a thin branch to reach the leaves. Why couldn't it see that was suicide? Then the branch broke, and the creature fell from my view. I dreamed on unaffected by its demise, but such dreaming strangeness still haunts the waking mind.

I learned to take the bed at the furthest corner of the room and tried to become invisible as I had learned to become invisible by the billabong. I escaped to the watery tresses of *Bridghid* in the school's swimming pool at every opportunity, finding solitude and comfort in her wet embrace for hours. It was a magical space largely devoid of bullies where gravity could be denied, and where I was sandwiched between the gaseous flights of my mind and the rocky terrain of my prison. Most days I escaped there for an hour before breakfast and at every other opportunity, my platypus yearnings strong. I learned to keep a low profile, which was hard being the tallest in the class. I knew the predators' eye has a habit of always moving and on this knowledge the terrified prey freezes and stakes its survival on becoming invisible. When that failed cigarettes were currency, as in every prison. I soon started buying them so I could buy my peace. Before long I was smoking them too as well as using them to placate the violent behaviour of bullies in nicotine withdrawal.

With thirty-five cents pocket money doled out every Tuesday I learned I could ransom my peace from addicts. Soon I was selling the cancer sticks to others also seeking to avoid a beating by paying for protection. The pack of twenty cost thirty cents so there was enough left for a bottle of pop once a week. But business was brisk and at five cents a stick I could quickly turn thirty cents into a new-fangled dollar, enough to buy three packs of twenty which equalled sixty 'fags' at five cents apiece (minus what I lost whenever I was shaken down by seniors) ...it was enough.

Too often the power of magical thinking failed me. There was nothing I could do to change the outcome. There was no logical connection between where I had been and where I now found myself, alone and far from my warm marsupial home. I had no ability to control this ugly thing that had come to roost in my patch of paradise like a septic *bunyip*. There could be no wishing the ugliness away. If I had been born of earth and wind and water this was surely my fire. When my worth was reduced to ashes my spirit rose miraculous like a phoenix and became the blue of the sky, the green of the grass and the red of the dry earth under my feet.

The best part of school (if it can really be called that for the learning was not in the classroom lessons) was escaping away at weekends to the remote homes of friends ...of fun-filled afternoons of impromptu polo matches in the shade of giant river gums; of moonlit rides along unpaved country roads after illicit beer-fuelled days of playful horse and rider gymkhana-fun; of foot stomping three-day two-night wool-shed parties and black tie events in remote station ballrooms where guests may have driven three hundred miles or flown in by private plane. On Monday we returned to our prison. Life was a banquet of such enigmas. We knew nothing else. It was as black is to white.

Some of my classmates only returned home to international destinations once a year. Mum, in her exuberance, embraced them in our home at every opportunity. With three sons at the same school my relationship with my brothers grew estranged for we rarely saw each other, except in passing at the assembly before meals when we were lined up two abreast to shuffle into the cavernous refectory, where the physical abuse could continue right under the noses of the teachers, engrossed as they were in their own meal. We became strangers, a condition which remained quite permanent.

Some students came from the far-flung islands that comprise this nation and others from as far afield as the United States of America. It had even been rumoured as a consideration as a school for Prince Charles to attend but the security of such an isolated campus gave the royals cause for pause and he went, perhaps thankfully, elsewhere.

My friend Tom was from the U.S.A. He was a year ahead of me but we both took private piano lessons which came with benefits …we had restricted access to the music rooms at the back of the auditorium on weekends. Here we became fast friends and spent many an afternoon below the radar of those who could terrorize our world. It was considered odd to have a friend outside your cohort, but Tom was kind and that (and his unusual drawl) made him stand out among the general bunch of miserable mean-spirited miscreates that seemed to comprise the majority.

We enjoyed our private cloistered den. Smoking cigarettes wasn't the only taboo we explored there. After school holidays I was always glad to see his face among the crowd of green blazers, crisp white linen shirts and grey felt Fedoras when I returned to the campus. Without his friendship I may not have survived the ordeal. I had "left home" and been forced to "grow up" in this extremely unsavory institution which my parents had paid dearly for while naively charging the New South Wales Department of Education with my care.

Tom only travelled home once a year but after one Christmas break, he didn't return. It hadn't occurred to either of us that our lives could be so quickly and completely severed. It hadn't even crossed our minds to have an address to which to write. In this galaxy of brutality, lies and dishonesty festering with every perversion imaginable, the intimate connections we had forged in that isolation had been deeper than, as children, we could have possibly appreciated. I would never again hear his voice …hear his laughter …see his face …nor feel the reassurance of his friendly touch. Something special, which I did not know I had until that dreadful moment, suddenly slipped like water through my fingers and in an instant, it was gone.

I struggled on alone with the terrors in this den of iniquity. I began to fabricate a cloak of 'otherliness' to make up for my aloneness. I created fictional characters to fill the lacking family structure of my life; parents who weren't my parents; friends who weren't there but with whom I held internal conversations. Lacking actual magic carpets onto which I could let my imagination wander, I saturated myself with the fantastic stories of other lives, whose lies lay neatly filed on the library shelves. I crafted myself a reality, a fetish, one word at a time. If all else failed I always had Garner Ted postulating his wordy truths alone into the insufferable darkness of the nights. I came to believe there was no *'God'* powerful enough to lift me out of the tsunami of muck where my spirit was mired. It was entirely up to me to seize any available buoy and try to float it out! Alone I had to navigate this shipwreck of my life, maneuvering between treacherous reefs and the invisible rip tides as best I could. There was nothing to be gained by giving in to despair. Despair was a poison that only gnawed at the soul.

Instead I buried my secret treasure …hatred …deep within my heart. It sustained my resistance. I survived by counting and being thankful for any small mercies. I watched the birds and noted their indifference to my suffering. *The Lord God Bird* looked out for them. They didn't treat each other so cruelly and after the occasional territorial peck in anger they could always escape. I watched and waited every twenty-eight days for the predictable loveliness of the full moon to appear. It brought some sort of order to my life and the vague reassurance that this same dewy moonlight also washed over the ruins of my previous privileged lot.

My young body and mind developed a relationship which worked best when the mind paid complete indifference to the state of the other. I realized there was an agent which inspired my mind to direct my body to solve the problems heaped upon it, but it could completely disconnect from the rest of my creature. Sometimes that agent simply had to leave the room when the mind and body were assaulted. Scared and helpless, I remained imprisoned by a government institution charged with my education. It was paid well to do it. I can still taste the legacy of fear. There was no one to listen to what I-knew-not-how-to-tell. I became quiet, not wanting to stand out. I learned to hear; to read between the lines; to become invisible; to watch the world like a hawk; and to act silently with the cunning of a dingo.

There was no joy to be found in collecting insults and burnishing offenses. I chose the bittersweet taste of the only low hanging fruit within my young grasp …revenge! The next best option to assassination was a well-placed origami paper water bomb dropped anonymously on any passing bully from a second-floor window. Such a futile gesture is often practiced by birds, and it fanned the flames of guerilla justice in my *'feathered thing'*.

I elected to walk an invisible path with manufactured hopes rather than acknowledge the darkness strewn about with misery and terror. If I outwitted a tormentor, it gave me the adrenalin rush I needed to feel I had at least some agency over my life.

I looked for pockets of joy in this dismal landscape; any bright thing…the leatherheads nesting in a Pepper Tree near the pool; a moment alone plinking and plonking my way through my piano practice; watching the full moon sailing freely into the sky out the classroom window as we served our two-hour evening 'homework' incarceration.

It was a time when I could project myself into the abstract and find small grace in the fading purple moments of the warnings of another bad day. It at least gave me something to look forward to that no one could take away. When the chips are down one must search out blessings to count.

My grades slipped. I went from straight As to Bs in maths and science only to discover that being first in 3B came with a lot more glory than being last in 3A.

Whipped, poked, punched and pulled I had little option but to become *'invisible'*. I drew a very clear distinction between my physical self and my thinking self. Only by learning how to vacate my body did I make life tolerable. It was a sense of detachment that permitted me privacy, a place where others could not see my thoughts when I was alone with them. I turned inward, like my father, in order to survive when the Maths Master shouted and thundered at me.

Any physical wounds had to be terrible before the embarrassment of presenting scarred teenage buttocks to the testy bark of the old biddy who served as Vice-Matron could be overcome. One always had to have ready a suitable *"I fell down an embankment"* story to snow any vague suspicions that may (or may not) have crossed her mind when we reported to Sickbay for the usual aches and pains of the abused. Showing her damaged private parts as she peered, always disapprovingly, over her gold-rimmed spectacles was not going to happen no matter how injured we were 'down there'. The worst brutality of this secret society was in the secrecy of the physical abuse hidden shamefully in plain sight by coercion and embarrassed silence …and the violent attacks on parts of the body where bruising would be hidden.

Like a nestling rudely upended from the only world it had ever known, I suddenly found myself having to defend myself tooth and nail, life and limb in a government sanctioned institution from which there was no escape. Oppression was inflicted with barbarous cruelty. But I remained the ultimate optimist. I see the future clearly but when I close my eyes the horrible *djinns* of my dark past rush in. I had to make the most of a terrible lot. I looked for the *God* we were taught to 'believe in' but found that space full of emptiness. Study of the Catechisms was just a safe place on Tuesdays with the added advantage of having a gulp of religious sherry before breakfast, the *'blood'* of this *Christ* I never found, washing down a dry wafer (*'the body of Christ'*). The fixation on torturous death and this odd ritual all seemed a bit too cannibalistic for me. Kneeling before a row of library chairs serving as a makeshift altar and praying that god's *'will be done'* on my earth *'as it is in heaven'* …if that was the case I wanted nothing to do with it.

My young mind boggled as it tried to string all these strange enigmas together in any kind of meaningful order on the short thread of my life, already a heady mix of feral wildness, and Rudyard Kipling/Ian Indress adventures now marinated in abuse and the study of the angers of *Lord of the Flies* served up with a side of Conrad Milton's *Heart of Darkness* and, for dessert and added drama, the study of *Julius*

In The Shadows of The Honey Trees

Caesar to remind me that even friends could be motivated to murder. It seems, in hindsight, the perfect recipe for producing sociopaths.

The cigarette trade was showing a profit even if I was shaken down now and then by teachers and older students. It was a percentage of loss I had factored in. To boost my income I designed a *'cuts with the cane'* contest, a pool of funds (five cents each to the pot with the winner receiving the most cuts from a teacher's cane at the end of the week taking all ...$1.50). The plan folded after I won three weeks in a row, the teachers perplexed why I seemed enthused to be receiving *'six of their best'*, as the ruthless assaults were affectionately called. The NSW Department of Education was supposed to log all such punishments in a special ledger. It now claims any such record is conveniently *'missing'*.

Among my peers I was by far the first to hit puberty. I shot up like a bamboo stalk with hair sprouting in all the usual embarrassing places. Being crowned athletic champion of my age group seemed almost fraudulent as I stood head and shoulders above the competition. It was a blessing and a curse. The Tuesday morning shot of sherry quickly morphed into an illicit trade with a country pub about three kilometres distant. It stood across the road from the deep river embankments, over which we could quickly disappear with our contraband once it had been sourced.

Whatever facial fuzz I could encourage would play an important part in my bootlegging business. Bottle shops did not exist at the time so I called the pub mid-afternoon one Friday from the school payphone and after a bit of put on farmer 'yabba', I enquired about the prices for port, sherry and beer so I could work out *'a bit of a budget for a party I'm having Saturday. I will call you in the morning with an order and get my boys to pick it up when they are driving home after football*.' I hoped I could lend the legitimacy of an eighteen-year-old 'driving' to the purchasing of illicit booze.

By Saturday morning I had enough orders from a gang of about twenty classmates who had paid their money. I called in the order and gave the first name that popped into my head: *'John Smith"* ...suitably generic and hard to forget. Any delays would not be my friend during this heist.

The plan was I would enter via the loading dock where logic dictated, I would have to park my imaginary vehicle. I had the cash in hand, not exact (that might be a bit obvious) and with the profits already secreted in my kapok mattress I couldn't afford a mutiny if I failed to deliver.

We set off across the fields after lunch, pushing our way through the wall of river reed's as tall as myself, and scampered up the high crumbly bank of the river about half a kilometre from the pub so we could approach unseen. We tried to dust the dried mud off our clothes, but it was useless. We looked like country boys who had been playing football. Before we had set out, I had used charcoal from the classroom fireplace to embolden the fuzz on my upper lip. Now, as we ambled along the dirt road shoulder toward our target, anxious beads of perspiration trickled down the back of my neck and I had to hope my charcoal mustache did not start dripping at the wrong moment.

After waving the waiting gang out of view I pushed boldly through the batwing doors that screened the loading dock from the bar. I put on my deepest voice and pulled my fedora (school band missing) down slightly too far over my eyes:

"Do you have an order ready for John Smith?" I asked as I fumbled in my pocket for the cash. Now the name sounded

In The Shadows of The Honey Trees

obvious but the answer I knew would be *"Yes"* and publican lifted three boxes of bottles onto the counter.

"Emmachisit?" I queried in my best country bumpkin accent. Without waiting for a response I handed him an adult wad of cash and waited anxious seconds while he rang the sale into the till.

"I will just take this one and get my little brother to help with the others," I offered blithely leaving the publican to count my change out to an invisible customer.

I was out in a flash and made a beeline for the corner of the building by the car park. I immediately handed the box off to the waiting hands then said: "Fatty, come help me with the other boxes."

Fatty was the shortest of the bunch and the difference in our heights would shed any suspicion my age might have raised. It worked like a charm. We made it back to the carpark with a great wave of relief washing over us. Everyone quickly shoved a bottle into their waist band, the boxes were flattened and discarded, and we moved off in twos and fours with everyone headed for the embankments by the river where the party could begin just out of sight and mind of the adult world mere metres away above.

Everyone settled into this sunny spot of hidden delights on the grassy ledge. None of us had any experience of drinking alcohol other than it was forbidden, except at *communion*. We bickered over which tasted the best for a couple of hours before realizing we had to now cross the river and stagger back up the hill to school and clean up before the dinner gong. Walking drunk was new to us, all three muddy kilometres of it.

We set off along the river, cutting through a lucerne field and crawling under an electric cattle fence, before stashing our remaining contraband in the school haystack. We just had time before the dinner gong to shower the river mud off and brush our teeth in the hope our table prefects wouldn't smell the plonk on our breath. We were all a bit heady but made it through dinner and then a movie screened in the darkened auditorium, with perhaps more than the usual amount of catcalling coming from our section.

The next day we were kept busy for the morning with some manufactured project but as soon as lunch was over, we headed out in twos and fours leading a zig zag track with the haystack as our ultimate objective. We were country boys who knew not to be too obvious in our crimes. We tried to act like we had no particular destination in mind in case we were being watched by predators.

With the haystack at our side to quickly hide our stash should we be disturbed we spent the afternoon seated on this sunny country couch imbibing in what was left of our booze. When the last drop was gone, we shoved the empties back in the bottom of the stack and hurried up the hill to brush up before dinner. The combination of sun, sin and sherry and warm beer was a heady mix we were a bit unprepared for.

The food at dinner felt good and helped stay our swaying heads. So far, we were under the radar. Church in the auditorium followed with the principal beating out his favourite, *'Joshua Fought the Battle of Jericho'* on the baby upright grand piano, evoking a newfound enthusiasm from our quarter during the chorus.

What followed was a return to our home rooms to write letters to family, a weekly obligation. Written words became not just the bricks and mortar of literature and geography but our mothers and fathers and the only outlet to express our emotions. Words became my fetish: …their form …

their cadence …their intonation …their suggestions …their excitement …their plodding …their pounding …their climax …their release …and the rebirth on the other side of every death. They left my head spinning in an orbit of its own.

Sunday evening was a time when we were lightly supervised with a single teacher wandering the corridors in case we had questions about the functioning of the universe. He was backed up by a second who rested, his feet up in the staff room. We continued to wheel about the classroom making paper airplanes and generally raising more than the usual level of disturbance while a look out watched for teacher. (Just why aeronautical experiments were so frowned on is still beyond me. Rocket scientists have to get their start somewhere).

We were feeling very full of ourselves thinking we had completely pulled a fast one over the world when the teacher on duty entered to dismiss us for the evening. The combination of too much sun, too much booze, too much food and perhaps too much fighting *Jericho* reached a tipping point and karma and coincidence collided head-on when Fatty could no longer contain it all and stood up and projectile vomited across the aisle in front of his desk, almost splashing the teacher. The reek of plonk was unmistakable.

The look on the teacher's face was nothing short of shocked disbelief. Someone was sent for a mop and pail while the teacher lined everyone up and gave us all a good sniffing. We were busted. This would not go down well with my teetotalling family. Then the inquisition began. We had rehearsed this scenario in advance with the premise that the school simply couldn't expel all of us. There was safety in numbers. We all confessed. We rallied behind Fatty (he was indeed dear to us all) and we stuck to having bought a bottle of sherry from a young guy in the village and that we had only had *'two sips each, Sir'.* It would be hard to disprove that improbable fact, but we feigned *'opportunity'* and *'temptation'* rather than the more egregious but true crime of *'premeditation'* and *'intent'*.

A second teacher and the mop and bucket arrived at the same time. We were lined up and sniffed again by the second teachers and we gave suitably quavering utterances of remorse (never underestimate the acting potential of a group of guilty teens) and took responsibility *"for our foolishness Sir! We don't want to bring shame on the school Sir!"* …Just to remind them they had some skin in the game. We feigned teary cow eyes while ruthlessly chuckling inside.

"It was just too much sun and the horrible effects of the plonk and… err... we will all deal with this so much better in the morning…" (It helps to provide people in shock with a solution and by morning the main evidence (drunk children) would no longer be in …err …evidence).

"I think Fatty is going to be sick again Sir!" I cried and by the time Sir had any opportunity to object I had steered Fatty out the door, and we fled to the safety of a toilet block two buildings away and then conveniently never went back. We shut the door of the end cubicle and proceeded to share a cigarette. They wouldn't come looking for us any time soon. The teachers wouldn't want to deal with something so messy so late on a Sunday night shift and I was pretty sure they had probably committed a similar type of crime at least once in their youth.

The next morning the headmaster had never seen such a group of carefully groomed and polished 3B as we were assembled in the quadrangle to receive our humiliation in front of the morning assembly. Sir was very *'disappointed'* with us and *"we are disappointed in us too Sir".* It was true. We were disappointed we had been caught out in the almost perfect crime. If Fatty had just held out five more minutes ..."*woulda/coulda/shoulda*". It was a year before we pulled the stunt again and were more judicious in the application of this new stimulant when John Smith started having more Saturday parties.

Surprisingly there was no marathon of hand whacking punishment and instead we were condemned to two whole weekends of detention, much of it doing badly needed maintenance on the half dozen tennis courts. Two weekends of freedom were eaten up by hot sweaty slaving. If it happened again parents would be informed ...paying parents (the only kind). I learned the price of admission to the world was high.

§

Whatever oppressors might have ruled our days our nights were luxuriously empty after everyone turned out the lights. By midnight everyone in our world would be asleep, including the teachers resident in their apartments at the end of the dormitory wings. A group of about five of us would carefully stuff our beds to look occupied in case of any late-night head counts and we would glory in the unfettered freedom night blessed us with. Once I shinnied around a four-inch-wide brick ledge on the second floor to access an open window in the staff room in order to steal an exam paper. With a flashlight I searched until I located the teacher's desk but, in my search, I leaned on a patch of papers and heard a loud *SNAP*! I had broken the Sports Master's pipe. (Yes, even the Sports Master, like most men in that day, was a nicotine addict). I pieced it back together and replaced the sheets of paper on top, then locked the window and departed by way of the self-locking door, leaving all the security in place and hoping the enigma of the broken pipe in the locked room would distract from an exam paper missing from the pile. I can still hear Mr. McErtry's words the following week:

> "You have surprised me 3B. Everyone scored at least ninety percent, far better than most of 3A."

It was a lesson in missed opportunity. It hadn't occurred to me that 3A would write the same test or I could have doubled my income from the death-defying midnight heist.

There was one other way to score a few hours of freedom. The school bus would transport us to the city about seven miles away every Saturday morning. Stores closed at noon Saturdays in Australia then. However, access was only granted if you were dressed in white linen shirt, school tie, grey fedora with school colors attached and college grey wool slacks and shined shoes, even in the heat of summer. Of course this made us all stand out in the crowded main street of this rural farm town, but it wasn't enough to curb our rebellion. Why pay thirty cents a pack for cigarettes when you could lift a whole carton from a depersonalized department store display in less than three seconds and shove it under your forest-green wool blazer with its deceptive gold piping and monogrammed pocket while saunter off innocently fingering other expensive merchandise which one had no intent at all of purchasing. The profit margin in my five cent-a-cigarette empire was greatly enhanced.

There was also the ruse of feigning an interest in the faith of the half dozen Catholic students who had to be transported into the nearby city for Sunday evening service.

In The Shadows of The Honey Trees

Freedom of religion could be claimed to qualify for the trip where we would be dropped at the front of the church at 6.45 p.m. to be collected at 8 p.m. The teacher driver would watch as we scurried up the stairs toward the door before he then took off. As soon as the minibus was facing the other way, we would immediately reverse course, hide our telltale school hats and ties and green blazers in the church hedge and spend a glorious hour of freedom wandering the empty park-like riverbanks in the thickening light. Magically we were all sitting in full uniform on the garden ledge at the front of the church looking well sermonized when 'Teach' drove back into view right at 8 p.m.

Another ploy to bolster extra cash for booze runs for the Smith's parties was a fraud we committed on the local department stores where we all had family accounts to which we were only supposed to charge *'necessities'*. We all took that term a bit loosely and I am sure the store clerks on commission drooled at the arrival every Saturday of the surge of teens in green blazers with charge accounts. The ruse involved selecting several pairs of pants and taking them to the dressing room and trying them on. The ones which fit best were left on and the baggy uniform college greys pulled on over the top to hide the contraband. We would then buy the other two pairs and put them on account. A good sale was hardly suspicious. However, the next Saturday we would be back at the customer service desk with a story that: *"Mum said they didn't fit right"* to have the charges reversed before our parents received their monthly bill, standing there boldly in the pants we had stolen the week before asking for our parents' money back on the cover purchases. *The gall! The stolen pants could then be sold to another student for cash for a fraction of their worth.*

Of course I knew all this was *"wrong"* in the eyes of the world but when your sense of *'right'* and *'wrong'* has been severely shaken one has very little concept of where the edges of all these shades of societal grey are. I suppose this *'acting out'* was a cry for help but no one person was ever allowed to see enough of the big picture to start putting the complexities of that kind of puzzle together. It was a survival instinct.

Closer to *'home'* we were often charged with helping unload stores for the school kitchen. The opportunity to access the food stores came quite by chance. The head cook had received a load of food, mainly gallon tins of fruit and big tins of Arnott's cream biscuits (a teacher-only treat) and I was among a group of friends passing the rear of the kitchen when we were commandeered by the cook to move it all from the loading bay into the storage room, a double brick fortress with solid metal bars bolted over the single large window. He treated us to left over desserts for our troubles. Wherever life finds you it never hurts to be in a cook's good graces.

Volunteering to help do two hundred and fifty sets of dishes was another safe place and was often rewarded with leftover teacher steak. While storing Cook's delivery (all in good cheer) I cased the nuts holding the window bars in place. The next week at the same time we watched for the regular kitchen delivery to arrive. In the meantime I had absconded with an adjustable wrench from the metal shop which now weighed heavily my pocket. As soon as the truck had been unloaded on the dock, I gleefully stuck my head in the kitchen door to ask if the Cook needed help again. He was delighted. While the others made a show of moving things in it was all in slow motion as I frantically cranked the nuts off the bolts holding the bars in place over the window, then quickly pocketed them. As I took the last one off, I held my breath hoping the rods holding it would be long enough to keep the heavy bars in place in the thick double brick wall. *Phew*! They were. I then joined the bucket brigade before we skittered off with our pockets bulging with cookies found in an open tin. It was a good heist, but we were only getting started.

For the next two years we made regular forays to the pantry, lifting the heavy iron grid out in the dead of night then using it as a ladder to access the high window to the storeroom (which we long ago unlocked). With a heavily barred window the lock was an easily overlooked aspect of the security by the short-sighted school Matron. On select midnight raids huge tins of Arnott's cream biscuits and gallon cans of canned apricots and peaches were handed out to that imposing barred window to the waiting hands below before we stood on each other's shoulders to jiggle the bars back into position. We then headed off stealthily to the school dairy at the bottom of the hill, far enough away from the rest of our world to safely light a fire and feast on the ill-gotten gains before returning to our beds (after burning the labels, crushing the tins and stashing them under a loose corner on the roof of the cow stalls to dispose of all evidence).

During our ramblings around the nearby countryside on weekends we often showed up at local farms offering to work. The pay was a pittance really but occasionally someone would be stingy after we had worked our butts off all afternoon in the sun that would rub salt in the wounds we had received elsewhere.

We worked one afternoon for a farmer who needed help planting his watermelon field. It was a hot day and when we asked for water, he told us we could drink from the river. It was more mud than water, but he told us we should have brought our own water. (This was long before the invention of bottled water). The interaction wasn't sitting well with the three of us, so we said our time was up much sooner than it was, took the measly three dollars each he offered us (it was usually five of the new dollars for three hours farm work) and headed home.

A few months later, carefully calculated and coordinated with a full summer moon, our usual gang crept out of our beds at midnight and stole the school tractor. It was left parked with its large trailer on a slope for easy clutch starting in the morning to transfer the cans of milk from the dairy to the kitchen. It was easy to just keep it rolling silently but slowly down the long hill before starting it once we were a kilometre away. We then drove around on the back roads until we found the patch of said watermelons, now glowing like fat little piglets in the moonlight. Within ten minutes we had loaded as many as we felt we could handle onto the trailer before enjoying a moonlit ride back to school with no headlights and stashing our take in the haystack near the dairy. We abandoned the tractor at the dairy rather than risk driving it back to the parking spot and waking anyone up. Its odd location became another enigma for someone else to puzzle over while we quietly slipped back into our pajamas and were found sleeping innocently in our beds in the morning. The melons, sold to other students who knew better than to look a gift horse in the mouth, proved profitable at fifty cents each but, unfortunately, the business model was not sustainable.

That drew our attention to the Tuck Shop, run by one of the teachers who sold assorted candy and sugary soda after school (unwittingly blighting us with acne). By calculating how much each person spent we figured that the till must be full of money. The shop door had a huge padlock which the teacher left hanging open in the hasp while the store door was open. When he closed the shop, the padlock locked without need for a key and he would then head up the slope toward the office never looking back. Someone found the source of these large padlocks in town and bought an identical one. It took a little group huddle at the door to hide the switch and we would then wait till closing time to retreat into the pool washrooms next door to watch for the teacher's departure. He headed off and the moment he disappeared around the corner we pounced, opened the lock, went in and closed the door, helped ourselves to the till (but left enough to make it not look too suspicious), took pockets full of our favourite candy and drank several bottles of pop and put the empties in the returns crate so the inventory would appear correct. Then we left putting the original lock back on. The teacher returned the next day to find all his security in place. It took a week or two before he noticed his accounting didn't add up. One day he was halfway up the incline when he remembered something and returned and tried to access our lock. Alert to something fishy when it wouldn't open, he hurried off and presently returned with the disbelieving principal in tow as witness.

Smelling the ill wind that could blow back in our faces we took advantage of his momentary absence, dashed from our hiding place, took our padlock off and then replaced it with the original and locked it. We then took up sunny positions on our towels by the nearby pool with front row seats to the drama we predicted would now unfold. The teacher, ranting to the principal, stormed up to the door to demonstrate the ruse; he stuck his key in the lock; and …it opened! The look of disbelief on his face was worth the price of admission and I am surprised the laughter stifled by our towels didn't give us away. It was the icing on our illicit cake. We had not only pulled off the heist but had hung an authority figure out to dry in front of his boss. We must be winning. It was definitely an *"us"* against the *"them"* issue with *"them"* "including everyone anyway senior to ourselves. I am pretty sure 3B was fingered as likely culprits of the unexplained Tuck Shop shortfalls during the ensuing discussions we imagined in the principal's office. Nothing could be proven. We went to ground and changed targets but not before returning the padlock for a refund because it was *'too big to go through the holes.'* This was crime on a shoestring. There was no learning these skills. It was the instinctive response to unreasonable oppression by external forces completely beyond our control.

I may have been cast into a mad wilderness of deranged victimhood, but I wasn't going to have my wings clipped that easily. I was built to soar, not just flap around. Through the ache of *'homesickness'* for the seclusion of that fantasy place called *'home'* I realized I had to create that warm fuzzy place in my core. A few days at home several times a year didn't heal the umbilical separation that had otherwise birthed me a kind and considerate independent individual. It made burying the wounds much more painful knowing the bandage of the comfort of home had to be ripped off again after two days. There I had faced down the most dangerous creatures on the planet. Now I had to find the glee of triumph over the much more slippery threat of institutional neglect, to which I had been indentured. As I had triumphed over the scaly snakes which had threatened me, the child, I now had a more invisible foe to contend with. I had learned well boldness from the gusto with which the Willie Wagtails defended their hapless unhatched eggs from marauding evil intent.

This 'education' was no carefully scripted drama where antagonists and protagonists took careful turns at center stage building to a predictable crescendo of tragic consequences. Instead I had to become inured to the random clods of muck thrown in my face as the flailing hooves of circumstance thundered through the landscape of my young life. I struggled on for four long years and left at the first opportunity.

I had no time for an all-you-can-eat smorgasbord of self-pity over the abuses I had seen and suffered ...I remain a survivor, not a victim. But there was no escape ...not even now. I cannot change what happened. I cannot unsee that which I have seen any more than I can unlearn how to ride a bike. I can only change how I view these things now with the shocking 20/20 vision of half a century of hindsight. I cannot live with the truth hidden in my heart. At times I had feared for my life. I wasn't a person; I wasn't an animal. I was reduced to being *'a thing'*. I can no longer collaborate with my silence. I knew not how real my fears were. I had no way of conceiving at the time that this was criminal abuse of power and criminal neglect at the hands of the N.S.W. Department of Education who willingly collected the ample annual fees from our parents and then completely neglected our care. That all children did not thus migrate to adulthood was lost on me. All those around me did. It was my truth. I knew not why I would pursue a world of words, while living in deep denial of much of this tale, only to find after retiring and beginning to write the story of my life, that fate had prepared me especially for this purpose. I blindly blundered into the realization that this is what my destiny had led me to, girding me enroute with the only tools to slay such a dragon of oppression when I finally met my *Fate* more than half a century later.This school had been my *Hell* or, at the very least, my *Purgatory*. *Mephistopheles* lurked in every corner. All I wanted was a sprinkle of humanity.

If my young soul had been a caterpillar feeding lushly on the raw terrors of the Australian *Never-Never* as a child, it had now cocooned in a form of solitary confinement. By some great unknown power innately invested in my spirit I transmogrified ...and emerged, inextricably transformed ...an ethereal *"flutterby"*.

CHAPTER 9

The Flutterby

"Happiness is when what you think, what you say, and what you do are harmony."

—Mahatma Gandhi

1968

Without much invested thought I spread wings I didn't know I had and drifted on the current of life. I had learned the first lesson of the butterfly ...looking back is fruitless. While I wished it had been different, I sloughed off the poison of my passage and became a troubadour; an outsider; an observer sitting on the fence holding hands with myself. I pursued I knew-not-what, but I pursued it none-the-less. There was only some vague idea that there was something greater out there waiting for me. By good luck, good looks or good management I found myself accepted to a cadetship as a junior journalist on a large regional daily newspaper. How I landed on those feet I really have no idea. I think it was having been president of the school Poetry Club, which, in reality, was only a shell group with an empty space (with a lock on the door) that I and a few friends took over as our hangout. The word 'Poetry' seemed to act as a bully repellant and we were largely left alone there. The room contained a collection of poetry books and it rubbed off enough that we read them, each reading aloud a page of an epic before handing it to the next person. It is still my favourite way to read poetry. It brings a special life to it. No conscious force propelled me into a life of words. I was equally interested in art school. When offered the journalism cadetship I went for the bird in the hand instead of waiting weeks for art school admission announcements. It was an alignment of bright lights, a syzygy whose importance in my life I was too naive to recognize in the moment. The wind of the wings of *the Lord God Bird* just seemed to push me that way.

I had emerged from the macabre world into which I had been cast and found myself welcomed into a close-knit group of kind, intelligent strangers who took me under their wing and made me feel like one of them without questioning my past. I assume they assumed my past looked roughly like theirs. That is human nature. We *are* how we treat others. We worked from 1 p.m. till 10 p.m. making it somewhat isolating for a young person, but I was used to that. This probably saved my *'feathered thing'* from falling into the trap of misspending my youth in hotel bars and gambling dens along with the rest of my mostly inebriated cohort. By the time I finished work everyone else my age was either drunk or heading to bed. I slipped instead between the pages of a book till the wee hours, continuing to live imaginary lives in unknowable places, then waking to an empty world where everyone had already disappeared to work. In a whole year I only saw my roommate awake about five times. It was a good arrangement.

The newspaper I worked for cast a wide web over a huge geographic area and transportation was facilitated by the company's chauffeur, Dudie, a diminutive man who perched behind the wheel with the front bench seat jammed completely forward (bucket seats were still only on the drawing boards) to afford him a view of the road (or perhaps so he could reach the pedals). Some road trips took hours with usually a photographer and me and often a senior writer jammed in the roomy backseat of his always latest model Ford Fairlane. No one ever volunteered to cram into the front.

We sat there, full-sized Smith-Remington typewriters balanced on our knees, hammering out our stories so the copy would be ready the minute we hit the newsroom. Dudie, the driver, had been ferrying reporters around for more than twenty years. He knew everyone we needed to know in every community, a veritable Who's Who of a geographic area larger than some countries. Most remarkable of all was his ability to tell jokes. He could literally keep us rolling in our seats for hours as we sped across the endless black mud plains, hurtling over hundreds of miles of perfectly flat parched countryside as emus stalked across the sky, floating mirages in the air which trembled with *Ra's* rage... With his shaved head poking out from under his too-small Fedora, Dudie cast a sharp contrast to the vacuous vista fleeing past our open windows (air-conditioned autos were also still just a pipe dream) as he revelled in his missed calling as a stand-up comic. By the time we arrived anywhere our sides hurt from laughing.

Back in the newsroom with a desk abutting the Social Editor's I only had to ask to get tickets to almost any event in the city from movies, theater and art shows to picnic race days. She had tickets to almost everything. She would gladly send me as her emissary to anything I volunteered for so she could cross it off her list. It was a case of *'who you know not what you know'* and I was accorded royal treatment wherever I went by the force of her grace. The sports guys could always use an assistant in the press box at any sporting event I wanted to take in on my days off …someone to go for more beer. They were heady days of living in a world where doors simply opened when I spoke the magic words and waved the magic tickets. I remained friends with most of this kind group of people for the rest of my life.

I remember being sent as a *'second pen'* to a luncheon for Queen. Elizabeth II. It was a sit-down affair at the University of New England where I somehow drew a seat beside the local Bishop. He couldn't have known my step great-grandmother had been housekeeper for the Bishop of Australia (or that said Bishop had married my grandparents. At that time nor did I). He was happy to coach a young blood in the etiquette of how to eat a whole roast Cornish game hen (or maybe it was quail) which arrived on the table in front of us alone in its own little woven wicker basket with a garnish of lettuce. I was more interested in the food than in the Queen. (The rule is you are allowed to use both hands to pull it apart but only use one hand when eating it off the bone. Who knew there was a rule for such things?)

Like the quail my words had wings. Good for short rapid bursts at first but with time I developed my stamina. Writers develop a cadence at which the words flow in concrete fashion, building soundly on the punctuation that come before, absent of split verbs and changed tenses. It is an act of flow, like swimming, only in words …one after another. There can be no getting ahead of yourself. When times were slow in the evenings, we cadets would have speed typing competitions. It made us sound busy from a distance and was our own brand of secret fun. It also helped as we sometimes had to take lengthy scripts over the phone from other news services. I quickly made sure I became a regular contributor. Cheques started appearing in the mail.

As I unfolded my word fetish, I began a life of traveling the world, pushed by winds of unknown yearnings; stringing words in gymnastic grammatical gyrations; singing for my supper; playing to an invisible audience behind a paper curtain. My words were delivered to the daily court of breakfast tables across first the country, then the world. I sought out far flung corners and earned the honour of humility from lessons unintended. I was many times left speechless by the kindness of total strangers.

§

Years passed.

The daily excitement of my everyday life I now try to weave into the web of my life's cloak with the raw honesty of an old spider who knows too much. Sometimes the names recede into the past, but the words and the faces remain fresh. Occasionally a television newsreel tweaks a string in the back of the sound box of my memory ...a name slaps like an old slipper dropped on the cold floor in the cottage of forgetting and I suddenly remember an orange cat with pea green eyes perched in a spot of golden sunshine on a painted window sill in a modest, nay frugal, red brick council flat in grubby East London, where the soot of the era of coal-fired heat still clung to the damp walls and chimney pots and assaulted my country bumpkin nose. It was here among these very dwellings that many babies born at the same time as I, had choked and died from inhaling some of the most poisonous smog to ever blight the industrialized planet.

The cat's kindly owner, an old lady with tightly curled grey hair, had granted me an interview. Days before when I had been handed the assignment Î had never even heard of *The Suffragettes*. No! It wasn't a pop band. Her name is still clear ...*Pankhurst* ...*Sylvia* perhaps (is this the start of forgetting?). My hair curled in horror as this diminutive old lady recounted her harrowing tales of chaining herself to the fence in front of the British House of Parliament with her mother, Emmeline Pankhurst, the insufferable leader of the British *Suffrage* movement for political and legal empowerment for women; a woman considered a political terrorist of the day. Hers was a whole family of women who simply refused to lie down and have the male dominated establishment deny them the power of their gender's suffrage ...their equal vote in politics and financial independence (the latter still a long time coming in places). Emmeline and her three daughters and others endured such indignities as imprisonment, hunger strikes and forced feeding (not the modern intravenous kind). Australia had largely avoided such a show down and had followed the global lead of New Zealand in granting women full political powers at the turn of the 20th. Century ...but it took more than another eighty years before Australian women alone could apply for a bank mortgage. (The movement also brought challenges to the status quo in North America, which in the US morphed into the *temperance* movement. Canada introduced the motion in 1878 but it took forty-two more years to finally be certified).

It was hard to imagine this grandmotherly lady fussing over a cup of Earl Grey tea and cookies for me spearheading a movement which had rolled out the brilliant carpet of political freedom that cushioned the sidewalks on which the young of the current day scuffed their shoes and discarded their cigarette butts without even glancing back to see who had borne the cost of their inclusion. It was thanks to women like Sylvia who bravely stood up against all odds ...thanks to thousands of women now invisible in their graves ...who stood together shoulder to shoulder and fashioned this carpet of freedom which has since been washed in the blood of millions to dye it in the invisible patterns of *'choice'* we now so blithely enjoy on today's Avenue of Freedom. Freedom always comes at great cost. It is all too easily now taken for granted by those who personally did not pay for the price of admission while enjoying the hard-won product. Old grey-haired women of every ilk *are* our goddesses. They all have moved mountains invisible to us.

As the sunlight slanted just so through the window it illuminated the eye of Sylvia's marmalade cat, which sat glaring from its perch on the windowsill, transforming it into a glowing droplet of liquid jade. As the creature blinked this gem flashed like a pulsing laser relaying a message in some secret code from a distant unseen galaxy.

Here was a woman who had first-hand shovelled the political excrement of exclusion from the corridors of power. She had bravely shone a bright light in dark places while seeking justice. She recalled the pain of a two-week hunger strike when the authorities would intervene, and force feed the strikers.

"The pain would stop for the next day, but we knew that we would then have to endure the great pain again when we again refused to eat. The only thing we had any control over was what we chose not to put into our mouths, "she said almost wistfully. Now she was content to live out her life in this little bedsit using a common bathroom down the hall where she had to put ten pence in the slot to get hot water for a bath. She shared a similar sense of economy as my father. There was an unassuming knowing in her presence ...her frugal freedom was political plenty.

She reminded me of her orange cat - happy; glowing; content in a private ray of sunshine others couldn't see; mantled in the holy grail of inner peace! It was a lesson in learning to recognize where my sunny spots were and to remember to visit them often.

Such raw and touching moments came from daily interfacing with strangers on an intimate level in order to be able to tell their stories. That was the great blessing of my life. For an hour or two almost every day someone would sit and answer my questions that often led the interviewee to new insights of their own when the information they shared was reflected to them. I had famous faces say to me:" I have told you things this last hour I have never told anyone ever before. Thank you for inviting me to tell my story. Get one thing wrong and I will sue you." Others would state:" I don't have anything interesting to tell" but each was an opportunity to fertilize my own growth as well as a chance for a human soul to brazenly leap out and bare itself just for me as if some greater wind had propelled me down their street with a piece of crumpled paper on which I had scrawled an address.

For Sylvia I had bought a bunch of daffodils as a peace token at a well-worn corner store enroute. I remember how the yellow glow from the flowers had illuminated her smile as she bent to smell them at the door. The flowers did their work. Her contented spirit simply radiated. I fell through a looking-glass and into the unassuming presence of a political goddess disguised as a little old lady complete with her own Cheshire cat. Such was not the only proverbial rabbit hole into which I unwittingly tumbled.

In The Shadows of The Honey Trees

§

Many months later, in a stone-built Italian hill village I was visiting one hot summer's day, an old woman shrouded in black and carrying a basket approached, stared into my eyes then fell to her knees on the cobblestone street, hands quivering in exaltation as she exclaimed: *"San Francesco, San Francesco."*

I was taken aback. Something disturbed my *Ioa*, and it moved within me in a way it never had before. Was it just my flowing hair or had she been touched by the sun? Had the sun caught the straw brim of my hat making it appear for a moment as a halo or ...? The earnestness of her epiphany left a deep impression on my atheistic mind.

'Saint Francis" was the patron saint of animals. I knew that much. Were the years of childhood immersed in the sublime animal kingdom to which I'd been born etched on my face? Did I carry my *anime* so plainly on my sleeve? Did I truly resemble some fanciful Saint Francis? Was she just nuts? She kissed my hand fervently repeating her salutation to *"San Francesco!"* It was a pleading cry ...as if for some kind of mercy.

I helped her to her feet, lifted her basket and, with the kindest of affection and my best Italian, bade her a pleasant day with a smile. She stood transfixed, watching as I retreated down the cobblestoned street. At the corner I turned and looked back. She was still standing there, rooted to the spot, watching. I smiled again, waved and then vanished around the corner. Had I as much impact on her as she had on me, two strangers caught in a sudden spurious up-pour of religious rapture in a public square? Did my face betray my allegiance with the warm fuzzy wilderness friends of my youth? Was I to be haunted by enigmas all of my life? I learned then it was always wise to pause and turn when departing any place to see who is watching.

Not long after I ventured to Sicily with Mariette, the woman who was to become my wife. Cash was carefully managed. We didn't know where the next safe source of water might be. We drank espresso or beer just to be safe. Wine was plentiful but not with ice in it. No fresh lemonade or uncooked food (strawberries are a perfect medium for cholera). Bottled water only existed in large five-gallon glass jugs. Armchair tourism had yet to be invented. Only seaweed littered beaches.

At a waterfront concession in Palmero two mute men befriended us. They were rather short and too entertaining to pass over in the sweat-soaked masses that seethed by the water's edge under the hot Mediterranean sun. At first, we thought they were comic mimes keen to elicit a few lire from us, but they beckoned us on, first to a hole-in-the-wall eatery (where of course we paid for the wine), then, with a combination of sign language and charades, they explained they had had their tongues cut out by a force of undetermined evil. With graphic oral demonstrations there was no question these men had had their tongues crudely removed. We were deeply shocked.

It was a horror too mesmerizing to look away from yet so disturbing as to send a rational mind into denial. Gazing into the gaping oral cavities so willingly displayed made my heart skip a beat. I realized I had only an inkling of the evil that lay hidden beneath the thin veneer of human *"civilization"!* Then again, they may have had twin cases of tongue cancer. We will never know their truth. I mustered my dignity, which had just been strewn across the acres of my mind by their

In The Shadows of The Honey Trees

dark revelations and followed the light of my compassion. We were together on the fringe of our respective worlds. For the moment we had each other.

They loaded us into two jellybean-sized Italian cars, each with only two seats. The journey continued along a rocky shoreline, Mariette in one pocket-sized car with one man while I rode behind with the second man in an equally tiny auto. We really had no idea where we were going. We simply trusted our instincts. These two seemed like outcasts from their own camp and being outsiders ourselves we at least had that desert in common.

The terrifying part was that the two insisted on speaking to each other using both hands out the windows madly conversing in sign language as they careened down narrow cliffside roads steering all the while with their knees. Never have I ever found my life in such peril and felt so completely incompetent to do anything about it. I dared not disturb the mind that seemed so content to conduct the business at hand in such a casual manner. Breaking the spell might have had fatal consequences. I could only take solace in my driver's confidence. I felt my life being handed over to the *Fates* …again.

We finally came to a stop in a remote spot beside a cliff. We were *'all in'* at this stage and had no real option but to play the hand as the cards turned. The two seemed quite gleeful and we had nothing worth stealing other than our passports and, we surmised, they had already had plenty of opportunities to rob us long before now.

We followed on foot as they led the way along the rocky shore. Eventually we came upon a niche carved in the cliff above the lapping waves. Here stood a simple white plaster statue of the Virgin Mary. Perhaps she was cement. The two quickly knelt, crossed themselves and proceeded to light candles clinging to waxy clumps where bygone votives had splattered the naked stone.

This was obviously their secret sanctum. They were overjoyed to share their holy place with us, and we dutifully bowed our heads reverently and crossed ourselves. (When in Rome…) We had much to be thankful for. We definitely needed some sort of divine intervention to bring this escapade to a close.

After revelling in their company in this odd seaside picnic-of-the-mind for perhaps another half an hour I started drawing clock faces in the sand and communicating that it was time for us to catch '*le autobus*'. (Their hearing was fine, but my Sicilian was poor). The disappointment on their faces was palpable. Their new-found friends wanted to bring the bromance to an all-too-sudden end. With my limited Italian (which I could never be sure Sicilians understood) I insisted. We must catch our bus in order to meet a boat-that-wouldn't-wait a hundred kilometres away tomorrow morning. They finally bade Mary farewell, snuffed out the candles and loaded us once more into their shoebox Fiats.

Enigmas aside, at the next township we all lolled in a courtyard taverna for an hour waiting for a bus to take us the last leg of our Sicilian journey into the port city at the island's westernmost tip.

Not wanting to disappoint our new friends I bought the rounds of beer until the bus hauled up moaning and groaning and packed to the rafters with fruit and vegetables and the occasional chicken in true rural Sicilian style.

With deep disappointment etched on their faces they had waited with us like long-lost family until the bus arrived. We took our leave as graciously as possible and with heartfelt farewells we left our friends to their fates, to which they both seemed confidently resigned. We returned their waves as the bus chugged away. We had again been granted a rare moment of odd truth, one that left us shell-shocked but grateful for the deeply personal experience these two odd characters had shared so enthusiastically with us, two total strangers. We all have a need to be heard.

It was late afternoon when we arrived in Trapani, and we already held tickets for the ferry to Tunisia departing in the morning. The first couple of inns we tried seemed inordinately expensive (go figure, with a captive audience of travellers?) After finding nothing else we returned to find those vacancies already filled and we had no option but to sleep in our sleeping bags in the town square. It was a rough night. It truly is coldest just before the dawn even in sunny Sicily. And the ground becomes harder as the night wears on. Needless to say we were delighted to be on our way aboard an unimposing boat the next morning with traditional Arabic tea served by young barefoot teens running about with huge copper kettles of sweet mint tea and a cluster of glasses providing on-the-spot Arabian hospitality where people sat cross legged on the deck. This was my first experience of that charming Arab custom of tea delivery, a new cultural epicurean delight.

The reception in Tunisia was much-anticipated but the tin-sided immigration compound was somewhat intimidating, more so when a border guard started removing everyone's passports. These disappeared behind closed doors and our names summarily alphabetized, and we were then summoned.

My future wife's name started with a "B", so she had been fully processed and had gone ahead to change money while

I languished, (as usual in all things ordered alphabetically for my whole life) with the Ws.

I was the very last name called. There was an issue with my visa. We had been to the embassy in Rome and were told we didn't need visas. My pleas for consideration fell on completely deaf ears. Mariette meanwhile was starting to wonder where I was. She returned and saw me from the other side of the gates. When she saw me hefted bodily into the air by six armed guards and carried off horizontally down the gangplank and back onto the ship, she started creating noise. Back aboard the ship the captain was instructed to lock me in a cabin and not to open the door until he was beyond the three-mile point. I was stunned. I had fallen from Heaven to Hell by the most direct route ...with the enigma being it was exactly the same place and the same players ...only going the opposite direction.

I couldn't have been more stunned (or relieved) when, minutes later, the key sounded in the lock, the door was flung open ...and Mariette was pushed into the tiny cabin to join me by a couple of burly border guards.

Perhaps because of her presence the captain, by way of kind non-judgemental courtesy, informed us that complimentary food and tea would be delivered to us. It was a much-appreciated pleasantness in a time of great stress. He also informed us that there would be no charge for the return passage. It was a deep lesson in the impact the manners of a kind stranger can have at a stressful moment.

The smiles of the kind captain sped us on our way once we reached solid Sicilian soil again and, with a high ambition of reaching the last ferry to the mainland at 5.30 p.m. we caught a ride with smoke-belching Coca Cola delivery truck loaded with empties, which jingled and clattered behind us as we contined, stopping every few kilometres to pick more empties for the whole length of what started to seem like a very long island. When we stopped for lunch, I invited the driver to join us and, using our by-now-enormous alphabet of Italian hand gestures, we held a rudimentary conversation. It was nice to break from the diesel excrement that belched from far too many overloaded vehicles that sped by us along the highway.

The entire fiasco of the morning had been emotionally devastating as it derailed our plans to travel through Africa requiring us now to travel and hop between Sicily, Italy then on to Greece to have a hope of accessing flights to Egypt, the only other access point to North Africa at the time.

This bottleneck was rife with tension. It meant we had to pass through two war zones. Turkey and Greece were deeply entrenched in the Cyprian military crisis while Egypt and Israel were heavily engaged in violent friction, all of which we had hoped to avoid via Tunisia. It required a wait of many days in Athens as the Cairo airport was closed due to clashes with Israel in the 6 Day War, when Israel seized the Gaza Strip and the Sinai Peninsula from Egypt and refused to vacate the premises. Also trapped in this political vacuum were another young couple who would become our life-long friends. That feather from beyond again pushed us yon into an unseeable future.

If I have learned anything in travelling it is that the language of the body and the tone of the tongue can tell you more than the words alone. I always travel with two rules: if someone comes under my suspicion once I simply watch my back. If there was a second instance of someone raising my inner eyebrows then I am out of there, no *'ifs'*, *'ands'* or *'buts'*.

The truck driver was extending the hospitality of the ride as a courtesy and gave no cause for any eyebrow-raising questionable motivations, having declined our offer to pay something for our fare. As the day wore on our truck seemed to be making more and more stops to retrieve empties and when he finally kindly dropped us near the ferry wharf in Messina, we were dismayed to find the final boat of the day had departed only minutes before.

Desolate, we heaved our backpacks against a concrete wall, sat down and consulted our *Oracle* - our flea-bitten map. We were so engrossed in trying to figure out the logistics of the next few hours until the first ferry the next morning that we failed to register that a sleek black Mercedes sedan had come to a stop at the curb beside us.

An elegantly-dressed middle-aged woman with her long hair caught up in a bun on the nape of her neck stepped out of the driver's seat and came over and spoke to us in Italian, or perhaps it was Sicilian. Startled, I begged her pardon. She repeated the request: "Where are you sleeping?"

I looked at Mariette and shrugged!

"Come," ...she said as she smiled and opened the trunk. We loaded our backpacks in and piled into the back seat. She silently drove us across the city, speaking only as we passed different landmarks, until we arrived at a well-appointed city villa. She beamed a welcome and showed us to a simple spotlessly clean suite on the second floor. There had been no discussion of costs, and it seemed a luxury beyond our means. She waved our protests aside. We were left resigned to what the ultimate financial outcome might be. It was a beautiful home. Glass transoms illuminated ornately plastered walls with fourteen-foot ceilings. Chantilly glass chandeliers sparkled with fractured incandescent light. The room to which we were shown held a comfortably outfitted century-old iron bed and spoke of another age. It was our first real bed in three days. Just the sight of it smoothed our ruffled feathers.

The woman, who reminded me of a younger version of my grandmother, then showed us to the bathroom at the end of the hall and informed us that supper would be served in an hour. With a sweet curtsey she announced:*" La mia casa e la tua casa!"* (my house is your house) and turned and left.

This was an obvious sharp left turn in our fortunes. From expelled fugitives thick with the grime from the hot, stinky Coca Cola truck ride, to being whisked away in a spotless black limousine by an enigmatic guardian angel who then showered us with that most underappreciated luxury of early travelling ...a soak in a hot bath. Our heads spun. When one door closes another opens.

Refreshed by a badly needed soak in the antique iron tub we arrived downstairs in our perma-pressed outfits (normally reserved for crossing borders) in time for dinner. We must have looked transformed.

Our host invited us into the kitchen where the smell of sauteed beef excited our by now long-neglected appetites. We watched as she served the meal and assisted in carrying the food to the table in the *'salon'* where floor to ceiling glazed French doors looked onto a patio garden with whitewashed walls, blue tiles and potted citrus trees.

She apologized for her husband's lateness but assured us he would join us soon. When he did arrive it was another surprise. The well-educated gentleman was an editor of a local publication and spoke fluent English. He began by explaining his wife's generosity:

"It started with Mussolini deciding to cast Italy's lots on the side of the German Reich when World War II broke out," he began.

"I was among a contingent of more than one hundred thousand young untrained Italian conscripts who were promptly shipped out to try and assert control over the Suez Canal as both sides in the war sought to secure access to middle eastern oil.

"A series of military missteps on the part of the leadership of what seemed an almost certain bloodless victory for the Italians led to the catastrophic rout and surrender of the almost unarmed Italians to a surprise British assault. The hundred thousand Italian Prisoners of War were promptly marched back onto their own troop ships and sent to internment in British-friendly South Africa."

The shock and the logistics of such a coup must have been mind-numbing. South Africa had considerable Boer political influence and was unenthusiastic in its support of either side in the war. However the British ties were strong, so the country agreed, no doubt for a fee, to accommodate the camp, or rather an impromptu shanty town complete with twenty-two kilometres of streets, which the prisoners were required to build themselves. The South Africans treated their captives with consideration, despite the enormous needs of this sudden population. The locals viewed them as much-needed manpower for local farms and once they had built their own shelters, they were farmed out under armed guard to earn their keep. In the evenings our host worked in the kitchen helping the head cook prepare food for one hundred thousand on a shoestring budget.

The gentleman paused to offer us sherry before embarking on his remarkable tale.

He was a slight man of medium stature and a dark Mediterranean complexion. Working in the fields in the South African sun only darkened his skin, he explained. The P.O.W.s were housed in a sizable-if-somewhat-rustic city which erupted suddenly like a mushroom on a farmer's field, with the prisoners building their own rudimentary accommodations with basic materials begrudgingly supplied by their unwilling hosts.

Among the entertainments organized by the inmates was a drama group which staged elaborate popular Italian operas. Our host had joined the backstage costume and set design crew and had access to simple supplies like makeup grease and fabric. The situation necessitated that the roles of the female stars had to be played by men in wigs made from dyed string and horsehair. Our host learned the transformational art of disguise behind that burlap curtain. In the course of his tailoring he secreted away three rectangles of used native fabric, a small, sealed tin of pig grease and a bag of fine ground charcoal. These he carried on his person whenever he went to the fields to work while hoarding his wages in a pocket he had sewn to the inside of his pant leg rather than spending it on cigarettes at the camp canteen like his friends. Inside the seat of his tattered pants he carefully stitched a ratty horsehair wig.

On returning from the farm work one day he took advantage of the guard dutifully studying the roll as they were checked back into camp from the back of a truck. Calling out his name in order as he leapt from the back of the truck the guard looked to find his name which gave him a fleeting window of opportunity. He did not not follow the man ahead of him. Instead, in the moment the guard searched the list in the fading twilight, he rolled quickly and unnoticed under the truck and hid in the oversized wooden toolbox under the bed of the transport he had just been unloaded from. The truck drove off empty of its prisoners a few minutes later and he passed undetected through the camp checkpoint. He remained hidden until the truck came to a stop several minutes later. He waited until it hadn't moved for some time before peering out. When he cracked open the lid of his hiding place it was dark. He slipped out and found some cover behind a building. There he hastened to grease up his face and lower legs then dusted on some charcoal and dirt then wrapped his army boots and pants up in one strip of cloth, wrapped another around his body in the style of a woman's body wrap, donned his wig of long locks, covered his head in the style of a native with the second cloth and then hoisted the cloth bundle of boots and masculine attire atop his head in the style of the local women and sauntered off barefooted down the road imitating the gait of the women on the dimly lit road ahead of him.

Thus he travelled all night afraid to stop because he needed to put as much distance as possible between himself and the prison before he was discovered missing. He then spent the day resting in the shade of a grove of trees to avoid any search parties looking for him. His half-hearted host nation really had little invested in his recapture, but he played it safe by remaining hidden from view in daylight, moving only in the early evenings as the light began to fail, then walking all night. He had been missed at morning roll call and a half-hearted search was launched by his captors. But instead of heading north-east toward the nearest Italian consulate in the neighbouring country (as prior escapees had done and been caught) he travelled north-west where no one would suspect his flight. He continued thus, switching between male and female identities when it seemed safe as he moved so as not to arouse suspicion. Once he chanced on a ride on a transport truck in return for lading services adding a couple of hundred kilometres to his escape in a matter of hours. By hook or by crook and one foot in front of the other, he made his way slowly incognito across the entire eight thousand kilometres of that hot, often sandy continent of Africa. His journey took almost two years. He walked most of the way.

His wife interjected and he translated:

"She says I could never have made this difficult journey without the incredible kindness of total strangers. Wherever I went I had to avoid the main centers of population. I had to walk this long road alone with not a friend in the world and very little money and a price on my head. The kindness shown to me by perfect strangers is the only reason I survived. I am forever indebted to help others on their journey."

We felt humbled to sit in the shadow of such giants.

His journey had continued via transportation routes, working his way as a caravan loader, tending to the kitchen camel and responsible for a string of sheep, one of which he had to slaughter daily to feed the large group nomads (as many as fifty men) who manned these 'ships of the desert'. He had helped his grandfather and father slaughter sheep as a youth so had some inkling of how to go about the task. He was grateful to be assigned the lowly position of slaughterman. He made his way north through Agadez, the heart of Tuareg/Berber influence, pacing out his days across the scorching sands in the shadow of the kitchen camel. The further north he trekked the more easily his Mediterranean features blended with the Berber locals and the further he travelled it was less likely anyone even cared at all who he was, but he knew most would sell out a stranger for pocket change. He had to become invisible, learning enough Arabic to survive but speaking as little as possible as he meandered through strange places driven by forces we simply find difficult, if not impossible, to imagine. Fear of being discovered retreated as his Arabic language skills improved but still he kept his head down as he travelled with camel caravans as they made their way through the Gates of the Desert under the Air Mountains before enduring The Great Desert for weeks as they wandered from oasis to oasis across the Djado Plateau, sometimes moving before dawn to beat the heat, then resting for food in their tents for the heat of the day before reloading the camels and moving on again in the cool of the evening, guided only by the moon and the brilliance of stars overhead. There could be no going back. He was drawn on like metal to a magnet, on through the dusty hamlets of Marana and Qotrun before arriving in Sebha, a drab city in the center of what seemed an eternal sea of shifting sand that could cut exposed flesh when the wind blew it through the drab mud town's sandy streets.

Sebha was a large oasis serving a population of thousands of inhabitants, a crossroads of goods travelling north and south along the camel tracks that connected the dots across these sandy wastelands. He began to feel the worst was over. He finally secured another position with a caravan of camels to cross the last leg of his long trek to Tripoli on the welcoming shores of the blue Mediterranean. He could hardly believe he had made such a journey alone, short on currency but fuelled by belief in himself.

There he boarded a boat with the last of his money for the final leg of his return to the arms of his anxiously waiting young wife who had received only one of the many letters he had sent along the way. She knew he had escaped and was alive but had no idea where he was or what might have befallen him until he appeared without fanfare at her door.

We tried to reciprocate with the telling of our pale-by-comparison Tunisian experience, assured them of our eternal grace and repaired to our room early for a much-needed sleep ...in a real bed ...the first in days. In the morning they fed us breakfast of strong coffee and honeyed marmalade on fresh hot bread in their sunny courtyard before returning us to the ferry landing in the black Mercedes. With kisses on either cheek like departing family, they stood together and bade us a smiling *"bon voyage!"* We parted friends though barely knowing each other's names. We felt we had been in the presence of angels who had dwarfed us with their grace. I remember her sudden appearance in our lives and the aching story of such a desperate journey of a lone man with a price on his head adrift on the ocean of Africa, as *the miracle of the Dona de Messina*. We had felt an angel's touch.

To this day I try to extend my hand and spare a smile and a courtesy to all. Paying it forward and back with as much grace as I can muster under prevailing conditions. Good manners and smiles are contagious and cost us nothing yet grease the collective cogs of all lives. Indeed they are a human's most attractive feature. Life is not about *"us"*; it is about 'them'. We are defined by how we treat others. We are all on a journey across the same ocean of our humanity, no matter how different our boats may seem at a quick glance when we pass like ships in the night.

CHAPTER 10

The White Dingo

"Each night, when I go to sleep, I die. And the next morning, when I wake up, I am reborn."

—Mahatma Gandhi

1975

On my return to Australia after several years overseas I took up residence in a simple beach house atop a headland that had one-hundred-and-eighty-degree ocean vistas. Here I lived content with little in the way of comforts and two adopted dogs, Don Juan and Carlos. Carlos was apt to run ahead while Don Juan followed closely at my heels …so close as to sometimes inadvertently step on my flip-flop catching it mid flap.

Carlos slept on the cool polished concrete floor in the foyer and Don Juan always slept right across the bedroom door. With such loyal sentinels in the Australian heat I left the doors all open and slept soundly on a mattress low to the floor. (It made the room seem bigger and was cooler than being elevated).

I had been living here for several weeks when I was awakened one night by the hair rising on the back of my neck. Dragged from my dreams it all seemed dreamingly odd for a moment until suddenly adrenalin kicked in and

In The Shadows of The Honey Trees

every hair on my body bristled in the darkness. I lay perfectly still trying to understand what was happening to me. I had to cast more light on this irrational creeping terror that ran riot now through my mind like a hot sword. There was another presence in the room. Knowing must be better than not knowing. I reached out slowly and jerked the chain on the bedside lamp.

I sat bolt upright. In the glare of the low watt incandescent bulb I found myself eye to eye with an enormous white dingo standing at the foot of my bed mere metres from my head and right at face level. We looked each other in the eyes. It was the moment of nightmares. I had fallen here straight out of dreamland and was having trouble rationalizing the apparition I beheld. Neither of us looked away. We remained in an eternal moment, our eyes locked with the other's mind. I was cornered. There was no way out. Disbelief coursed through my body like an electric surge.

From the corner of my eye I could see Don Juan sleeping soundly across the door. This could not be! Dogs are territorial creatures of scent, and a stranger should have sent them both into an overboard reaction. I questioned whether I was really awake, or had I simply fallen into another dream?

The ghostly canine at the foot of my mattress had unbelievably leapt boldly over both my sleeping sentinels and stood a good two feet tall at the wither. It was a big dog. Far larger than either of mine. He had jaws which could have torn my throat out in a second. Shock set in, hitting me like a club to the back of my head. No fear flashed through me. Fear had awakened me when even my dogs had slept but it now dissipated, leaving me in a state of solid absolute awareness of the impossibility of my vulnerability. Gravity was vacuumed away leaving two alien entities facing off in a crushing silence on a dark night on a lonely road. I lived three lifetimes in the passing of those seconds. Such time hallucinates. Time alone can be the protagonist.

Suddenly the big dingo looked away to the door, swiftly leapt over still sleeping Don Juan and then Carlos and disappeared into the wild hedge of banksia at the end of the garden.

I sat there stunned and began to tremble. I was very alone here despite the dogs. The only neighbours were often away, and I had no telephone. People contacted me at work. It was just the way things were then. I rose and closed the doors, the dogs waking but showing no signs that they registered any foreign scent. It all seemed so impossible.

I was suddenly exposed when I had least expected to be vulnerable. That my inner Ioa had stirred gave me an odd reassurance that indeed I may be more than the sum of the parts that I thought I comprised.

The next day I recounted the event to an incredulous friend who suggested I talk to one of the native locals. When I shared the experience, they wanted to know exactly where this had happened. Their origin story told of the spirit of a great white dingo ascending on the headland where my home was and propagating the local tribes. It was sacred ground on which I had trespassed. The hair rose on the back of my neck again and that flapping crow of trespass made the rounds of my thoughts for more than a couple of days.

I had been struck by another such illuminating terror once just months prior when I had returned home to *Platypus Flats* after years of wandering the globe. I insisted that my parents take the opportunity to enjoy a vacation. I could manage anything that needed managing. It was a rare chance for them to get away.

In The Shadows of The Honey Trees

On the first day the gaggle of about fiftty geese came hissing and squawking at the garden gate. I walked out to investigate what the fuss was about, and they hissed and squawked even harder. When I opened the gate, they all turned and ran a few steps down the hill. Nothing odd about that. I closed the gate and made as if to go inside and they returned, making a terrible racket. I opened the gate again and they again turned and ran down the hill. I followed them for a few steps then stopped. They turned in unison and fifty orange beaks made their displeasure known.

I finally figured they wanted me to follow. So we set off on this odd turn of the tables where the geese led their master. I followed the now silent grey and white army down past the vegetable garden and the strawberry patch, by orchard near the creek and then up the hill on the other side. We had hiked a good kilometre when we reached the crest of the hill I could see, sitting in the distance, a lone grey female in the middle of the lucerne patch.

I couldn't imagine what might have befallen her here in the smooth field of green, but I hurried forward with my comrades-in-wings until we finally approached the trouble.

The trouble was not with the mother goose but with one of her offspring who had flipped onto its back. Unlike most young birds, goslings are unable to get up if they fall onto their back. Without my intervention it would perish. That the geese haven't figured out how to resolve such an evolutionary failing remains a puzzle, but they had made a collective decision to leave a single guard while everyone else trekked home to communicate the trouble to HQ and to lead me back. As I reached out to play *God* and bring about the youngster's reprieve, I was about to experience the wrath of the *Lord God Bird* who looked over these matters.

The surrounding gaggle immediately attacked the arm with which I was righting junior. To suddenly have my troops set upon me unnerved my feelings of allegiance. I wandered home alone to nurse my bruises, which were surprisingly considerable. The goose bites left my arm black and blue to the elbow ...still, nothing I couldn't handle. But in years of living with this flock it was a unique confrontation that leaves me to wonder what else is not written yet about such clearly thought-out farmyard interventions. It was a shade of George Orwell's *'1984'* but the day was still young ...and this was the *Never-Never*.

At five o'clock the horses arrived and hung their heads over the garden gate. I had skipped the milking-of-the-cows routine in the morning so had to make less-than-optimal offerings of bread and some scrappy carrots from the vegetable basket. They were satisfied but not impressed. They then led me with gentle nudges toward the haystack. I was a bit slow to catch on as I hadn't done this for a while, but they went expectantly to their mangers were soon happily munching on their allotment of hay.

The chickens cawed their displeasure as roosting time fell and they hadn't been fed, coming like the horses to the garden gate to see what the delay was about. Once that was attended to and they were safely locked away from the foxes I only had to share out some kangaroo meat for the working dogs and chain them to their kennels for the night and then feed my parents little terrier a haunch of rabbit.

At bedtime I crawled back into my childhood bed tired from all this communing with the animals and fell into the familiar deep *Never-Never* silence filled with starry dreaming. At some ungodly predawn hour I awoke to what I surmised was the small dog moving around on my bed. I sat bolt upright to grab it and settle it down when I grabbed something very large and very hairy. As I blindly felt my way upwards, I realized I was dealing with an invisible hairy monster …as far up as I could reach.

There is a bright terror which infects the darkness when one's world gets tipped upside down in the middle of the night and one is at the end of miles of dirt road where the nearest human is far away and something unexpected happens. In a piercing moment you realize you are totally alone. It is a pinnacle of terror for there can be no calling for backup.

As my mind raced through the cosmos of possibilities, I remembered other monsters I had confronted. There was the enormous two-legged creature which had charged down the dirt road toward me as I sat terrified in my jeep trying to figure out what kind of creature would be so bold out here in the wilderness. As it gathered speed in my direction it had suddenly unfolded two-metre wings and soared up over my open roof …it was a giant Wedge-tailed Eagle with a rabbit in its beak. Head on (and completely out of context) …and with the rabbit disguise …I had failed to recognize it.

The other fright had been when I went to investigate strange scratching noises coming from the iron roof of the veranda one day. I had fetched a ladder and as I climbed my eyes crested the eaves. There I found myself eye to eye with an enormous goanna holding a dried rabbit skin in its mouth. Up close and in disguise it had turned all my knowns and unknowns in an instant. It was this blind momentary terror which I was now reliving again in the darkness of the absolute wilderness night.

These scenes raced through my mind in seconds but still the enormous hairy critter I now confronted made no sense.

Like a blind man being handed parts of an elephant and asked to identify the subject confusion reigned. I sprang for the bedside lamp to shed real light on this unknown foe. In the flash of light the assailant was revealed, standing full on the bed with both huge feet, his hands pulled up in a defensive stance as he rocked his body awkwardly back on his long tail as the bed springs wobbled under his weight. It was an adult kangaroo standing almost two metres tall upon my personal sanctum.

I recognized him immediately. This was Joe ...a pet raised from infancy (male or female, they were all called Joe). He obviously thought he owned this place. That he had wandered in and found my parents missing and found someone sleeping in *his* bed was not lost on me. Despite the familiar face the hair on the nape of my neck was still trying to calm itself down. I wouldn't mind betting Joe had slipped in silently on his big, padded feet every night for years to use my bed but was always up and away by the time my parents rose in the morning. Having fur instead of hair there would be no tell-tale shedding on the quilt. There is no photographic evidence of this, but I have my hunches he was asserting himself over his sleeping spot.

Joe leapt off the bed and I followed him. As he tried to exit the back door, which I had left ajar, his long foot caught the door and pushed it against his head. He repeated the action several times, looking to me for answers. Perhaps he had only come to wake me up because he couldn't get out? I scratched his head as I opened the door, and he bounded out across the veranda into the garden and off into the night leaving me to scratch my own head in wonder.

Old pets often returned to visit during droughts when they would bring this year's baby in the pouch and last year's as well hopping alongside. They knew the garden grass would be green, but this was the first time in a century that one had come right onto the bed to rouse the forces when he confronted a problem he couldn't solve by himself. There was nothing predictable about the *Never-Never* life.

Chapter 11

The Land of We

"Our greatest ability as humans is not to change the world but to change ourselves."
—Mahatma Gandhi

1978

The launch pad for my many adventures become my new home, Canada, a country of great compassion and kindness where my wife and daughter and I now settled. Here I felt *'comfortable'* in every way. For someone who had grown up believing that running water couldn't freeze, it was a rude awakening to arrive to find myself in a land of frozen waterfalls, ice roads, rivers of solid ice and lakes frozen solid enough to drive vehicles on. The ice was so clear one could see the trout swimming about more than a metre under one's feet. It was a land gripped for months on end in the icy fingers of terrifying winter chills that could see temperatures well below minus forty centigrade when the fingers of the Arctic Vortex made itself felt. It made *The Wet* of my homeland seem like a warm bath. Also I didn't have to be so watchful to avoid the adults whom my abusers had now become while walking the streets of Australia. I felt complete here …I felt safe …I felt I belonged! It helped that

In The Shadows of The Honey Trees

the figurehead of the local indigenous circular cosmology was an all-powerful but invisible spirit ...the Thunderbird.

Perhaps the frozen Canadian political mists have fostered the spirit of cooperation in the life and death weather. This has resulted in there being a general improbability in Provincial and Federal politics in Canada of many outright majority governments. With that comes a certain sense of *'We'* rather than the more decisive *'Them'* and *'Us'* mentality of two-party politics. It is quite a unique political balancing act which generally embraces inclusion and sets the country apart from most, that and its vast uninhabited spaces and unique winter wonderland.

I fell into logging with my brothers-in-law in a part of the country which unabashedly calls itself *'Beautiful British Columbia'*. It was a place I had daydreamed about as a child, perhaps inspired by a picture map in an old magazine with snowy peaks and streams full of fish and loggers in red and black checked shirts riding rafts of logs down raging rivers. I felt confused. It hadn't looked this cold in that long-ago journal.

Every morning we rose at 4 am and ate a hearty breakfast, squeezed ourselves into woollen long johns and heavy wool pants and boots lined with inch thick wool felt socks and headed off into the darkness for a two-hour drive into the mountains.

As we trekked up the valley we often had to stop while huge herds of elk *(Wapiti)* crossed the road. They would winter in the valley away from the deep snow further up the mountain range and gathered in herds of hundreds on the flats, gazing at us in the pale early dawning as if to demand an apology for our impertinence at disturbing their frozen solitude.

The final leg into the peaks was on roads of solid snow carved into drifts many metres deep. These were more toboggan chutes for our pick-up trucks than roads. We fishtailed through this pre-dawn winter wonderland with the knowledge that at this time of day we were the only vehicle on the road that led only to our camp.

The first chore was to start a chain saw and buck up an entire dead tree into pieces about a metre long then set the pile ablaze. This would burn all day and served as a warming station for the rest of the long, cold day. By the end of the day we would have burned the whole tree, and the bottom of the fire would have sunken many feet into the frozen ground making it necessary to start tomorrow's fire at a new location.

Sometimes overnight snow would have blanketed the camp and equipment requiring some shovelling before any work could start.

My job was "choking" fallen trees with steel cables to ready them for collection by the "skidder" - a broad tracked engine with a powerful motor under which we had to light a fire first thing on arrival to warm the engine oil sufficiently for it to start.

The utter silence of the land blanketed metres deep in snow is spellbinding. Hour after hour I often sat in the ceaseless snowfall holed up among the fragrant fallen fir boughs heady with the smell of terpenes, waiting for the skidder to return. The constant chaos of snowflakes falling exerts an eerie hypnotizing power more silent even than a long *Never-Never* Milky Way night.

The endless downward movement of falling snow hour after hour causes one's mind to hallucinate. The mind levitates, a surprising sensation of 'floating upward', invoked by the stimuli of a billion white spots moving downward

In The Shadows of The Honey Trees

ceaselessly hour after hour, sometimes for days. The mind begins to soar. Knowing that you can't possibly be floating doesn't stop the hypnosis from being complete. One's head seems to disconnect from one's feet.

If the sun came out, we risked losing our vision entirely as the intense ultraviolet light ricocheted off every crystal flake of snow overwhelming the eye so the pupil closed so tightly one can become painfully blind as your retina screwed itself into an impossible knot trying to escape the overwhelming ultraviolet assault. Wearing a good UV screen and snow goggles and lip gloss were important safety measures for loggers even if you couldn't see the sun through the frozen clouds.

There were days, especially in the spring, when whole mountain sides of snow across the valley gave way under the sun's rays sending great waves of snow crystals billowing hundreds of metres into the air, frozen shards of water swirling, crashing silently, almost dreamily in slow motion, into the valley below. Such avalanches of floating frozen crystals are thick enough to drown anyone who breathes it in. Such catastrophic events can instantly bury one alive and, sadly, in alpine terrain, many still perish every year in such a way.

It was an extraordinary experience but extremely dangerous work. After three months of tossing a forty-five-pound chainsaw around all day I was in incredible physical condition but a couple of close calls had me hang up my hardhat and return to mining words for a living.

One would think we would have enough of snow, driving and working in it every day, but on the weekends or on moonlit nights we would strap on cross-country skis and head out into the wilderness for more of this magical, frosty delight or take to the local mountains to don downhill skies and fling ourselves off towering snow cornices into the pillows of snow below just for the fun of it. Snowboards had yet to be invented.

The family was cross-country skiing one night under a full moon. There was at least three metres of snow on the ground and under the icy moonlight you could almost hear the ice crystals growing in the minus twenty-five-degree air as we slid across the slightly crusty surface, the only sound being our two-metre-long blades slicing the snow. It was an unforgettably beautiful night, the eerie glow cast by the full moonlight on the unbroken whiteness rendering the world in mauves and whites, sparkling here and there as perfect ice crystals fractured moonbeams.

As we silently cut across the hushed valley floor on our long slender slats my sister-in-law turned and held her finger to her lips and pointed to a dark patch near a thicket of bushes. I suppose they were young trees but with the trunks buried in the deep snow only the bush was visible.

As we sidled up to the dark hole, we were greeted by a remarkable sight. Standing in the moonlight at the bottom of the hole were two enormous elk. The full-antlered bull eyeballed us warily through his shield of sharp pointy antlers, but the cow continued to munch on whatever marsh plants lay exposed at her feet, unfrozen at the bottom of the well in the snow, as if we didn't exist. The wall of snow separated our two worlds. There was no alarm. Had we been a wolf pack the huge rack of razor-sharp horns may have been intimidating enough but the elk, having no real retreat in snow so deep, embraced this universe of their own ingenious device with Zen confidence.

These majestic creatures can spend the winter in such wells which they create when the snow starts to drift deeply. As it accumulates, they maintain their hollow, their bodies there shielded from the frigid wind that often swept across the icy surface while they were able to slowly scrape out sedges and rushes from the swampy floor where the insulation of many feet of snow trapped the heat of the decomposition of the swamp buried underneath preventing it from freezing completely at that depth. There could be no escape from their cozy den. They would live here the whole winter, or they would die here. It was yet another haunting enigma, a rare moment when *Fate* seemed to have nudged me into a secret world of frigid ice and snow where houses can be drifted in snow to the windowsills on the second floor. Something greater than I propelled me on that moonlit night to head out into this twinkling winter glory, gliding silently through the *dreaming* which is nature's majesty. What a magnificent planet we call home.

§

Many years later I found myself in a remote village in the mountains of British Columbia on assignment for the provincial art school.

My curiosity always led me to seek out local *"colour"* in my off time in a strange town. I was referred to a Mr. Brown. The directions to his domicile I was given by a pair of locals outside the non-descript convenience store, a place whose windows were decorated much like corner stores the world over …with the faded promises of delectable, frozen treats.

"It wasn't far," they insisted. "*Down the main street two blocks turn right and continue to the house at the end."*

Local directions the world over are always suitably vague but I saw no other vestige of human life as I trudged down the narrow street overhung with enormous trees that invited an early twilight into the late afternoon air. It was a deserted public street but being a total stranger I felt a fleeting flap of *"trespass"* as I walked, dodging low slung boughs. After the heat of the open summer sun on the main drag it was a tunnel of beautifully cooled shade.

At the end was a house so overgrown with bushes that the entrance was almost completely obscured. The green paint on the door peeled and it stood ajar. I could see into the entrance hall and was aware of a light shining from a farther room, which was hidden from view.

I knocked loudly …but it brought no response. I rapped again …with similar results. At that point I called out.

"Hello! Mr. Brown?" Invited by the open door and the light shining from just beyond my view I considered the possibility that something might not be quite right with this picture. I ventured forth. Perhaps he was just out of earshot in the back garden. As I stepped into the darkened hallway I called again.

The yellow light fell across a worn-but-beautiful Afghan runner that carpeted a hall which had three other darkened doors. When I reached the lighted doorway, I drew a deep breath.

It was a sight nothing could have prepared me for. An elderly gentleman lay sprawled across a table strewn with broadsheet newspaper, his glasses still on his face akimbo. I was immediately taken aback. The half-seated body lay as limp as a rag doll tossed aside by an errant child. Was I a witness to a crime scene? He lay as a dead man collapsed among a newspaper shroud.

In what seemed like an eternity I stood frozen in the hallowed glow of the bare incandescent bulb which protruded

In The Shadows of The Honey Trees

beneath an ancient green plastic shade above his unkempt, lifeless head. I felt frozen in time. Suddenly I felt the instinctive sensation that I was being watched. It was my inner hunter's *"third eye"* sending me a warning.

An electric sensation crawled up my spine and I felt my hackles raise on my neck. Fear arrested all my senses in a terrifying flood of uncertainty.

The man lay sprawled across the headlines, his pale profile seemingly uninjured but ashen against the glow of the paper. It was a scene completely of another world, an equal but opposite universe from the one I just stepped out of.

In the shadows in the far recesses of the room a single yellow eye caught the glint of the light that illuminated the corpse before me. As my eyes adjusted to the lighting the hair on the back of my hair rose again instinctively.

It was a single unblinking yellow eye. I stood transfixed under the double spell of fear and curiosity …What I saw before me made no sense. The piercing eye sat about eighteen inches above a visible shelf where several hardcover books lay dishevelled. It seemed to rest atop a yellow twig crowned with a white mass that melded with the shadows. Then again, it could have been my imagination …then it blinked.

The next two seconds were the longest of my life. Seconds took on an elasticity that defied the tenure of time. My brain struggled to construct some known creature form with insufficient information.

Then my attention fell to a pair of dark eyes staring at me from a shadowed recess in the cabinet a little further down the wall. It was a large black crow - no, a raven. Its arresting stare was directed at me – accusational eyes of jet. The pale-yellow light glanced off the thick plumes of steely gun-barrel blue.

I looked again to the remains of Mr. Brown upon the table but saw no sign of any allegiance - no lifting and falling of life's breath; no slumbered stirring; no mortal signs. None!

It was a quantum moment. Time was vacuous. It imploded like a death star. It assumed the texture of mud, the type that roots one to the ground in a dream and from which one seeks to, but cannot, escape - a black hole where neither flight nor fight were an option. I had been here before and it had not ended well for me.

The world could no longer be measured in time but rather by space; a space filled by the unwavering gaze of two silent witnesses to a felony and to my part in it.

If you want to believe that the world is made of snow, go ahead but convincing others of that will demand solid answers. Proving you had nothing to do with the death of another human over whose body you were found standing might well be another matter.

The yellow eye blinked again. The raven continued its riveting stare. It looked through me as if assessing my bones. Only my eyes moved, darting about the room like terrified bats seeking an exit when there was none ...no telephone fixed urgently to a wall, no visible means of consultation, no chiming clock to indicate the passing of the minutes. Nothing ...just empty space filled by the corpse before me and the dark accusing stares.

Somehow, I jerked the ripcord of reality and the parachute of my mind popped open again. I bent down on one knee and placed one hand gently on the cold back of the old man.

"Mr. Brown! Mr. Brown!"..."*Excuse me*" seemed redundant. With the other hand I took his bony wrist searching for a non-existent pulse. Suddenly there was a blink of life. His right eyelash quivered momentarily then flickered to life like a waning antique fluorescent tube.

He sat up, puzzled by my presence. The raven of *trespass* flapped on my shoulder again. I don't know who was the most shocked. We both stammered a moment trying to find our social footing, me confronting the resurrected and he waking to a strange face bent over him as he roused himself from the depths of slumber in the privacy of his own dining room.

"Are you ok?" I gasped.

"Yes, yes," he mumbled, still looking around shocked by my sudden presence, trying to find his bearings.

"I must have fallen asleep," he stammered half apologetically.

I tried to explain myself, but reason seemed to lack traction. I was, by law, a trespasser, who had entered his private space uninvited, if well intended.

"Can I get you some water?" I spluttered. It seemed a hopelessly inadequate gesture, but I had nothing else to offer in the moment.

"Thank you ...in the kitchen" he replied with a directional wave of his hand as he straightened himself in his chair, appearing somewhat embarrassed. Through another doorway I found a glass and brought water from a single brass faucet over a sink in an untidy kitchen. It was a moment that gave us both time to assemble our dignity again.

Returning, I explained that I had been directed to his home by neighbours, as I was seeking information about the local history of the town. He brightened on that note, as do most people when it is suggested their knowledge might be worth hearing.

The owner of the yellow eye interrupted suddenly, unfolding itself like an intricate origami and with three wide flaps of its white feathered wings it landed on its single yellow stilt on the table in front of us.

It was an egret. It bent forward, its single beady yellow eye luminous in the overhead light as it cocked its head to glare directly into my soul with an intensity unique to the one-eyed. Then it pecked sharply at the paper spread on the table in front of the gaunt figure of its guardian, impatience obvious in its actions.

"*He's hungry,*" declared a now-alert Mr. Brown. "*If you look in the refrigerator there is some ground beef.*"

I retreated to the kitchen again where I found a plastic bowl containing finely ground beef.

Mr. Brown took a pinch and offered it to the egret. For a moment I became invisible. It was as if I wasn't even in the room, that I had never walked into this stranger's home and found him first lifeless upon the table but now engrossed with feeding his friend.

Mr. Brown turned and began to explain but was interrupted by the awkward flapping of the raven who was determined not to be left out of the gastronomic dialogue between the egret and the old man.

"*Someone brought him to me with a broken wing,*" he explained of the raven as he fed it a worm-sized slice of beef.

"*He must have been hit by a car. The egret was one of a rare flock that made the lake here its home one summer. I had never seen them here before. When fall came they left, all except this one who I found half frozen on the lake shore in mid-October. One leg had completely frozen as was one eye, but he has managed well with just one of each.*"

The bird hopped deftly about the table on its single yellow stilt vying gamely with the raven for the attention of their saviour. The Lord God Bird or the Thunderbird had had a hand in this.

For the moment I had completely forgotten my mission. I didn't have to ask. The world was unfolding before me as it should. I had stumbled down a proverbial rabbit hole again and found myself looking deeply into the well of a living moment. It was a touching scene of true intimacy…an ancient human extending compassion to the less fortunate regardless of their species, sharing his frugal repast. This considerate act cast him in a shroud of glory, a wizard casting a kind spell on his universe, the love so completely given returned in spades. His kingdom was defined by the halo of light in which these three friends were gathered. It was a rare intimate grace to behold. I savored the honour. I had again peered into the workings of the inner sanctum of the world.

The twilight was gathering outside the windowpane and the light from the lone bulb seemed to intensify, casting its circular spell over this odd trio of friends whose most personal moments I had just witnessed. We chatted for an hour like old friends while the birds refused to leave the table, remaining in the circle of light as if engrossed in our conversation.

As I took my leave all eyes were focused on my departure. The egret looked piercingly at me with its one amber eye (still a remarkably confronting experience) and the raven darkly glared as if it had never trusted me with its master and was glad to see me leave. Mr. Brown waved his farewell having not moved from where he sat enthroned before his subjects. I suspect he lay his head down upon the table again after I left and continued into his dark night as I had found him. I gingerly closed the green door behind me as if departing a dream and retreated down the by-now-dark deserted street.

I hastened to pull my jacket tight against a chill wind which had crept down from the surrounding snow-capped peaks while I was indoors. I paused and looked back at the yellow light falling from the window into the quickening dusk and wondered at the ease with which I seemed so blessed to step between such parallel universes.

§

This scene reminded me of another experience on the banks of the beautiful Bellinger River in Australia years earlier in 1975, where I had stumbled upon the simple home of a Mr. White. He was well into his 80s and lived alone in a simple bungalow screened from the road by a towering clump of giant bamboo whose stems as thick as a man's leg towered more than thirty metres into the air.

It had been the bamboo that had stirred my curiosity and on finding the hidden home behind it I ventured forth and introduced myself to the large Sulfur-crested White Cockatoo which sat defensively on the veranda rail challenging my presence. The bird leaned forward, flashed its yellow crest, flapped its wings at my approach and screeched raucously, a reproach more than a welcome.

The white-haired head of Mr. White appeared in a darkened doorway. His creased face belied his age, and a look of surprise broke into a welcoming smile when I introduced myself and begged forgiveness for my trespass. He was a talkative old gentleman. He was happy if I wanted to salvage some bamboo but warned me it would be almost impossible to disentangle the huge stalks from the mass. He had planted it long ago to provide water pipes and gutters and warned to only cut the stems that seemed least entangled lest they never come loose from the crown of the plant.

I could have as much as I wanted but in return he had a request: Would I help him harvest the guavas from the tree in the garden and make him a guava pie? He still had his dear departed wife's recipe. How could I refuse?

I followed him down to the bottom of the garden and picked a couple of buckets full of fabulously fragrant fruit and the following day returned with the pie, this time armed with a cassette tape recorder. I explained that I would like to conduct an interview with him to record his story and explained that I would like to tape it.

"Tape?" he queried ...This interview was going to be different. I began to explain and clicked the record button. After a moment Mr. White pointed out that my radio didn't seem to be working, for despite clicking the button no sound was emitted. I rewound a few loops of tape and hit *"play"*. He looked incredulous as the conversation of the previous few minutes rolled out verbatim.

"Who is that talking," he demanded to know, hearing his own words but failing to recognize his own voice. It was obvious he had never encountered such magic.

I explained the basic concept of tape recordings and the light of illumination fell across his brow. We chatted disregarding the lazy spinning of this new invention and I regret that in a lifetime of international peregrinations I seem to have lost this record and retrieve it here from my brain. My mind recorded the detail, so I suppose subconsciously I knew I didn't need the tape.

Mr. White had been granted this *"selection"* by the river by the government of the day keen to see entrepreneurial farmers turning out produce. He had worked hard to clear the land of its stands of rainforest and at times he had felt overwhelmed with the task of eking out what would become a small dairy venture. It was isolated and with no nearby township for his milk produce he was primarily involved in churning the cream into butter, which he could pack down to Port Macquarie for sale while raising pigs on the milk by-product. It was an isolated place and lonely and so he had posted an advertisement for a wife in the Port Macquarie newspaper of the day. This bustling hub was a good four-hour ride away, but it was his only hope of finding a wife. He had carefully written out the ad and visited the newspaper office in person in the hopes it might fulfill his wish.

It was about two weeks later that he received a response by way of a letter. If he could travel to Port Macquarie, a young lady in search of a husband would be happy to have him meet with her and her family for dinner on the Friday evening.

He immediately made arrangements and prepared his Sunday best outfit, carefully packing it in his saddlebag, and set off on horseback with his weeks' worth of butter and his hopes high. He arrived with an hour to spare before dinner allowing him to sell his butter and to freshen up at the only hotel before searching out the address of this potential spouse.

Finding the home of his prospective in-laws wasn't difficult and he spent a pleasant evening over dinner with the young lady and her parents where the conversation focused on his life in this far flung but beautiful valley of which he spoke glowingly. The next day they all adjourned to the local racetrack to watch the horses race and by evening things had reached a point where an agreement had been reached that the young couple should marry at church the next day. Suffice to say, speed dating is not new.

In The Shadows of The Honey Trees

The bride arrived at church the next morning in a hastily-refitted gown in which her mother had been married twenty years earlier and Mr. White wore his by-now-becoming creased suit and a new shirt he had purchased for the occasion. They were married before the congregation at the regular Sunday service and spent their first night of wedded bliss in the narrow bed in his room upstairs at the hotel.

On the Monday morning his wife bade her parents farewell and, riding side-seated behind Mr. White, her skirt spreading over the rump of his horse, they ventured off into the wildness of the bush scrub, two romantics on the adventure of their lives. They had lived happy and content in this solitude for fifty years before she had passed away a few years earlier. He still cherished her guava pie recipe and I felt included for having baked the magic spell into such a delectable treat on my first attempt. Mr. White was overjoyed.

As we shared tea and guava pie on his veranda, he made my hair curl with his tales of survival in this remote but beautiful corner of the planet, now known locally as *The Promised Land*. However, its history is sullied by his memory of times when there was a bounty on aboriginal scalps and other outrages which passed for colonial indignation in the day.

I left him standing on the simple veranda, his white feathered companion sitting on his shoulder, wiser for the wisdom not written in books and wondered at what other truths of colonialism have been lost in the mists of wilful blindness brought on by shame.

CHAPTER 12

Temple of the Dawn

"God has no religion."
—Mahatma Gandhi

1984

More years passed. I had wandered from Europe to Africa then back to Australia then to the life of an expat living in Canada, with numerous trips to South and Central America as well as Asia and frequent returns to Australia.

The worst thing about the tropics is the restless hours spent quietly sweating it out in bed at night trying to sleep as the heat continues to assault you by degrees, seemingly egged on by, or perhaps in cahoots with, a bevy of unseeable mosquitoes which maneuver in ever-diminishing circles around your ears, continuing to advertise your invisible whereabouts with their confounding buzzing, even if outside a protective net. They are still the most deadly creature on the planet. They seem to work in a partnership with the heat to deprive the sleeper of the maximum number of hours of restful respite possible. Air conditioning was still a dream in most places and even ceiling fans were a rare luxury as I spent a childhood living under such invisible tyranny while spending summers at my family's beach cabin, sandwiched as it was between a golden stretch of sand on one side and a festering mosquito swamp on the other. Was I doomed to be caught between polar opposites all of my life?

The necessary protective netting (malaria is always just one bite away) seems to suck the oxygen out of the air and trap body heat just when you need it least …and there is always that one mosquito which penetrates all defenses and haunts you from one ear to the other until you thrash out at as if at unseen demons and bury your head under a sweaty pillow just to escape the sound of the menace while offering free blood from exposed parts …a waking nightmare from which there is no escape. It is the very definition of a *'black hole'*.

Their buz-z-zing irritates more than their bites …it is the constant threat which keeps one swatting at phantoms through the night. It is a toss-up …sweat it out in a puddle of your own juices; be ravaged by the insects, whose haunting buzz in the darkness breeds an anxiety worse than the gnashing teeth of a snarling dog, or itch in a puddle of your own blood as you scratch yourself to pieces? For this reason I am a fan of ceiling fans in the tropics. It is the best escape possible from that dual nocturnal curse and far preferable to sleeping in air con.

After one such night spent batting at invisible monsters I embarked on a journey to enlightenment. Everyday *Ra* in his *Barque of Millions of Years* sets sail across the sky whether it be in outback Australia or in the very centre of bustling Bangkok where a quiet monument silently awaits the moment *Ra's* crimson orb emerges glowing from the smog of the million two-stroke motorcycles that idled through the city the day before. The first rays strike the very pinnacle of the *Temple of The Dawn's* tall spire setting it afire against the cotton wool clouds laid out in the porcelain sky over this bustling city of millions.

Platypus Flats

Our boatman had been organized in advance and met us in the semi predawn darkness on the *klong* near our hotel. For the next half hour we had an incidental tour of the people of the city waking up, stretching on their verandas, which extended over the waters of the *klongs* where families swam naked or sat on steps leading into the water from their abodes, washing themselves shamelessly in the cool early air. It appeared a world without pretensions.

We were the first of many to arrive at the temple, so the boatman did not have to jockey for the best observation point. After securing his long skinny craft to a pole in the water he came up to where we were sitting and unpacked for us the most delicious breakfast of sliced mango, melon, monkey eyeballs (a smaller member of the lychee family) and paprikaed pineapple and proceeded to quietly regaled us with the story of the temple as we sat sipping sweet syrupy coffee while drifting gently in the flow of the river as the sun slipped slowly into the sky, illuminating the scene of ultimate tranquility laid out before us. A more deliciously spiritual feast I am yet to behold. The whole was an apparition of loveliness, a credit to any genie!

This Buddhist temple, *Wat Arun*, in the Yai district of Bangkok, sits on the west bank of the Chao Phraya River, but derives its name from the Hindu god *Aruna*, a deity personified as the radiations of the rising sun, proof enough for me that *God* has no religion.

Ra's first gleaming light of the day broke across the smoggy horizon and gilded the tip of the temple spire before beginning a promise of the heat of the day (and more mosquitoes to come at night). My head throbbed with the memory of swimming in last night's bloodied sweat. These memories were quickly swept away by the delightful host; the beautiful food; the freshness of dawn on the water: the slithering cascade of life's breath down the impossibly steep spire; the dawn light refracted by a mosaic of a million shards of porcelain glinting in the sun like the scales of a rainbow serpent. Every family in the city is rumoured to have contributed porcelain pieces to this inspiring edifice which was erected as part of a temple reconstruction two centuries earlier. Whole dinner services are set as concave mosaic jewels on the exterior of the temple walls. It is a sight to behold.

It sits across the wide river from the gilded royal palaces where the king's sacred white elephants idle in their fairy tale stables, which are similarly topped with beautiful golden spires. These also are set ablaze by the blush of light as the sun crests the horizon an embarrassed shade of orange, casting creeping fuchsia shadows among the gilded facades of the exotic palace peaks. Last, but not least, the pink rays finally wash down to the water's edge, there illuminating the life-sized carved white marble crocodiles standing silent sentinels on either side of the white marble stairs into the river making them blush an embarrassed shade crimson as they welcomed the day's pilgrims. After stepping ashore from their flimsy watercraft the arrivees paused to hang fragrant leis of frangipani blooms on the stone creature's snouts. Oh holy place!

Had we arrived twenty minutes later we would have missed this sacred awakening. It was a truly spiritual moment unfolding like a lotus, bursting forth from the mud of night, heralding the throng of a city crowded almost beyond belief. As we drifted for a fleeting moment in the sunrise on the metaphorical *River of Life*, turning gently in currents drawn on only by grace of gravity, the Ioa of my personal Rainbow Serpent slithered out and sunned itself in the glory of it all.

Platypus Flats

§

By some metaphysical umbilical vortex of the dawn this sacred place is connected to another rare place on the opposite side of the planet ...another of my most-loved *Edens* ...the tiny Caribbean Island of Tobago. Mere kilometres off the coast of Guyana and Colombia at the mouth of the Demerara River it is a speck of land approximately ten kilometres wide by thirty-five kilometres long. It is the smallest and western-most of all the many islands of the Caribbean and is home to an extraordinary range of flora and fauna and another dawn phenomenon.

A tiny uninhabited rocky offshore outcrop on the ocean side of the island is home to a colony of majestic red and black frigate birds. As the sun rises out of the Atlantic the birds are roused from their slumber on the rocky cliffs and they prepare to depart for the long flight to the delta of the Demerara River, in Guyana, to feed for the day before returning here each night. As the first rays of the sun warm the rocky isle the air above it starts to rise. The birds simply step out into the updraft with their wings spread wide and one after the other they follow each other in a soaring, silent spiral on the upward column of warming air without beating a wing. It is a spellbinding sight. Hundreds of wide-winged birds are silhouetted in a upward vortex of air, motionless like pterodactyl kites painted on the blue canvas of the awakening sky. Then, when the birds reach a certain altitude, they are sucked into a jet stream which shoots them off toward the delta ten kilometres away at extraordinary speeds, the birds completing this aerial journey having barely beaten a wing. For how many eons have they known this secret place? Did flying dinosaurs know this roost? Has this knowledge trickled

In The Shadows of The Honey Trees

down through evolution for a hundred million years? How they came to make this discovery asks more questions than mere books can possibly answer. It felt like watching the edge of time.

In the nearby seaside village of Speyside we shopped around for a birding guide to take us birdwatching in the jungle. We were told *Parrotman* was the best but first we would have to find him. Each afternoon when the successful fishermen returned from braving ocean currents, they announced their catch by blowing a conch horn which always waits on the long table under the palms by the beach. Here they deftly butchered their prize with a machete, selling it off slice by slice. On hearing the haunting bellow of the conch everyone hurries down from the hillsides to make their selection for supper ...no refrigeration needed. No conch call means stomachs will have to be happy with only *kal-il-oo* in the village tonight. If *Parrotman* had *"caught a fish"* (i.e. had found a client and made some money that day) he might want fish for dinner. This was a hand to mouth economy. It seemed the most likely place to find him.

I was sitting on a palm log with a few of the locals watching the action of the fishermen. I noticed three large scars split wide and angry on the left upper arm of the young man sitting beside me. I enquired what had happened.

He replied:" Somebod-*ee chop me ...wid a machet-ee.*"

I must have scrambled to pick my jaw back up off the sand.

"Who did this?" I demanded, agog at the thought of such savagery.

"My friend there." He indicated a man two metres further down the palm log on which we all perched. Believe it or not, all had been forgiven. With a population of only about

forty thousand people, playing fair means due respect to the privacy of others and the forgiveness of sins.

The 'chopper' had been sentenced to jail time for *'de choppin'* but the 'chopped' also got time for marijuana possession (related incidents perhaps) and was sentenced to lashings across the back with a split cane in spite of having sustained the *'chops wid de machete'*. Then, in an odd twist of *Fate*, they had to serve their time in prison together. The scales of justice in which these lives hung seemed somewhat skewed but the social rifts, along with the gashes, seemed healed. It was an eye-opening adventure, but we didn't have any luck finding *Parrotman*.

Being the only person around with a camera I was invited to officiate as photographer at an island wedding. We would be departing by boat. Dress was *"island casual ...don't wear shoes"* was the official verbal invitation. The reason for this became obvious when we arrived at *No Man's Land* by way of an old, small, wooden-framed motorboat. It is a brief peninsula sporting a few palms, where we had to disembark by slipping over the prow into about a metre of water before wading ashore. The band was already in place perched high on platforms built in the trees. The reason for this later became obvious.

No Man's Land is a point of low-lying land that falls below the high tide line of the highest tides, and, in the old slave days of Tobago, it was the one place where the island slaves could congregate for social occasions since it belonged to 'no one', British law dictating that private property ends at the high tide mark of the highest tides. By its tidal nature it was a sacred gift of the moon, a show of grace to the enslaved. Centuries after emancipation (the first island in the Caribbean to do so) it is still considered sacred.

In The Shadows of The Honey Trees

The bride and groom arrived to much acclaim amid much steel drum beating. They, like the guests, were barefoot and dressed in colorful sarongs and, like the rest of us, waded ashore. In an hour or so we were reminded that we stood at the pleasure of the moon who, soon enough, sent the tide licking at our toes. The colourful formalities completed, the party began to rock as the tide slowly crept in ...until everyone was dancing knee deep in water with no escape other than to slide back into the waiting boats as the band played on in their stage built in the branches of the trees, above the waterline ...the rhythm of natural events dictating the deepest cultural tides I could ever hope to witness ...a culture that reached back to the darkest days of its isolated enslavement of Africans in the Caribbean.

When the tide swirled in over our toes as we danced that moment away, a blink of time when reality was suspended like a jewel of dew on a gossamer thread, we entered a magical realm which left a deep imprint on my soul. With the turning of the tide the portal into that other world closed, leaving us wanting. The band finally stopped playing and climbed down from their perches amid laughter and cheer, abandoning their instruments in the trees to return for them when the tide receded, and they were again sober.

The tide reached its peak. Like those foot-stomping nights in the long-lost colonial ballrooms in which I had grown up, we had just surfed an amazing human wave of spirituality, tied in this case directly to the moon and her power to grant these peoples a sprinkle of freedom, of belonging, of the right to drift in and out, coming and going with the freedom of the tide.

We clambered into the waiting boats wet to the chest and sang and clapped our way home back across the bay.

Tears of appreciation rolled down my cheeks on bidding our new friends farewell (and wedded bliss) at the dock before handing over the precious film that had been our price of admission to the magic of this moment ...to a sacred place where the landless had for centuries gathered for fleeting momentary freedom, the few square metres nature had granted for a brief escape from their enslavement. It was a powerful moment of *kingdom*. The moon giveth and the moon taketh away. Ah! Paradise Lost!

When the British colony emancipated the enslaved, each received a share of the copra estates they had slaved to establish. The island became a beacon as a model for nature reserves and national parks the world over. The many small holdings now held by family groups discourages sales and development is usually done by long-term lease. The ebb and flow of humanity here is palpable ...weddings, births, deaths ...all have a place in daily island lives ...as did the sea turtles who dragged themselves out of the ocean to dig holes in the garden of the home we had rented to lay their eggs.

I was invited one day to help secure the funerary pots, large community cooking cauldrons, which simply made the rounds of the island funerals as needed. It took me into many private gardens as my friends searched for these sacred vessels. These were necessary for the preparation of a special dish of *"dollymander... a big liz-zard from de fore-est"* which, in hindsight, I understand might be some island form of giant "salamander" whose consumption is reserved there solely for one's celebration of life ...only served at funerals! I have also read that the skin of many salamander species is hallucinogenic. I did not partake of such honour here despite, in that moment, being swept up in the embrace of a cultural wave of acceptance and in a manner of *"bread'er'in"*

In The Shadows of The Honey Trees

... (in other words, accepted as family ...welcomed to family hospitality as *"a frien' ob Iguana's"*), hosted to family meals and events – celebrations of births, burials, weddings and wakes. It was genuine, human, warm acceptance, the welcome of being included authentically in the island's inner circle. It left an impression that, as its final societal honour, this culture served up the sacrifice of its rarest creature (hallucinogenic to boot) to mourn one's passing.

This cultural was a mesh of religious and cultural beliefs, ranging from the true Rastafarian adherents living as holy men in caves in the mountains, to strong Voodoo beliefs and the power of curses incanted, overlayed by a contrasting veneer of fresh-faced evangelism.

The next day the pots were finally located, and we returned with them in the back of the pickup truck to the home of the deceased where the wake was under full steam. The children played outside in the street and the women busied themselves serving tea and biscuits and preparing the open wood fires for the pots in the garden while the men seemed content to suck on their cigarettes as they sat around inside playing cards on the kitchen table. It was one of the most shocking kitchen table experiences of my life. Old Fred, who had passed away the previous morning, was laid out in his Sunday best, unshrouded, slap bang right down the middle of the kitchen table. Dead, plain as day! Around him his friends gathered drinking home-made rum and playing cards on what remained of the surface of the green painted rough-hewn surface not occupied by Fred. This was a personal relationship with death I had never encountered before. In fact I had never seen a dead person before. Any dead person I had been around before was safely sealed in a coffin. I had that feeling of trespass that had flapped so raucously on my shoulder as a child delivering granny's note to Ol' Edith in her haunted wood. I was witnessing something very personal.

I was set at ease with a tin cup of rum and expressed my condolences to those present and my appreciation about how good Fred "looked" there on the table; how I was sorry I hadn't met him sooner; and what a wonderful man he must have been to have so many caring friends to help him on his way. Crooked smiles were cracked then cards were shuffled, cigarettes smoked, money changed hands, neighbours arrived from their tin-sided shacks painted every color of the rainbow ...not by some quirk of artistic expression as I had wrongly assumed but because *"dat de only colour de paint shop had."* I should have known better.

Hands of cards were tossed hard in disgust or triumph and a couple of times, when someone thumped the table particularly hard, Ol' Fred moved just enough for me to wonder if I wasn't witnessing some macabre *theatre noir.*

As I left, I discreetly tucked a twenty-dollar bill into Fred's hand so he might buy his friends a last round of rum before they all gathered the next morning, somewhat hungover from the celebration of his life, to gather him up in his shroud and convey him to the glen beneath the fabled Silk-cotton Tree. There are only several such trees on the island, but it is the consecrated ground of whatever ancient belief system was rooted here by the first people. Centuries of burying island residents among the roots of these enormous sacred trees have fertilized enormous limbs luxuriant with aerial vegetation of incredible diversity; orchids of every color; vines and bromeliads literally cascade from the overcrowded branches while countless beautiful butterflies flit about the branches, bright flashing halos in their sun-splashed orbit.

In The Shadows of The Honey Trees

The Silk-cotton Trees are the quintessential *Tree of Life*, true guardians of the souls.

As the sermon by the church official dressed in purple droned on rainbow-coloured Bee-eaters fluttered back and forth to their nests in the adjacent embankment, their brilliance reflected in the colorful dress of the people gathering below, where those who rest among these roots live on in the branches. The parade of mourners, each as resplendent as the birds and the butterflies above, gathered in the still dewy jungle, flashing beads of color in the sunlight filtering through the fronds, alerting eternity that Ol' Fred was on his way. In such a sweet place might we all be so fortunate to lay at our final rest. It seemed that here the world was turning as it should, the cycle of human life a cog in some greater, grander whole.

§

It is impossible to hold a grudge in an isolated community. On Tobago everyone on the island shows up at Bucco Beach every Sunday after church for *"Su-unda-ay scho-o-ol"* where all sins are forgiven. Church is not something to be missed on Caribbean islands. Like the island birds of the forest the women of the island (and many men) are skilled at making their own plumage and on Sundays everyone steps out of what may be a simple cabin all looking like they just stepped from the pages of *Vogue*. It was our ritual every Sunday to sit in the cafe by the church to watch this gathering of finely feathered divas under extravagant hats whose creations were inspired by the plethora of spectacular birds and butterflies that peopled their world. There could be no doubting any God's great pleasure in this sight.

Platypus Flats

Su-unda-ay scho-o-ol started around 3 pm Sunday afternoon when crowds had finished their religious duties and they gathered with their fastest goats for the first event ...the Goat Races. Anyone with a goat is there hoping their animal could win some beer money. If they lose, they will have to pass by the bootlegger's backyard still where bananas and mangoes and sugarcane are enticed to exude an extraordinary home cooked rum, a form of fiery liquid spirituality ...the true flavor of a Caribbean hangover.

With religious zeal the goats are trained to run to their owner at the far end of the track. Every inch of fencing was occupied by tethered goats who gazed out at passersby through their strange rectangular irises, which give them a far-away-devil-may-care kind of expression that bears no love. The events were all pretty much dog and pony show stuff, except with goats.

After a couple of hours the racing was finally over, the crowd was tipsy, and bookmakers marked their tallies amid a swarm of worthless butterflied betting slips which now carpeted the ground. Only the book makers seemed to be winning. Suddenly a truck hauling a pair of huge two-metre-high sound speakers pulled up and without a word the driver hopped out of the cab, wrapped a climbing belt of colored cloth around the nearest electricity post, shinnied up, took two leads and simply applied the clips directly to the main community overhead electricity wires. My jaw dropped again.

The speakers crackled a bit before a sweet liquid bath of Latino Carib beats started to wash over the fun of the fair. Soon I could feel my diaphragm pulsing to the volume, squishing the beer I had drunk around uncomfortably. As if cued by the rhythm of the electric tin drums roadside vendors start appearing out of nowhere to feed the by now hungry hordes who had been drinking beer all afternoon in the hot island sun and were now jigging and jiving on the same grassy verge where once the goats had raced.

The Caribbean sun slunk into the horizon, a galactic fried egg for a moment before being consumed by *Tan*. The lights of the food vendors and the smoke of their fires added to the atmosphere and with diaphragm-pulsing music raising the collective blood pressure of everyone from grandmas grooving with their grandkids to young couples barely able to contain their explosive sensuality as they undressed each other with their eyes as they danced.

In the gathering dusk I *'limed'* (relaxed) with a group of young men when one returned from a vendor's stand with a paper cone (a page from an old elementary school maths workbook) stuffed with French fries. He offered them to me, and I reached out to avail myself of the treat. Midway to the offering my eyes registered that these were no ordinary fries, they were fried chicken feet. I probably paused too long, but my brain quickly made the necessary adjustment, and I was introduced to a crunchy delight I otherwise would have had difficulty bringing to my lips. When in Rome...

As the party wore on into the late evening word spread that *"de beer is runnin' out!"* The news shot around the fairground like a bolt of greased lightning and there was a sudden mass movement toward the bar which stood to one side of the field, it's back to the beach.

We decided it was late and made a break for it, bade whatever friends we had made that day goodnight and walked back along the beach, past the beached shipwreck of a fishing boat that now served as a home for old *Rock*, to our temporary home ...a large, old, now-less-than-grand beach

Platypus Flats

house that stood some half kilometre down the beach. We need not have bothered. The music continued to rock the pictures on the walls even at that distance and we were only able to lie on the bed pulsing to the music and listening to the rapture of the mosquitoes buzzing succulently just beyond the stifling net over the bed until the din finally died down around 6 a.m. when the Ra arrived and somehow, magically, simply by his presence, evicted the remaining stragglers. The party was over for another week. After the libidinous throbbings of the night before the people of Bucco Beach rest on Mondays, having fulfilled their weekly responsibility to the rest of the island to provide entertainment after Church ...Church as a proper noun ...a place of that importance. A place where the community joined in spiritual rapture every week ...before retiring to the goat races and reverting to their sinner ways ...and the beach-side electric-marimba tin-drum symphony that slowly eroded the evening every Sunday here in Bucco since before anyone could remember. These are the knots in the visceral cultural web that is Tobago!

I almost started a fight one day when I stopped to pick up two hitchhikers. It was island protocol to pick up anyone needing a ride if you had space in your vehicle. The further man was an old gentleman, and the nearer fellow was a young Rastafarian with a lifetime of dreadlocks folded neatly on his head like a blanket. I stopped somewhat nearer the older gentleman who was comfortably seated beside me before the young *Rastaman* drew up a bit annoyed I had made him walk so far. He sat in the back but was sullenly silent. We reached his destination shortly and he departed with a minimum of good grace. I drove on with the old gentleman as company. Never one to ignore a human story

I started out the conversation about *"family?"*... It is always a good ice breaker.

"*Oh yes. I 'uv twelve child-rin on de inside and two on de outside,*" he volunteered. I must have looked blank.

"*Congratulations!*" I managed.

The look of puzzlement on my face was recognized and he explained further: "*I 'uv twelve wid me wife on de 'inside' and two wid me gilfren 'outside' me union.*"

I struggled to keep my boat of disbelief afloat. Here was a gentleman who knew no manufactured shame who had taken the rudimentary life he had been born to and had learned to recognize and maximize every opportunity. He lived near the top of Patience Hill, so named before the advent of the automobile. Here I was invited in. The hut was made of ancient rainforest wood, obviously cleared from the land when the plantation was established two centuries earlier. It looked just as it had when his enslaved x2 great-grandparents were ceded this section, along with their freedom. He had woven himself a fragile happiness with the world he had been granted. I stood humbled by the candor with which this man had played the cards he had been dealt quite successfully and without apology nor complaint. He not only supported everyone with his copra crop but had a lucrative government contract to keep the grass verges of the road clear of grass. This he accomplished with a small herd of placid cattle, which he tethered with ropes each day at a different place along the way. He had thus used his cleverness to become a cattleman without the need of acreage. I had to admire his resourcefulness.

This tiny island paradise is home to hundreds of species of brilliantly coloured tropical birds, butterflies and flora. It is surrounded by coral gardens and has wisely limited mass tourism development to a strip of land directly across the road from the airport, conveniently leaving the rest of the island almost untouched. It is one of the last surviving windows into such a paradise lost. It was a complex place, shaped by Rastafarian roots washed over with African Voodoo overtones and a sprinkle of surface evangelism.

§

We eventually found the eccentric forest-dwelling gentleman named *Parrotman* and hired him as our birdwatching guide. To make for an early start we stayed in a simple half open room he had built in a tree by his house. In the morning we found a large boa under our bed ...no kidding ...attracted, according to our host, by the heat our bodies cast through the bed. I hesitated to think what may have happened if that wasn't warm enough for it. We were miles from any outside contact as telephones of any stripe had not intruded into the hinterlands of the island at that time. *Parrotman* had no phone and to find him we simply had to watch for *"de guy wid de dreads in de red jeeep"* ... We put word out on the street that we had *"emplo-oyment"* for him. (Tobagonians speak English *swe-e-etly* ...the rhythm of an ancient language translated to a new tongue, with every utterance imbued with a social grace that matched a long subverted linguistic thread, the invisible foundation of an ancient humanity uprooted centuries earlier and transplanted here into slavery, not entirely unlike penal Australia).

Parrotman must have had another name but as with *Floaty* and *Limey* and *Razorblade* and *Greeny* and *Blow* and *Mira* and *Fruitman* and *Iguana* and *Fingers* and *Hacksaw* no one bothered to use it.

In The Shadows of The Honey Trees

Resources were never squandered here. As the few street lights in the villages spluttered to life when darkness fell families would pull their tables and thrice-repaired plastic chairs into the circle of light on the street verge under the streetlamp and eat watermelon and play cards under the glare of this rare utility until the inevitable eclipse of moths attracted by the light eventually drove everyone to seek solace in the darkness of their simple homes until only a handful of young men remained handing a *"spliff"* back and forth now that the adults had retired while arguing over whose grandma knew whose grandma.

The other option at this hour was to go to *Floaty's* place and watch television. *Floaty* had rows of folding chairs in his one room home, the better to share the good fortune of his television set with his neighbours. The picture was such a blur of snow I found it difficult to watch so *Floaty* went outside and adjusted the *"Sesame Street satellite dish"* ...the skeletal remains of a large metal-ribbed beach umbrella wired to a long bamboo pole and then wired to the back of the television set ...and, to my doubtful surprise, the image improved slightly. I watched for half an hour so as not to offend his generous hospitality before departing with *Razorblade* to the local bootlegger's house where we stood in the dark garden calling softly through the open but dark bedroom window to try and score some homemade rum from a bootlegger, who was obviously already in bed. I fully expected a shoe to be thrown at us but here everything was flavored with certain *eau de enigma*.

After some muffled exchange a hand thrust a corked rum bottle through the dark opening of the window and a large note was exchanged in silence.

Platypus Flats

§

In the morning the village water was turned on. It happened once or twice a day, gushing from central faucets which were always left 'on'. Those who could afford houses with roofs capable of channelling water into tanks at the corners were the independent elite.

Each village's water was only delivered intermittently by a single faucet atop a slender pipe in the middle of the dirt road intersection. It was left turned to 'on' all the time for a reason.

"Ow else we gonna know de water is here if de tap not be turned on?" I was chided when I suggested turning it off to avoid wasting the supply. Of course! How stupid of me.

This was a community where you could order your chicken *"pluck 'n' gut"* or you could take it home squawking and do the *"pluck 'n' gut"* yourself. But beneath the silky surface of tropical tranquility rivalries ran deep. Anyone making a good business move was viewed with suspicion ...that it must somehow be *"il-legal"*.

Parrotman had cleverly invested in fifty pairs of rubber boots costing $10 a pair. He waited by his bundle of boots at a mountainside bus stop where tour buses carrying birders arrived with regularity. Given that these jungle birding trails are wet and greasy all the time it didn't take long for dismayed tourists in their new white holiday scuffs to shell out $5 for boot rental. I had to hand it to him for cornering a market. He was making an obscene amount of money by island standards, but the envy of others saw him always wary of being a victim of a ruthless tall-poppy syndrome, which seems to permeate islands everywhere.

I hired him as our guide and the following three days were as wondrous as any I have spent. A tropical cloudburst interrupted one afternoon and had us struggling up steep greasy pathways through the jungle. *Parrotman* went on ahead. The birds had vanished to their hides to ride out the storm and it felt a bit like any other parade that had been rained on ...overly moist!

I stopped to rest by a small stream and sat for a moment on a wet log watching the fresh in the rill tumble over the rocks. Out of nowhere the least extraordinary looking bird imaginable - small, buff and bedraggled (like me) from the storm - flew down and alighted on a thin branch not a metre from my face.

We stared at each other for a moment, unmoving. The bird looked at me eyeball-to-eyeball and then fearlessly threw back its tiny head, opened its beak and broke into a song so spellbindingly beautiful that I instantly fell into its spiral of rapture. In that moment I was witness to the power of the *Lord God Bird*, and there, in this most unlikely place, I had heard the voice of *God*.

The bird took its own song for granted and as it sang it was lost in the power of its own glory. It demonstrated something I could never have learned from books. Together in the forest, tired and wet and weary, it showed itself as the "elephant in the room". It sprang from the "cup half full" theory of human thinking and simply filled it up with itself- being-itself, celebrating the moment so selflessly and without conceit, until both our cups *"ranneth over"*. It reminded me of my favourite myth, the Mayan story of *Zit Zaat Zooon* ...the tiny hummingbird.

§

The Story of *Zit Zaat Zooon*

Zit Zaat Zooon was the drabbest little brown bird in all the forest. Her spectacular dizzying flights set her in a class of her own in the size-to-speed division, but for all her zooming grace she was a simple drab, brown bird the same colour as the dirt. For Zit Zaat Zooon's wedding, Pachamama the Earth Mother, asked all the forest birds to contribute their best feather for the creation of Zit Zaat Zooon's dress of love.

Feathers collected, Pachamama commissioned a crafty old spider to tailor the gossamer gown. Using long-forgotten magic stitches and invisible thread he created a tiny gown of unimaginable iridescent loveliness reflecting the very best all the other birds had to offer. So astonished were the birds at the sight of their now dazzling friend dressed in such glory that they begged Pachamama to permit Zit Zaat Zooon to wear the new gown in perpetuity. And she and her kind still illuminate the forests to this day with their brilliant plumage as they speed about their lives.

§

Like the old spider we all surround ourselves with a cape of beliefs, friends and support systems. From this we select that which we most admire in those people who have touched us deeply and, if we possess enough magic, we weave our own fabled cloak.

In The Shadows of The Honey Trees

One such Tobagonian gentleman who contributed a feather to my cape was Mr. Loving. We were staying in a tiny cottage in a village responsible for supplying Tobago's demand for chicken. These were small troops of chickens maintained by almost every household in the village. Every morning, one by one, the roosters begin their crowing starting about 4 am until the din was impossible to ignore and one simply had to surrender to such a force and get up. Roosters also don't know the rule about sleeping in on Sundays. By 5 a.m., as the first grey fingers of the day crept across the sky, hundreds of roosters would be screeching their territorial claims, however small. It was why rent was cheap in this village. Tourists failed to appreciate the predawn rooster choir.

Each morning, as we had coffee in the garden fronting the street, we were daily regaled by *Fruitman*. (That is pronounced *Frrr-oot-mon*).

"*Ello. Gud mornin'! I is Frrrootmon. You be needin' mango fer breakfas? ...pineapple? ...no banana but I can bring you later. Do you ne-eed any other diffffi-cult to oob-tain sub-stan-ces?*" I'm sure he could have filled any order.

Every morning a young woman would also walk the streets with a large tray of home-baked goodies balanced on her head to tempt our fast. She one day asked if Mr. Loving could pay us a visit. He was a village elder, she explained, who had heard some Canadians were staying in town.

Curious, we agreed. Later when the sun was high a grey-haired elder with a broad smile on his kindly face arrived at our door supported by a sturdy staff. I offered him a cane chair on our porch and brought lemonade while he fanned himself with a broad palm frond.

He wanted to thank us personally for Canada's *"enormous"* kindness and caring for treatment he had received after he was terribly injured in a nasty accident that almost cost him his life.

He had been riding his best mule, he explained, high on the hills behind the village dragging logs. He was mounted on the animal at the end of the day and had begun his weary way back down the mountain when something startled the animal. He was thrown from its back, but his foot had caught in one stirrup. The animal bolted for home and by the time it reached the stable gate Mr. Loving's leg was shattered in thirteen places. He was so badly injured that his family despaired for his life. He was assessed as urgently needing radical medical intervention and was quickly airlifted thousands of kilometres to Canada where doctors pieced his leg back together and helped him through the long rehabilitation.

"Canadians took care of me wife too so she could be wid me while they put me back together and didn't charge us one penny. You Canadians didn't even know us, but you gave us back our life. I cannot say enough thank yous to express my grace." The old man shed a tear of gratitude as he sipped his drink.

"You Canadians is wonderful people. You is always welcome in our village. You is brethren to Tobagonians." The intimacy of his language was moving. It was nice to hear that my country of choice was doing good things in the world for others less fortunate when no one was necessarily watching.

He eventually took his leave after we had listened as he elucidated his life and loves with a candor my wife and I seem gifted at inspiring in strangers. His gratitude was thereafter reflected in the village (word had passed around there were Canadians afoot). We were no longer tourists but guests of honour. We were invited into homes for meals

In The Shadows of The Honey Trees

(it was always *"po-light"* to discreetly leave $5 each on the side table (handing it to the host would offend) but for all intents and purposes we were accepted as if we were visiting members of the family. Ruby's *"chilli-ee prawns"* at the local restaurant built in the branches of a tree by the beach (to be out of reach of King tides) were legendary and became our island favourite.

One evening after an afternoon playing cricket on the beach with the children (the only way to play this game), the waves fielding in silly-mid-on (or was it mid-off?), we had finished the delicious meal of spicey hot prawns and spent an hour counselling Ruby on how she might deal with the witchdoctor down the road who put a hex on her son so someone else's son would be smarter at school. She confided that the old witchdoctor had been paid off to curse her child. She knew this because the witchdoctor suddenly had four new goats and she *"recognized one o' dem"* as having belonged to a woman whose son was in competition with hers at school. Her belief was so strong she was truly troubled. Being outsiders she could confide in us in a way she couldn't trust those around her. As outsiders we were in the suitably remote position to hear her fears confessed.

It was undeniable, she said. The four new goats in the witchdoctor's compound had previously belonged to the other boy's mother. That her son had been cursed was *"as plain as de nose on yo' face."*

We cautioned that paying more goats to have the hex reversed was unlikely to improve the outcome and that she should encourage her son to overcome the curse by facing it head on and studying hard. That would show the other mother that she had wasted four goats. Revenge is always sweet. I never did hear how that all turned out, but it plays in my imagination sometimes. When it came to depart Ruby's hospitality that night, I realized I had left my wallet back at the house.

"Oh don' worry!" was her flippant response. *"Yo-ous can pay me nextime."*

We walked home past *Razor Blade's* place, through ol' Mrs. Williams vegetable garden (*"Good evening Mrs. Williams"* was the secret password for cutting through her veggie patch), past the farm store advertising *"chicken pluck 'n' gut"* on a huge chalkboard before we were cornered by Adam at the *"fruit stand"*, a solitary wood plank triangle built around a light post where he radiated hope into the early hours from his 'stand' on the edge of a scruffy three-way intersection. Armed with a blender hooked up to the street light power lines and a supply of fresh goat milk he was not going to take our being penniless as an excuse for not *"enjo-oying de worl's bes"* smoothie. We could also pay him *"to-mor-row."* We sat on a split palm log and surrendered to the colour of the character. Adam knew everything. Everyone gave up parts of a secret to him he said and each customer who returned would be asked another related or the same question - *"jes to see if dey remember deir li-iess".*

He was the epitome of the expression: "When life serves lemons, make lemonade!" In the face of dire necessity and armed only with an old second or third-hand blender hooked up to a streetlight and a good measure of enthusiasm he was making a go of life as it had been dealt to him and spreading joy while he was at it. I consider his raw contribution to the human spirit places him among the giants.

CHAPTER 13

"Celestial"

Seek not greater wealth, but simpler pleasure, not higher fortune, but deeper felicity.
—Mahatma Gandhi

The moments which stand aloft in my life are not the meetings with the rich and famous, of which there were many, but the confirmation of humanity by unpretentious strangers in candid moments in forgotten corners of the globe …places without pomp and fanfare. One poignant moment occurred in the jungles of The Sacred Monkey by the Usumacinta River, the frontier border between Southern Mexico and Guatemala.

The area is shrouded in thick tropical jungle inhabited mainly by indigenous people, descendants of the original monumental Mayan civilization, now living, much as they had forever, in simple thatched dwellings scattered through the forest in an area rich in the awe-inspiring ruins of their ancestors. Many stone edifices survive in remarkable condition casting unparalleled colourful graphic insights into the minds of the inhabitants of a thousand years prior.

Language divides this planet, and it is never so much in evidence as when one visits the largely Spanish-speaking South and Central Americas. Despite abject material poverty the libraries in these cities are oasis of calm and grace and elevated to places of worship. To my delight, they were full of books rarely seen by English eyes and I became acutely aware of how having only focused on English language books had crimped my information base. It was akin to discovering another world.

The ruins of Central America make those of Egypt look like a small rural village. The scale of the Mayan, the Aztec and Inca civilizations is staggering. At its zenith the population of the early Americas must have numbered in the mega millions. Today Mexico City alone is home to more than thirty million people. Social scientists have calculated that the central American indigenous population is only now recovering to its pre-European contact numbers, five hundred years on. While the locals speak their many indigenous dialects everyone also speaks Spanish to a greater or lesser degree.

Far from the capital we had wandered into the jungle marvelling at architectural wonders time has forgotten which have only recently been wrested from the clutches of the thick choking undergrowth. The Bonampak ruins still sport frescoes of remarkable alacrity with visions of dangers and delights and warriors bedecked in colorful pigments with a surprising element of fantasy mixed with these ancient hallucinations.

We arrived in a tiny village where we had made prior arrangements for overnight accommodation. There we met two young British men travelling independently who likewise had planned for overnight room and board in this remote hamlet.

Our hosts were an indigenous couple and their three children, one a young girl about seven years old. The children

In The Shadows of The Honey Trees

found us curiosities and in our limited common Spanish we embarked on conversations. The young girl in question was intrigued when I pulled out my pencil and sketch book and began to draw.

These beautiful olive-skinned people were remarkably open in their hospitality. We invited the child to sit at the table with us while her mother prepared our meal (with a baby slung across her back) and to draw in my sketchbook. She was delighted. For her it was an extraordinary moment of discovery.

She was a striking exception to the usual tribal features of glossy, perfectly straight black locks. Her hair was instead completely blonde, a genetic deviation approximated by the phenomenon of red hair among Europeans. With her golden complexion, dark Mayan eyes and her tow-colored hair, she was, in a word, striking.

For a time she was completely focused on making marks with the coloured pencils and looking at my drawings. Then suddenly, completely without warning, she looked straight into my eyes. She clasped my face between her tiny hands, gazed deeply into my soul and proclaimed in a wonder possible only in the innocent: "Ojos *celestial!*" (*"Heavenly eyes!"*). It was a simple exclamation. Just two words but coming from a place of utter innocence. I had glanced at these eyes in the mirror every day of my life but realized now that I had never really *"seen"* them.

In half a century of wandering the world I had never been on the receiving end of such a sweet and heartfelt compliment. It had taken the clear-eyed observations of an innocent jungle princess to point out the two most obvious gems in my crown ...not as any kind of polite compliment or false flattery, but as an unadulterated statement of fact, an indisputable truth, nothing more, nothing less ..."*celestial*".

I had wandered, seeking grails, holy and otherwise, without noticing to look back and *"see"* the windows into my own soul (what else had I missed?). I had confronted them daily and I had taken them utterly for granted. They may have been the first blue eyes this young girl had ever encountered up close and kind, but I am forever humbled by her purity of spirit. It shines still decades later, a human pool of limpid *felicity* in the surrounding darkness in the soggy jungle of memory.

I had seen a similarly illuminated moment of the spirit once before when I had the opportunity to teach printmaking to two youngsters who were deaf. I approached the lesson with cut-out character silhouettes that could be repositioned against changing frames of color, to tell a visual story in comic strip style. The lesson was necessarily very visual.

At a certain stage of the instruction the young lad suddenly began to pump out images of a white duck on a yellow ground with ever changing backgrounds. The duck was swimming, then walking, then flying. The boy's spirit at that moment took wing and soared ...and mine with it. His sister, looking on, grasped the flame of illumination from her brother and they both began to churn out their visual stories. To be able to clearly elucidate our thoughts is a priceless craft. To see that door thrown open in such joy in my presence was truly humbling. It is a magic place beyond mere words where, unfortunately, few get to tread.

After our Mayan repast of squash and corn and beans our jungle hosts showed us to our thatched room. It was spacious but we had to laugh. The room contained two double beds. One for my wife and I and the other for the two young men, who were complete strangers. It was an exercise in negotiating the minefield of cultural ambiguities and privacies which left us all giggling through the darkness after the compound's generator was shut off at 9 p.m. sharp.

The next day we took our leave of the little blonde jungle girl and soldiered on up The River of the Sacred Monkey cramped in a long skinny wooden boat replete with a cargo of several motorcycles, which were loaded by driving them up a wooden plank and jumping them into the craft with a short, sudden burst of power. It required a special skill. The boat owner himself conducted this mission. We were accommodated in what space remained. We had no clue as to where this might lead us for we followed blindly a dog-eared map which had excited this adventure now leading us on via crocodiles basking on the steep muddy banks up which there would be no hope of escape for any ship-wrecked adventurers. The head of each of these great reptiles, remarkably, was surrounded by a fluttering halo of brilliant butterflies, which bobbed about seeking the minerals excreted from the great reptiles' eyes. Oh crazy world! We *'arrived'* miles up the river in Guatemala, dragging our wheelie suitcases up the muddy, muddy banks of the mighty Usumacinta into a tiny village of about six buildings where we were greeted only by a swarm of snorting pigs. There was no customs office, no one to stamp our passports …nothing. Just a few huts without any barriers to keep the animals from the door. No stores. No signs of life other than the pigs. But word travelled fast, and it wasn't long before someone with a car hauled up to see if they could be of help. We hired him on the spot to drive us to the nearest accommodations an hour or two away and began a trek across open cattle country, which had obviously been hewn from a now depleted jungle that had once matched the forest in Mexico on the other side of the river. It was confronting to see the loss. We were informed by our driver, a middle-aged cowboy with an easy laugh, that we would have to report to the authorities a hundred kilometres away. He could take us that far for a price. Freedom always comes at a price. It is always worth paying such fees in most Spanish-speaking countries where all drivers involved in an accident are usually considered guilty till proven innocent. Hiring drivers is cheap insurance. We had thus followed a hopscotch of pilgrimages around the globe, through revolutions and sweaty jungles, past wonders our eyes could scarcely believe, over rivers and stark plains and brutal deserts.

This adventure through rolling grasslands ended when we arrived at Tikal, the center of the extraordinary ancient Mayan culture, arriving via the back door. The Spanish conquistadors, who trekked here on this route half a millennium earlier, had gifted the head honcho of a nearby lake-town a horse, an animal beyond the comprehension of the early American population. In reverence they had fed it only flowers until it died of starvation, (or so the legend goes).

We were road weary by the time we passed through the Tikal staging area for day tourists on our way to check into the limited hotel space we felt very lucky to have secured in advance with the help of our driver. Tikal is a popular destination with thousands of day trippers to the ancient city ruins, which spread over more than twenty square kilometres. As our driver nudged his way through the bustling crowds heading toward the food outlets for breakfast my wife declared she saw an old friend from afar (and from behind) across the crowd. I mocked her. How could that be possible? We had been crawling along through remote unknown backwaters for weeks not even knowing ourselves where we were so how could such a coincidence occur? But *'occur'* it had, for three hours later, as we reached the peak of 'Tower 3' (one of the highest vantage points in the whole ruins) who should be sitting there but our friend George, whom we hadn't seen or had contact with in years. The wings of the Lord God Bird work in mysterious ways.

A few days later we arrived in La Antigua, a city of ruined splendor, the 16th Century papal center of the New World trashed by an earthquake in the mid 19th Century, then abandoned. It is a city of resolute beauty, the ruins of large Franciscan monasteries, now reinforced and serving out their days as five-star hotels or splendid private enclaves.

Guatemala is a rampantly beautiful landscape littered with thousands of years of grand cultural ruination but now overrun with crime and abject poverty, which sadly is commonplace in Central America today. To add to this enigmatic chaos the landscape is littered with active and dormant volcanoes, a coarse reflection between the *"haves"* and the *"have nots"*, surrounded by a lush canopy of tropical rainforest, home to thousands of exotic flora and fauna … some of the planet's most exquisite living gems, all overlaying the stupendous ruination of ancient cultures.

One of the planet's most macabre human civilizations …the Maya …had abandoned their awe-inspiring vainglorious cities, once home to hundreds of thousands and where thousands more were often sacrificed to appease their gods. Stupas of ancient stone sit cheek-to-jowl with a rainforest of such diversity and temples and churches of such architectural wonder that together they take your spiritual breath away.

Jewelled birds compete with clownish butterflies for wing space in the jungles while some of the world's most dazzling orchids trail from the trees which attempt to strangle the acres of still-buried-little-understood civilizations which stretch the length and breadth of Mesoamerica.

Amid this cacophony of colour lies the raw underbelly of the remnants of the brutal Mayan culture, now masquerading under guise of the Holy Roman See. Everywhere are evident the ruined human bodies, the cost of brutal civil unrest of only decades past.

When the Spanish arrived Cortez, in his chain mail and ostrich plume-topped medieval metal helmet, was mistaken for the incarnation of *Quetzalcoatl*, the feathered serpent god of the indigenous population. It was an almost bloodless coup. The Spanish brought with them another powerful marvel ...the arch.

The Maya, and other Mesoamerican cultures, were superlative stonemasons and, with ruins galore to provide an endless immediate supply of ready cut stone, the Spanish dazzled the jungle dwellers by building new sacred buildings. Here not just the priests could convene with the gods atop a pyramid but under arches, which seemed to almost magically hold aloft great towers of stone, the common man was able to venture into the sacred space. The locals came in awe and brought their Mayan practices with them.

I have witnessed live chickens sacrificed in village churches and offerings of rum poured around the smoky tallow votives stuck to ancient stone floors by more than five centuries of wax. The floor may already have been laid centuries before Cortez arrived and simply been repurposed. We will never know.

Modern day civil wars have raged across many of these tiny mountainous countries, fueled by a bad combination of drugs, greed and evil, often fed from afar by forces outside the imagination of a poorly educated huddled mass of humanity left in the wake of the tidal waves of social change and violence which have pummelled their sunny shores for the last five centuries.

The price of this dysphoria-in-paradise is written on the faces of the locals. I can never forget the deep tremors in my soul when my eyes first fell upon the battered human remains of the brutal clashes between political extremists ...of mere remnants of humanity dragging their all-but-obliterated bodies around on little wooden trolleys with small metal wheels, eking an existence by begging or polishing the shoes of others to put even a little food in their mouths.

There were days when I had my shoes polished three times for to simply offer money was to offend the dignity of a hardworking shoe-shiner and to undermine them by condemning them to the lower position of beggar. Everyone has their pride.

Not all shoe-shiners are born equal. In Guatemala, for example, grown men who have had their bodies destroyed in the civil wars that plagued the country can be found plying their trade on their established corners while street urchins as young as five work on an ad hoc basis in cafes and parks. These children are quick to demonstrate their linguistic capabilities to deliver the service with formal business banter in your language of choice.

According to shoeshine boys I consulted, one cannot have a girlfriend if you shine shoes, for to aspire to a relationship is beyond the earnings of a shine boy. Most able-bodied ones moved on to something better paid after turning eighteen with the goal, of course, of amassing sufficient attractiveness to attract a wife.

I remember inviting one young boy of about six to join us in our meal in a cafe since it looked like he hadn't seen the other side of an empty plate in a while. As he perched awkwardly on the edge of the chair, I had the premonition that it was the first time he had ever sat at a table. I served him a plate of food and he began to eat, ignoring the cutlery and using his fingers.

We continued our conversation to allow him the space to eat before plying him with questions. He had seven siblings, and his mother was a single parent who spent the day working at something he couldn't quite translate. He didn't know where his father was, and he couldn't recall his family name or at least he wasn't going to tell us.

Once he finished eating, he was keen to be on his way and we didn't press the point. We had earlier had the waiter prepare a whole roast fish *"to go"* and presented it, wrapped in aluminum foil, to the lad who left in haste ...beaming from ear to ear. I'm sure he made a beeline directly home with this prize. After he departed, we glanced down to see a pile of vegetables which he had discreetly discarded under the chair. So much for good intentions. The scars of war run deep and cut through all levels of society. Visitors are not exempt. We must act as if we own the places where we wander and take some responsibility.

La Antigua is one of the most breathtakingly beautiful and oldest European-style cities in the Americas. The architecture is stupendous, mind-boggling even in its ruins. Its original beauty was fashioned by an unquenchable appetite for the local gold and the souls of the local heathens! The city's ornate facade flourished for almost three centuries before it was severely dented by a catastrophic earthquake in the mid 1800s which brought much of it crashing down. After being abandoned for more than a century today's majesty was rebuilt from the ruins into private residences and luxury

In The Shadows of The Honey Trees

hotels, a true phoenix rising from the ashes which threaten it still. At night one can sit in the main square and watch the sparks flying out of the volcano which overshadows the town, a subtle reminded that the gods of destruction were always only one earthquake away.

The beautiful city dreamed into being by the golden riches of conquest is still ringed by active volcanoes which the villagers face down the same way we faced down snakes at *Platypus Flats*. They laugh in the face of fate. After the 19th Century quake the city was promptly abandoned and the new capital of Guatemala City, now one of the ugliest and most dangerous places on the planet, was established a mere modern hour away. The two cities are like chalk and cheese - one the ruinous wreck of dreams gone wrong and the other a ruinous wreck of humanity driven to the edges of despair.

I remember a radio interview with the chief of police for Guatemala City who said there were an average of eighteen murders a day there but the challenge was always which one to investigate as the police department had only one fingerprint kit so only the murder most likely to be solved would be investigated. The other seventeen just fell through the cracks ...every day. At the time the rumoured local price for a hit man to dispose of anyone you didn't want to share the planet with was $25 US. Life was that cheap.

Everyone carried concealed weapons. I remember entering an airport and passing a sign that read: *"No firearms beyond this point"*. That was shocking enough but on entering the departure area there was another ominous sign which read: *"Guns beyond this point will be confiscated"*. In other words ...we know you ignored the last sign, but we mean business this time ...if we catch you. Here one can also expect to be

239

'wanded' when entering a shopping mall. One short flight we were taking was overbooked so the last passenger to board was simply seated on her bag between the pilots ...I kid you not! As we later disembarked at a regional airport a nearby volcano was belching plumes of smoke and ash skyward ... but no one even glanced its way.

Friends who lived there recommended carrying my money in my sock, while keeping five one-dollar US bills in my pocket.

"If someone pulls a gun on you, throw the money on the ground and run. Don't worry about being shot. These people are too smart to kill their golden goose. They won't chase you. They will be too busy picking up the money, "was their wise advice. I opted for a whole pocket full of local *'mula'* as well to make the picking up slightly more time consuming. "Don't bother," the friends said. " They don't want local *mula.*"

My friends said they never bothered reporting such robberies to the police, considering it a total waste of time. They would instead call a friend to commiserate over the trauma and to laugh it off so they could get on with their day. And all avoided that particular spot for a while.

Highway robbery was a daily occurrence with the favourite strategy being to drag a log across the road then rob the drivers and passengers of the vehicles forced to stop on either side. I remember rounding a corner one day to see my first "log-on-the-road trap" ahead. Without even waiting for the car to come to a stop the driver jammed it into reverse and sped away backward up the narrow mountain road. I'm not sure which course of action I would prefer if confronted so again ...handing over my money and my camera or another perilous hair-raising reversal up a narrow, winding, mountain road?

In The Shadows of The Honey Trees

Of course the brave action of our driver required a generous honourarium. He said such highway robbery strategies were most often applied to busloads of people because the heavy vehicles lacked the opportunity to escape as we had.

I decided to celebrate our survival by getting a haircut, but the barber had obviously had a liquid lunch. He almost sliced off my ear with his drunken scissor craft. Once bandaged, we decided to call it a day and take refuge in a local house of hospitality. We were directed to an establishment known as *Casa Perez*.

The three-wheeled *quickshaw* took us through a maze of narrow streets all named *Una Via* before he deposited us at a blank wall on a dangerously deserted cobbled street of definite antiquity. The driver indicated a chain hanging from a hole in the ancient wooden wall, really a giant gate with a smaller human sized door within the larger door, which had once opened to give entry to the courtyard to a horse and carriage.

We tugged on the chain and heard a bell jingle somewhere on the other side and watched anxiously as the *quickshaw* sped out of sight taking with it any last hope of a fast retreat should things go sideways at this strange abode. The log-on-the-road escape was still fresh in our minds as was the scissor attack on my ear. Anything could happen. We felt momentarily naked …exposed and vulnerable …on a deserted roadway, veritable sitting ducks in this crime-ridden landscape where every house presented a fortress facade to the street. The street-side rooms of homes here were often the chambers of business, either as windowless family storefronts or spectacular galleries of local art accessible by appointment only. It was a housing mix which has served the Spanish culture in the Americas well but from the street it presented a solid unbroken wall of buildings should things go pear-shaped.

Eventually a grated portal within the smaller door within the enormous door opened and a sweet face peered out and assessed us as harmless *gringos*. A heavy hasp rasped in its confines and the smaller door within the larger one opened and we were shown into an overgrown courtyard.

Central American courtyards, many of them unchanged in centuries, are oases of tranquility though the modern-day razor wire coils atop the high walls always had me questioning whether I was a prisoner no matter how delightful the prison. The young woman who had shown us in busied herself for a moment securing the door again as we took in the surroundings.

It was an enormous courtyard in a country of courtyards of often staggering beauty. This one followed the line of an outer L-shaped building and an overgrown jungle separating a grand but eloquently shabby mansion in the opposite corner from the long colonnaded wing. The house presented a solid but unremarkable facade to the street and the huge gates were designed to mean "fortress", in a nod to their Moorish influences. The door-within-a-gate continues to afford efficient pedestrian security centuries after its design. One home we frequented had three connecting courtyards each with a beautiful fountain at its centre into which the downpipes of the inner roofs of the complex spouted their rainwater feeding underground cisterns whenever it rained. No detail was too trivial not to serve a purpose here in grand houses designed before the Industrial Age.

This one was a riot of overgrown exotic vines with a rambling *copa d'oro (solandra maxima)* that reminded me of home and trumped all the other spectacular flowers with a

In The Shadows of The Honey Trees

show of plate-sized golden blooms. A gaggle of shiny blue-black birds squabbled over the offerings on a large, elevated feeding station and every column in the long veranda was festooned with clumps of flowering native orchids.

After settling us on a wooden bench by the entrance the woman harvested our information and informed us of the charges for a room by the day. We enquired about a weekly rate, and she quietly excused herself and disappeared down the arcade leaving us watching the large overhead fan slicing futile circles in the steamy tropical air, unable to relieve the sticky heat.

The woman appeared a few minutes later with a quote for the weekly rate and we asked to be shown the room. She led us through the tangle of vines to the entrance to the shabby mansion and proceeded down a darkened hallway without bothering to turn on a light.

The place had the smell of stale air but otherwise the room she led us to had glazed French doors that once had opened onto a private portico but now seemed rusted shut.

She apologized for the staleness of the air and busied herself opening windows and airing the place out. It was obvious that we were the only guests in that part of the building, which also sported a kitchen we could use, as well as a library whose decaying pages were the source of much of the pervading mustiness. (Humidity makes it hard to keep a library in the tropics). It was nothing that running a few fans couldn't solve, especially given the spaciousness of the accommodations and the delightful jungle courtyard view …we agreed to the deal.

When we began to count out the required sum, she explained that we must pay Señor Perez directly. Somewhat reluctant to leave our bags unattended in strange surroundings we nonetheless followed her back to the garden then down the airy arcade where she stopped before an open door and ushered us in.

Nothing could have prepared me for the sight within. Señor Perez was an elderly gentleman, perhaps in his seventies, with a grey balding head, who peered at us from behind gold rimmed glasses. He wore a simple white sleeveless singlet over his upper torso and sat beneath a whirring ceiling fan that failed to ease the sweat from his brow. He was propped up in a bed obviously shortened to better accommodate the office function of the room. He sat surrounded in paperwork which stirred demurely in the air moved by the hardwood blades of the antique cyclotron that wheeled overhead, moving the overheated air without really diminishing its stickiness.

I wasn't prepared to be introduced to someone who was in bed. The young woman who had sized us up initially, introduced us to our host. He sat looking slightly dishevelled (like his papers) and peered up over the rim of the spectacles perched like a gilded bird on his nose. He extended his hand in welcome as I tried hurriedly not to notice that Señor Perez was only half there ...physically ...he was completely missing everything below the navel. Shock is an involuntary reaction. Stunned, I remembered my manners. Smile! Everyone has a right to their past and I think in this gentleman's case he also had the right to try and forget whatever tragedy had befallen him without apology. Only a catastrophic car accident or a volley from a submachine gun or a land mine could have inflicted so much damage. That he had survived his tragedy in such a colonial outpost was certainly nothing short of a miracle. That he had carried on as unaffectedly as possible in exercising his life in a successful and cheerful way that accommodated the hand he had been dealt was nothing less than utterly extraordinary! The wind from the wings of the *Lord God Bird* had again pushed me this way.

He mouthed the stub of a Cuban cigar that sat un-smoking on his lip. The housekeeper extracted a cash box from under the far side of the bed and unlocked it. We completed the transaction. He counted the money twice after holding it to the light to check the watermark for counterfeit. It was a crime to pass it on if you found it in your till. He showed us what to look for and warned:

"One *cannot be too careful. Counterfeit paper money is a daily obstacle,*" he warned. "*Tourists especially must beware because once someone has passed it on to you it is your loss as it is a serious offense to knowingly pass it on again.*"

He made no meal of self-pity. He shifted the weight on the stump of his trunk …*"would you like tea?"* He motioned for us to sit while the silent housekeeper disappeared, returning a short time later with the steaming beverage.

Señor Perez spoke English fluently (also German) as well as his native Spanish and some local Mayan dialects. He had been born here in this house and lived here all his life. He enquired after our interests. When I expressed admiration for his chaotic botanical wonderland, he confessed to not being able to resist buying orchids brought to him from the forests by the woodcutters.

"*If someone who doesn't know how to care for them buys them, they are lost,*" he bemoaned. "*If you really want to see a fine orchid collection you must go to the mountains and visit my friend who runs the International Orchid Sanctuary.*" Who knew such a place existed?

I expressed an interest in visiting the mountains in hope of catching a glimpse of a Resplendent Quetzal bird, a shimmering green iridescent avian rarity with flowing tail feathers as much as a metre long whose plumage was a key feature of Mayan fashion.

"Before the Spanish the Mayans caught the birds using glue painted on branches. They would pluck the tail feathers out and let the bird go. With the advent of guns it was easier to shoot the birds in order to acquire these shimmering status symbols. The population plummeted," he explained.

"So I shouldn't bother," was his advice. "I know a gentleman who spent three months up there hoping to catch a glimpse of one and didn't so much as find a feather. But go for the orchids if you like that sort of thing."

We thanked him for his hospitality and took our leave, still somewhat gobsmacked by this genuine gentleman who presided so pleasantly over his empire from the trainwreck of his life. He had organized his world in such a way as to maintain his independence without having to apologize to anyone for it. His friends the birds came daily without fail to the large feeder outside his window so he could watch from his bed and outside on the portico posts clusters of rare orchids spread their special brand of joy. He rarely left this sanctuary. His world was largely restricted to a visual circle ranging less than ten metres in any direction, but he had made it one of the most fascinating circles of life on the planet.

After a week or so we did venture into the mountains and found the World Orchid Sanctuary where, instead of jostling with anticipated crowds of botanical buffoons, we found ourselves wandering completely alone, the only guests all week, amongst what is rumored to be the most complete collection of orchids on the planet, all carefully arranged on trees along jungle paths. It was akin to inadvertently stumbling into a department store of paradise. Señor Perez's

In The Shadows of The Honey Trees

friend offered us accommodation for the night in the official garden residence, but we already had arrangements in an ancient hacienda where the sky could be glimpsed through cracks in the ceiling, but the charm of the elegant colonial architecture radiated when it wasn't raining.

We did, against Señor Perez's better judgment, trek through the mountainous *Biotope de Quetzal* where we spent a long, futile day staggering around the steep cloud forest with a guide in search of the illusive birds. True to his word we saw nary a *feathered thing*.

Walking home tired and dejected down the long dusty dirt road that led to our tiny cabin in the woods we were rewarded with the flight of a group of quetzals just metres overhead. They then landed in the *aguacate* tree right beside our front door. At that moment I felt I had again been pushed hither by a feather from yon. I am sure I heard a far-off chortle from someone who had schemed to reward us but not before we had worked hard enough to truly appreciate the show now performed for us on our doorstep by these amazing iridescent marvels.

§

Years later on another journey in the Americas, we found ourselves in Guayaquil in Ecuador where we needed to change $1000 US each into local escudos to pay for our charter boat when we arrived in the Galapagos Islands.

Being tourists we got priority service at the bank to change this amount into local currency and did not have to wait for the two-hour line up that stretched down the block. In a bank with people standing shoulder to shoulder in line at other tellers, we slid twenty $100 US bills under the plate glass partition to the teller and asked for local currency. She disappeared with our cash returning about ten minutes later with three stapled shut brown paper supermarket bags stuffed with about sixty million escudos. A bit shocked we had to take her word for it. She then proceeded to stand up on her chair in front of the whole crowd and hoisted the three bags over the plate glass partition behind which she usually sat. Nothing to see here folks. Nothing abnormal about this transaction!

We left quickly observing ourselves being watched by every eye in the room. We jumped into the first taxi we saw, went four blocks and jumped out, flung 1000 escudos to the driver and flagged another cab going back in the direction from which we had just come hoping to give anyone who might follow us the slip. They don't call me *el Dingo* for nothing.

The Galapagos experience was one of absolute wonder. There was only one sad creature experience there and it was the human failure to keep things even remotely organized at the airport. From the main town it was some thirty kilometres of dirt road on an antique bus to reach the end of the island, after which everyone had to clamber down the rocks to the shore with their bags to board any of several small boats taking passengers five at a time across the narrow inlet to repeat the rock-climbing-with-suitcase scenario on the other side, there to pile into the back of open pickup trucks for the short jog to the airport, an iron-roofed pavilion with chain link walls. Inside several hundred people seethed because an earlier flight had been cancelled.

"But we re-confirmed our reservation with the travel agent in the village this morning," I pleaded. It wasn't going to fly. We had to now return to the main island, doing the rock climbing with wheeled suitcase trick again twice then thumping and bumping all the dusty way back to our hotel in the capital, a sleepy seaside berg comprising two streets where you had to tip an iguana off a chair if you wanted to sit down in the local outdoor waterside cafe. Thankfully, because of the cancelled earlier arrival we were able to get a room again. We then tracked down the travel agent who had confirmed our seats that morning. Her response? ..."*Don't worry...go again tomorrow...*". Easier said than done.

The next morning we did the bus-rock climb/ boat/ rock climb/pick-up truck routine again. The airport, little more than a large open-sided shed, was a scene of the same chaos that ensued the previous day. All these people left behind yesterday must have simply camped out here overnight.

At that point I realized the only way to get on a plane was to make myself such a pain in the butt the airline's people would shoehorn me onto a plane just to get rid of me. Being unpleasant was unpleasant but it worked. From the trip of ten days of witnessing the spectacular natural wonders working in harmony to such a scene of human chaos was a frightening contrast. There is no hope for humanity. I can think of eight billion reasons why we are doomed. The contrast was unspeakably obvious to the dullest mind. After snorkeling with crowds of manta rays, dolphins, penguins and turtles all moving in harmony the utter chaos of modern humanity at its worst was like running fast into a brick wall ...on a dark night ...*again*! It made painfully clear to me that we are our own worst enemy.

If it hadn't been for the wonderful hospitality of the locals and the abundance of passionfruit it might have been a really concerning disappointment but the crew on our charter boat were wonderful, entertaining us with their guitar and harmonica and stories in the evenings and preparing delicious *'catch of the day'* meals. On our "ashore" day the host of our horse safari in search of giant tortoises truly made the experience unforgettable. The contrast between the creature calm and human chaos was sobering. You can't make this stuff up. There could be no doubting the *Lord God Bird* had pushed me here just to witness that.

CHAPTER 14

The Swan with Two Necks

"Do not judge others. Be your own judge and you will be truly happy. If you try to judge others, you are likely to burn your fingers."

—Mahatma Gandhi

2005

As Galileo had pierced the heavens centuries ago with two lenses affixed to a cardboard tube, fiber optics now makes it possible to peer back through history without leaving the room. The age of time travel has arrived if we can but recognize it for what it is, rather than for what we had fantasized it to be. Magical backward facing portals now await those curious enough to explore them. With the aid of advances in fibre optics the past has never been nearer.

One such portal led me to the story of William Singleton, father-in-law of my x3 great-grandmother. His link to my history is somewhat circumstantial but is a colourful story about *The Swan With Two Necks*, which mirrors much of the penal realities of early Australian colonialism.

Anyone who has had the opportunity to watch swans courting cannot but be bewitched by their grace and beauty. Long necks intertwine and wings are set as the sails on a ship as the birds dance their silent, zithering dance of lifelong love while reflected in the placid waters. It all looks so effortless and belies the large, webbed feet paddling furiously below the waterline. Once the rites are completed the couple *'swans off'* side by side and in profile, from a distance, it appears without a doubt, as a single bird with two necks.

It was the actions at a London ale house of this name that one fateful day changed the course of the life of William Singleton, and for better or worse, for richer or poorer, the lot of my x3 great-grandmother who married his son Joseph in Singleton, N.S.W., Australia in 1829.

William's trial transcript casts a light on the events in London. on May 30, 1790. It took a week to reach the bench of the magistrate of the Fifth Sessions, Major J.A.C. Boydell, in June. I found no record of bail being asked for nor posted but the judge issued this finding:

To Witt:
"Case 257 William Singleton was Indicted for feloniously stealing (there is another way?) on 30th May last, 27 yards of Callice (sic) the property of Matthew Pickford & Thomas Pickford:

The case was opened by Mr. Garrow.
Joseph Buckley sworn: *"I am porter to Mr. Miller, Manchester Warehouseman No. 28 King Street, Cheapside: I picked up some goods and delivered the goods at the usual place, The Swan with Two Necks,* Lad's Lane, at the warehouse door: I delivered them Monday 16 of May.

John Martin sworn:
"I am head porter to this wagon, they have several packages: on the 30th May *last I was at the Crown in Lad Lane, having a pint of beer and the prisoner went up the Swan Yard and turned*

to the right hand: I went up in about two or three minutes and could not see him. In half an hour he was coming down the yard with a bundle under his arm":
I said: *Singleton, what have you got?*
He says: *"Some linen"*:
Says I, *"let's see"*: they were tied up in his apron:
I said, *"pretty linen, indeed"*:
Says he, *"Master be as easy with me as you can"*:
I said, *"damn me, where did you get them?"*
He said, *"I took them out of the wrapper."*

COURT: *"Did you promise that in case he would confess, you would show him favour?"*

"No Sir, I sent for a constable and carried him to the compter (s (sic). On the Monday, we rummaged the warehouse and between the warehouse and the stable there are some iron bars to give light: behind some straw in another house we found the wrapper, that was a place it should not have been in: it had been opened and sewn up again".

Wrapper was produced and disposed of.

Dixon sworn: *"I received these goods from Martin, this is the same apron, I saw nothing of the wrapper".*

Court to Miller: *"That is the same wrapper you saw in the stable?"*

"Yes."

Robert Manton sworn: *"You are in the employ of Mr. Miller?"*

"I am."

"Look at some of these things and tell us whether they are the property of Mr. Miller?"

"When I took it out of the sheet that contained the goods, when it came up from and? (sic) I saw this remarkable stain upon it: I called ? to show it to me."

"Are you sure it was one of those delivered?"

John ? (Sic) sworn: "I prove that the names are properly spelled in the indictment."

The prisoner called four witnesses to his character.

GUILTY — transported for seven years tried by the London Jury before ? Merrin William.

(That is the verbatim auto translation of the court record '?' indicating name illegible. Punctuation mine.)

In the space of ten minutes, perhaps fifteen, the direction of this entire family was suddenly sealed for what today might be considered a minor shoplifting offense and an awkward one at that. This was the official line but there is much to read between the lines. Twenty-seven yards of calico is no small bundle, and I simply cannot imagine it being hidden in any "apron". It is a bolt of fabric almost a hundred feet long and probably forty-eight inches wide, long an industry standard. He made little effort to conceal the matter, and since his wife and young children travelled free with him on the same ship to Australia, one can only guess at the motive for the crime, something conspicuously absent in the trial. Like a swan with two necks the pair zithered off to Australia where William was *"assigned"* to his wife to serve his seven-year sentence [...good work if you can get it!]. He was one of the one hundred and sixty-two thousand people thrown into British courts on often flimsy charges and sentenced to "transportation" between 1788 and 1868. Many were unwanted political "influencers" on trumped up charges. Others were gamblers who figured they had nothing left to lose. It was usually a ticket of no return and provided the new colony with more than two million human years of "unfree" labour. It was less than a *romantic* experience.

William Singleton, was one of four hundred and four convicts transported on the *"Pitt"*, departing London a year later in June 1791. Nothing is said about where he was detained during the intervening year. They must have been crammed in like sardines. The new Australian colony was in its infancy. He arrived in Australia on 14 February 1792 after eight months at sea. Napoleon was rampaging around Europe following the fall of the French monarchy. Britain was in turmoil with internal political strife and an angry Ireland. William's wife Hannah and two young sons (Benjamin and Joseph) came with him with free passage on the same ship. (Their older son James arrived later in 1809*)*.

At the end of his seven-year sentence William and Hannah received a grant of ninety acres in 1799 on the river near Freeman's Reach, which they farmed. For what seems like a very well calculated caught-in-the-act risk they had started a new life on the far side of the planet and been enriched beyond their wildest dreams, an illicit bolt of cloth transformed into a landed fortune in the space of eight years.

From my point in history it looks very much like a calculated gamble. By the 1806 Australian *'muster'* they had two hundred and thirty-two acres. William was a signatory to various petitions that circulated during the Bligh period. He was shown as a landholder at the Hawkesbury in 1827, although he later (according to historical records) sold much of his land owing to indebtedness caused by floods.

Five years later the family settled on a ninety-acre (36 ha) grant at Mulgrave Place (near Windsor), where his eldest son, James, then aged 30, joined them. Benjamin, then 19, and James built watermills at Kurrajong, Lower Portland Head, and on James' fifty acre (20ha) grant at the Hawkesbury, where they ground wheat for the government stores. Joseph tried his hand with an illegal distillery but was quickly shut down. As a first offender the penalty was light. It wasn't long before he found a more legitimate, though somewhat related, calling as an innkeeper.

While it may have been a land of opportunity for many it certainly was not for young single men. As the two younger sons grew into adventurous colonial entrepreneurs there was a dearth of young women, with the ratio of colonial men to women being 6:1.

Benjamin was 41 and Joseph 39, considered princes of the colony, before Joseph wed my x3 great-grandmother Agnes Neal months before her 14th birthday. People grew up fast back then and it inspires one to ponder the original rationale for child brides in cultures where it remains the norm. It is not so easy to be indignant in hindsight.

Joseph died eleven years later leaving Agnes a 25-year-old widow, pregnant again and already the mother of three. Within here months she remarried Mr. Green the shoemaker in Singleton town (which had been founded by the first husband and his brother on a grant of land for that specific purpose) and had three more children including John Green, my paternal grandmother's grandfather. The shoemaker passed on and Agnes married a third time to Joseph Canavan and bore another son. Canavan too died and she married a fourth time to Joseph Morris. She bore eight recorded children and died of typhoid fever at 48-years-old, the same age as her first and last husbands when they died. Her son John grew up to operate a hansom cab service in Muswellbrook before marrying Caroline, my paternal great-grandfather's widowed mother. John and Caroline produced a daughter, Ada, who was my paternal grandmother's mother, making my grandparents first half-cousins. This was proof beyond all doubt of my colonial hillbilly pedigree, hidden in plain sight in an old photo on the living room wall at *Platypus Flats*, of Caroline bedecked in Victorian black *widow's weeds* (or perhaps that was how you broadcast your new availability in those days). 'Swiping right' may not be such a recent invention.

CHAPTER 15

The Bunyip and the Beached Whale

"Your beliefs become your thoughts,
Your thoughts become your words,
Your words become your actions,
Your actions become your habits,
Your habits become your values,
Your values become your destiny."

—Mahatma Gandhi

2007

I had long left my oasis in the Australian hills and forged a life for myself in Canada with my Canadian wife when one day I received an unexpected call from my cousin ...the homestead at *Platypus Flats* had been razed by fire.

It was a pivotal moment. My octogenarian mother, now a widow and living there alone, had noticed a brilliant orange light coming through a frosted glass door leading to her sewing room on the western side of the home. Thinking it must be a spectacular sunset she went to investigate and found the room ablaze. Closing the door hurriedly she retreated down the hallway collecting the framed family photographs from the walls as she fled, pausing only at the telephone to alert the local volunteer fire brigade. She then retreated to a bench at the bottom of the garden with her little dog and wallaby and could only watch helplessly as a dream a century in the making perished before her in the blink of an eye.

She was very stoic about it all. She had escaped unhurt with her photographs and waited by the horse trough where she could do nothing but sit alone in the wilderness with her little animal companions and watch as the flames consumed a hundred years of solitude. By the time the far-flung volunteer fire brigade could be marshalled little but cinders remained of the beautiful home and all its haunted history.

Being in such a remote place there was little she could do but sit and watch her universe go up in smoke.

Generations of bush living had bred a canny sense of creative resolution in us, and Mum seemed to take the devastation of the fire in her stride, though, in reality, it was a heavy blow that she refused to acknowledge. She simply turned the other cheek.

I returned home as quickly as possible to offer support. She was staying with a friend in a nearby city and together we drove out to the site of the blaze.

As always, she looked on the bright side of things. She had escaped unharmed and seemed content with accepting her escape as the most positive outcome one could hope for under the circumstances. There were others worse off by far. Tragedy, like lightning, had struck and there could be no putting the cat back in the bag. She simply bravely let every day bring with it what it may.

With her usual stoic face she was grateful. Had it started during the night she might have perished in her bed. She had taught me to always see the silver lining of dark clouds and now she clung to the strength of her convictions like a drowning rat in the monsoon flood. I could do little more than feel for her and assist in helping her come to matters that needed determination.

As the miles slipped away under our wheels, I realized I was on the journey of a lifetime, rolling backwards through a life I had left a half century before. During those earliest teary-eyed departures enroute to boarding school I had never reflected on the fact that they had spelled my expulsion from paradise. Yet in all my global wanderings, no matter where I hung my hat, this place to which we now journeyed had always been an almost fictionalize *"Home!"*

It had been the cork that had helped keep my head above the water in my many human floods - those times when the human condition tried its best to erode me. The warm marsupial moments of my youth here had given me the tenacity to cling to the last scraps of hope at the worst of times when hope had to be a manufactured pony I could trot out to distract myself from the hopelessness of any given moment.

We rolled past fertile lucerne fields following the course of the river where I had caught many long-ago-trout. Then the road angled steeply up the cutting hewed by hand into the orange rock face of the steppe more than a century earlier by the convicts. I was reminded again of the high cost of that commodity called *freedom*. Those men really had earned their pardon.

Beneath the surface my Mum had changed since my last visit. During the journey she had told me the same story about her friend Nita three times, all the while rubbing her thumb and index fingers on her right hand together, a medical symptom aptly labelled "pill rolling". The stories made sense; it is just that they were often repeated ...and in much detail. Several times I reached out to hold her hand to try and short circuit the anxiety, but the pill rolling would begin again the moment I let go. Her brow was tired, and she had adopted a severely moussed hair style for the grey locks that had previously spent a lifetime floating around her radiant face. She had exerted control over what she could control though it pained me to see the severity of the change.

At the point where the road leading to the homestead veered off from the main track stood a tangle of one of the world's most remarkable botanical specimens - a giant century plant. It was not native here but had obviously been planted with singular purpose as a landmark, an unmistakable sign in the wilderness that could never be missed by someone following the wheel ruts or bridle trails as a sign that human habitation lay nearby.

The rumor of its name is somewhat deceptive, but it does take as long as forty years for the giant spiny coils of fleshy leaves (many metres long and the size of a man's leg and striped a bizarre aloe-green with brilliant yellow variegations) to work themselves into the orgasmic skyward thrust of a flower spike that towers more than ten metres into the air. It is a testament to the power of patience. I saw my mother reflected here. At its apex the flower bracts bloom like large flat brilliant yellow plates the size of coffee tables taking many months to mature. These plates grow smaller as they mount the central spire and as they age, they change color until finally, many months after blooming, the "seed" falls already a miniature clone of the original plant with tiny leaves barely an inch long. It then slowly but surely insinuates itself on the unforgiving landscape in an imperceptible way perfectly suited to being completely ignored. It unfolded its secrets as nature intended, slowly unfurling its sinuous beauty to the applause of none.

As a child I marvelled at the quiet determination of this creature-plant that seemed a law unto itself, transforming its landscape in a process so remarkably slow that I grew old waiting for it to reach its reproductive performance. It now reminded me of Mum.

Opposite it, the double iron gates stood open (as always) in welcome. It was spring and the fields were lush, the horses and the cattle were sleek, and the parrots wheeled and screeched overhead in breeding pairs as we wound our way through the ribbon of trees that shaded the way.

The car pulled up the pinch from the bridge built by my great-grandfather a century earlier along what remained of the long avenue of Kurrajong trees that led to the iconic homestead, which stood now forlornly silhouetted against the jarringly blue robins-egg sky, a charred skeleton arching skyward like the tragic remains of a beached whale incinerated on a verdant shore by a sad spell.

The great fronds of the date palms were severely scorched on the house side but remained defiantly green on the other. On the blackened rafters of the homestead the peacocks perched vainglorious in iridescent indifference to the tragic remains of a century of dreams that lay now in crumpled, silent ruin at their feet. The golden rams' heads on the garden gate were as bright with promise as ever but beyond the rampant garden the magic was unquestionably gone.

The wisteria, completely covering the still standing meat house, bloomed in a vigorous display as if egged on by the smell of the nearby ashes. The roses over the entrance arbour had spluttered to life again for the hundredth time and the Crepe Myrtles cast their flashy skirts of blooms in the shelter of the Grevillea trees now bowed heavy with combs of golden blossoms. The contrast of nature's indifference to our loss made it that much more poignant. The universe to which the garden had been merely an adjunct for so long was now departed yet the life breathed into this garden by a century of *'dreaming'* continued around the creature corpse of that dream, flowering joyously without pause. The humans had roosted here for a hundred years but now the branch was broken. We would have to perch somewhere else; somewhere without the fragrance of orange blooms and jasmin and moonflowers which now vied vainly to trump the rank, dead smell of charcoal.

The fire had burned ferociously in the century old hardwood baked dry by a hundred summer suns. We toured the ruins in silence. Mandarins and oranges still hung heavily from the trees in the citrus grove and tiny sky-blue fairy wrens darted frantically back and forth to their nests hidden in the tangle of the wisteria and passion vines, as they had for as long as any living human could remember, with complete indifference to our tragedy.

In the wood-panelled hallway the old piano, which had trilled its joyous songs into the wildness for almost a century, now stood scorched and blistered, its strings snapped by the heat and its silky ivories curled and charred. The violin, once the bearer of so much love and lively joy, now lay gutted of its strings, its beautiful woods burned through, its loveliness destroyed. It now lay alone …remote …in its corner from where no escape was possible. I saw in this blackened beauty a sad personal enigma playing the last notes of that *'tune without the words…that never stops at all.'* In living we must learn to lose.

Amazingly the verandas had escaped almost unscathed. A small table stood by a charred door frame. It supported a large open leather-bound volume, the leaves of fine French linen whipping back and forth in the stiff breeze. A sheet of lesser manufacture would have torn and been whipped away into the wilderness.

"What is this? "I asked.

"It is your great-grandfather's journal. I can't make any sense of it," Mum replied. I was surprised I had never seen it before. I had to remind myself I had left here more than half a century ago.

The pages of the old ledger rifled restlessly in the wind. I closed the cover to console it in its mourning. The dream hidden within its cryptic confines was dead.

I tucked it under my arm as we reviewed the devastation. The roof had burned out and collapsed in on everything. The tome had survived sandwiched in a closely packed bookcase where the complete lack of oxygen had sheltered the secret incantations bound within. Only the spine had been destroyed. I would look at it later. My mother, who had mothered every creature in its hour of need, now needed the mothering.

A pretty-faced grey mare saw she had company and cantered over through a field of purple-flowering alfalfa hoping for a little companionship and perhaps a treat. She missed her humans. She embodied everything one could want in another creature …as Robert Duncan so aptly wrote of the horse…." *friendship without envy; nobility without pride; beauty without vanity"* …and perhaps above all, an air of regal independence. She didn't really need us but just wanted to chat.

Mum fished in her bag for an apple core saved out of long country habit for just such occasions and offered it to the mare who deftly picked it up with butter-soft lips. We left her munching and gathered a bucket of oranges and mandarins from the citrus grove and a few lemons from the orange trees (which Dad had once cut down, but which grew back bearing only lemons ...another haunting enigma).

We passed the long water trough, now strangely empty of birds. The fairy wrens peddled furiously from bush to bush. The singed date palms were forlorn but would survive. The pink rose clambering over the iron fernery carried on regardless, its cascading boas of blooms a compliment to the black funerary backdrop of ruination, an enigmatic undertaker's offering at this crematorium of dreams. How cruel the wrath of a vengeful *God*. I was watching the final scenes in a slow-motion epic; a never-ending story into which I had inadvertently tumbled another lifetime ago. The saga encrypted in the tome I cradled in the crook of my arm held a nakedly feral record of nation building. To be holding it at this moment as we stood among the ashes surrounded by the palpable sense of loss was a rare *Phoenix* moment when the record of a life I had never known miraculously leapt back from the ashes of his dreams to land in the arms of the only person on the planet who could possibly decode it. I realize now, looking back, this was perhaps the greatest enigma of them all. What were the odds that I would unearth these tales I now tell? That I should be the instrument that joined all the dots flung far like stars across the cathedral of the night sky? That I had long ago been pushed by the wings of *the Lord God Bird* into a life that had simply been the preparation for this task now at hand? That this enormous responsibility should choose me? In following my curiosities I had simply arrived at my fate ...and *'the story of my life'* in every sense of those words.

Why had this record, never before seen by me, escaped the gutting blaze? Why had someone left it here thrashing in the wind in the wilderness for me to find on an altar to the destruction of the very dream it dreamt?

In the zest of such moments I didn't always fully appreciate the full sum of the parts. It takes time and space warping just a little to bring things into true focus.

Not the echoing emotional truth born of the faded canyons-of-the-mind kind of focus but fresh views now seen with the clear dry eye of a lifetime of hindsight. This most enormous enigma was lost on me in the moment of mourning the passing of an age. I had fallen down another magical rabbit burrow of the mind and I wouldn't be satisfied until all my questions were answered.

The bees, fresh from a hard day's work at the blossoms of the Honey Trees *(eucalyptus melliodora)*, murmured as they drank where horse trough overflowed and the Crimson Rosellas continued their occupation of the nesting hollow in the trunk of the ancient Pepper Tree, where they felt safe sharing the tree with the bees, whose hive was hidden in another hollow.

It was a bright day. There was just enough blue sky visible among the clouds to make a cat a pair of trousers, a forecast for the outcome of the rest of the emotional day …cloudy with a few sunny patches.

As we stood on the empty veranda the stench of charred wood was overwhelming. There lay the shattered vessel which had for a century cradled our souls in this solitude. Time marched on to the silent music of those frosty nights when dancers had whirled here in rhythmic undulation, strutting as elegantly as sure-footed gazelles, while the ghost of a musician drunk on the rapture of his own making played

In The Shadows of The Honey Trees

on in the distance. Ashes to ashes. Dust to dust. We stood silent in the wake of the passing of a realm. There could be no turning back. All other life continued as it had for a million years. We had only been transients in this place of unbearable loveliness.

We walked to the car in silence, each engrossed in our own thoughts. We drove down the long avenue of leafy trees, crossed the bridge of a hundred years for the last time, and pulled past the iron gates and onto the main track, where we surprised a grey kangaroo and her joey. They hopped off into the bush as we drove by in silence. After a bit Mum spoke.

"There is someone I want you to meet when we get back to town." And she began her tale of meeting Letty again:

"I was at the church picnic one day when a tall woman approached and noticed my name tag asked if I was a Weabonga West. I replied I was by marriage.

"She then sat down and explained that we had met more than fifty years ago when we were the only two new mothers in the local maternity hospital who gave birth that day. That was when you were born."

She paused as if configuring the words, She silently gazed out the window. A quiet sigh of sadness crossed with resignation escaped her lips.

"Fifty years! And there we were talking again. What a coincidence. If I hadn't worn my name tag, we might have passed like two ships in the night."

I didn't try to stop her. I knew to go to where she was rather than seek to constrain her memories. I put my hand over hers. She was pill rolling again. I pulled the car over into some shade by the shoulder and turned to comfort her. It was going to be another day of enigmas. They seemed to flourish here.

Platypus Flats

§

Later in the comfort of a cane-bottomed chair on the veranda of some other family's *'dreaming'* I puzzled over the entries in the ledger. There were accounts for things that seemed incongruous ...Jockey Clubs; assorted business names and organizations; Individuals ...the list stretched on for pages.

Had Eagle purchased the journal at an auction and turned it upside down and begun afresh from the back when he founded *Platypus Flats*? Did he operate other businesses before he had come here?

Turning the book upside down I realized that in the reverse were the journals for *Platypus Flats* but from the front it was a ledger for another business. Then I noticed a familiar name - Sam Brazel - my maternal x2 great-grandfather. That gave me a geographic location for the puzzling entries. I combed the pages mining information. It was the ledger of old Eagle's livery and carriage business in Walcha's early days though nowhere was that declared. Here was the history of the foundation of the life I had lived carefully laid out in neatly quilled cursive executed in that seductive sea-green octopus blood ink popular - if you could afford it - a century earlier. An old scribe's motto struck me in that instant.

"I was here, and you were not. Now you are here, and I am not."

Here was his annual shopping list for the station store in 1902:

6 pairs work boots
200 lbs of flour
120 lbs of tea
150 lbs of sugar

In The Shadows of The Honey Trees

Here was his Last Will and Testament neatly scripted and then obviously transcribed to the loose-leaf document with each word marked out with pencil as it was transcribed to guarantee the accuracy of the transcript. A few pages on there was another and then another. Each in order echoed Eagle's life and changing allegiances. First Bob was to inherit everything, then my father and his brother and "any challenge" to the will would trigger a "charity clause". In the end I know Bob and Violet bought him out, but the relationship became so acrimonious that when he left, he had set the original homestead ablaze but not before leaving a note in the margins in the journal which he conveniently left in the carriage house where an inquisitive great-grandchild might find it decades later:

"*If I have to leave, I will leave the place in ashes....*" he had written as an afterthought for me to find three generations on. The written words echoed through the canyons of silence a century in the making. It suddenly made clear a puzzling offhand comment made by my father decades earlier in response to my boyhood enquiry as to why a wisteria tree stood out in the cow paddock. He had replied:

"*That is where the corner of the old house used to be.*"

When I asked what he meant he trailed off saying: "*Oh there was a fire*". He was a man of few words and said no more and even as a child I knew better than to press the point. I must have seemed an incorrigible to him. Despite a very strong physical resemblance between us we had personalities as different as chalk and cheese. Or perhaps not...

I realized this journal was a map of the buried family *bunyips*. The reading ended there but it connected unknown dots of information gleaned as a child that I had filed away in the "makes-no-sense-but-remember-this" department;

things spoken, and odd notations suddenly sprang anew from memory with fresh currency. While it quenched a special thirst for knowledge of who came before I knew that kind of longing could be quickly sated if too much information was suddenly uploaded. I took my time connecting the dots.

I felt life pulse through the thin red veins of the animal tracks of the mind as they converged, thirsty, on this odd watering hole of the heretofore unknowable.

CHAPTER 16

──●◉●──

The Reckoning

*"The weak can never forgive.
Forgiveness is the attribute of the strong."*

—Mahatma Gandhi

October 2018

When one writes autobiographically there is a certain requirement to take each stage of life and turn it this way and that to see just what came out of that set of circumstances. That leaves the writer vulnerable for whatever is unearthed in the box of memory for once released it cannot be put back, nor quickly forgotten.

There came my own day of *'reckoning'*. It was an out-of-the-blue unexpected thunderclap on an otherwise bright sunny Canadian late autumn day. I was sitting in a cafe reading the news on my phone when up popped this bulletin:

Melbourne, Australia (CNN) — Australian Prime Minister Scott Morrison broke down in tears Monday while making a national apology to thousands of victims of child sexual abuse in institutions in a scandal which has spanned decades.

In a speech which was broadcast live across the country, Morrison said the trauma suffered by victims in institutional settings from church orphanages to youth groups and schools had been "hiding in plain sight for too long."

Destiny swooped down unexpectedly and slapped me sharply across the face with her raven wings. I sat dumbfounded, completely 'thunderstruck'. Until then I only had an inkling what that word meant. Living on the other side of the planet and not seeing that much news from Australia there had been no preamble to this sudden revelation. It had dropped like a rock from the heavens into a tranquil pond in my soul I had spent a lifetime soothing. A quick Google search brought evidence of the continued practice of secret abuse at my old institution.

The Gods of Guilt crushed me in an instant for having not spoken sooner. The adult in me saw myself in the tens of thousands of other abused people, a recent study claiming as much as sixty percent of the population having experienced abuse in at least one of its many disguises. My silence had in part failed them all, not the least myself. I felt remorse for having buried the denial of those events so deeply it had remained beyond the view of my moral compass. I felt remorse for having stilled my young voice when I had feared for my life if I spoke up. I had buried the memory of the abuse along with the shame and toxic coercion.

Evil prospers when the good say nothing. I finally found the oxygen to speak the words buried more than half a century but am aware that recounting one's abuse can trigger unprocessed trauma in others, spreading it like the overlapping ripples of a handful of pebbles cast casually into a seemingly placid pond …distinct yet even but troubled where they clash together in their silent passing. I have tried not to say anything ugly in conveying the atrocities which happened without resorting to brutality for the sake of brutality. It is a challenge for me to speak to ugliness without walking through your mind with the crap on my shoes. So I choose the high road and take a broad view in the hope that in this process my personal ugly will fade when it is weighed against my joys without soiling your moral core. When my particles eventually disperse and return to the universe from whence they came, I know my heart will balance with *the feather of truth*. We are all untold stories but there are some things others don't need to know in detail. We must all walk our own road, but destiny has singled me out to render it here. I had the luxury of reading the following message without the theatrics:

§

"Full text of the apology speech for institutional child sexual abuse as delivered in parliament on Monday Oct 22, 2018

Scott Morrison

Mon 22 Oct 2018 00.15 EDT

Whether you sit here in this Chamber, the Great Hall, outside elsewhere in the nation's capital. Your living room. In your bed, unable to rise today or speak to another soul. Your journey to where you are today has been a long and painful one, and we acknowledge that, and we welcome you today wherever you are.

Mr Speaker, silenced voices. Muffled cries in the darkness.

Unacknowledged tears. The tyranny of invisible suffering.

The never heard pleas of tortured souls bewildered by an indifference to the unthinkable theft of their innocence.

Platypus Flats

Today, Australia confronts a trauma – an abomination – hiding in plain sight for far too long.

Today, we confront a question too horrible to ask, let alone answer.

Why weren't the children of our nation loved, nurtured and protected?

Why was their trust betrayed?

Why did those who knew cover it up?

Why were the cries of children and parents ignored?

Why was our system of justice blind to injustice?

Why has it taken so long to act?

Why were other things more important than this, the care of innocent children?

Why didn't we believe?

Today we dare to ask these questions, and finally acknowledge and confront the lost screams of our children.

While we can't be so vain to pretend to have answers, we must be so humble to fall before those who were forsaken and beg to them our apology.

Yours was a 'sorry' that dared not to ask for forgiveness …a 'sorry' that dared not to try and make sense of the incomprehensible.

In The Shadows of The Honey Trees

It was a 'sorry' that insults with an incredible promise ...a 'sorry' that speaks only to your profound grief and loss ...a 'sorry' from a nation that seeks to reach out in compassion into the darkness where you have lived but briefly.

Nothing we can do now will right the wrongs inflicted on our nation's vulnerable by official neglect.

Even after a comprehensive royal commission, which finally enabled the voices to be heard and the silence to be broken, we will all continue to struggle.

So today we gather in this chamber in humility. Not just as representatives of the people of this country, but as fathers, as mothers, as siblings, friends, workmates, and in some cases, indeed as victims and survivors.

Ngunnawal means "meeting place". And on this day of apology, we meet together.

We honour every survivor in this country, we love you, we hear you and we honour you.

No matter if you are here at this meeting place or elsewhere, this apology is to you and for you.

Your presence and participation make tangible our work today – and it gives strength to others who are yet to share what has happened in their world.

Elsewhere in this building and around Australia, there are others who are silently watching and listening to these proceedings, men and women who have never told a soul what has happened to them. To these men and women I say this apology is for you too.

And later when the speeches are over, we will stand in silence and remember the victims who are not with us anymore, many too sadly by their own hand.

As a nation, we failed them, we forsook them. That will always be our shame.

This apology is for them and their families too.

As one survivor recently said to me, "It wasn't a foreign enemy who did this to us – this was done by Australians." To Australians. Enemies in our midst.

Enemies. In. Our. Midst.

The enemies of innocence.

Look up at the galleries, look at the Great Hall, look outside this place and you will see men and women from every walk of life, from every generation, and every part of our land.

Crushed, abused, discarded and forgotten.

The crimes of ritual sexual abuse happened in schools, churches, youth groups, scout troops, orphanages, foster homes, sporting clubs, group homes, charities, and in family homes as well.

In The Shadows of The Honey Trees

It happened anywhere a predator thought they could get away with it, and the systems within these organizations allowed it to happen and turned a blind eye.

It happened day after day, week after week, month after month, and decade after decade. Unrelenting torment.

When a child spoke up, they weren't believed, and the crimes continued with impunity.

One survivor told me that when he told a teacher of his abuse, that teacher then became his next abuser.

Trust broken. Innocence betrayed & power and position exploited for evil dark crimes.

A survivor named Faye told the royal commission: "Nothing takes the memories away. It happened fifty-three years ago and it's still affecting me."

One survivor named Ann said: "My mother believed them rather than me."

I also met with a mother whose two daughters were abused by a priest the family trusted. Suicide would claim one of her two beautiful girls and the other lives under the crushing weight of what was done to her.

As a father of two daughters, I can't comprehend the magnitude of what she has faced.

Platypus Flats

Not just as a father but as prime minister, I am angry too at the calculating destruction of lives and abuse of trust, including those who have abused the shield of faith and religion to hide their crimes, a shield that is supposed to protect the innocent, not the guilty. And they stand condemned.

One survivor says it was like "becoming a stranger to your parents."

Mental health illnesses, self-harm, and addictions followed.

The pain didn't stop with adulthood.

Relationships with partners and children became strained as survivors struggled with the conflicting currents within them.

Parents and siblings felt guilt and sadness for what they had missed, for what and whom they chose to believe, and for what they did not see.

While survivors contemplated what could have been.

A survivor named Rodney asks the question so common to so many survivors, he wonders about "the person I may have become, or the person I could have become if I didn't have all of this in my life."

Death can take many forms. In this case the loss of a life never lived, a life denied.

Another survivor, Aiden spoke of not getting justice because his abuser had died. He said, "I was bereft because I was robbed. I was robbed of my day in court. I wanted to tell the world what he did. That was stolen. That was him again, taking control."

In The Shadows of The Honey Trees

Mr Speaker, today, as a nation, we confront our failure to listen, to believe and to provide justice.

And again today, we say sorry.

To the children we failed, sorry.

To the parents whose trust was betrayed and who have struggled to pick up the pieces, sorry.

To the whistleblowers who we did not listen to, sorry.

To the spouses, partners, wives, husbands and children who have dealt with the consequences of the abuse, cover-ups and obstruction, sorry.

To generations past and present, sorry.

Mr Speaker, as part of our work leading us to this day, I recently met with the national apology survivor's reference group – as did the leader of the opposition – who are with us here today.

I want to thank this wonderful group of people, brave people.

Many are survivors; they have all worked so hard to make today a reality.

They said to me that an apology without action is just a piece of paper, and it is. And today they also wanted to hear about our actions.

It is a fair call.

In outlining our actions, I want to recognise the work of my predecessors, former Prime Minister Gillard, who is with us here today, and I thank you for your attendance. Former Prime Minister Rudd, the Member for Warringah, who continues to serve us here in this place, and the former prime minister, Mr. Turnbull. I want to thank them for their compassion and leadership as they also confronted these terrible failings.

The foundations of our actions are the findings and recommendations of the royal commission, initiated by Prime Minister Gillard.

Acting on the recommendations of the royal commission with concrete action gives practical meaning to today's apology.

The steady compassionate hand of the commissioners and staff resulted in 17,000 survivors coming forward and nearly 8,000 of them recounting their abuse in private sessions of the commission.

We are all grateful to the survivors who gave evidence to the commission. It is because of your strength and your courage that we are gathered here today.

Many of the commissioners and staff are also with us today and I thank them also.

Mr Speaker, acting on the recommendations of the royal commission with concrete action gives practical meaning to today's apology.

The commonwealth, as our national government, must lead and coordinate our response.

The National Redress Scheme has commenced.

I thank the State and Territory governments for their backing of the scheme.

The scheme is about recognising and alleviating the impact of past abuse and providing justice for survivors.

The scheme will provide survivors with access to counselling and psychological services, monetary payments, and, for those who want one – and I stress for those who want one – a direct personal response from an institution where the abuse occurred.

It will mean – that after many years, often decades, of denials and cover-ups — the institutions responsible for ruining lives admit their wrongdoing and the terrible damage they caused.

The National Office of Child Safety is another big step forward to ensuring the prevention and detection of child abuse, wherever it occurs.

It was announced as part of our government's response to the royal commission and was established from July 1 of this year within the Department of Social Services.

As prime minister, I will be changing these arrangements to ensure that the National Office of Child Safety will report to me. It will reside within the portfolio of Prime Minister and Cabinet, as it should. The minister for social services will assist me in this role, including reporting to me on the progress of royal commission recommendations and the activities of the Office of Child Safety.

The office has already begun its work to raise awareness of child safety and to drive cultural change in institutions in the community – to ensure that the systemic failures and abuses of power that brought us here today are not repeated.

Our children must be heard ... they must know who they can tell, and they must be believed.

Importantly, children themselves are being empowered to participate in these initiatives – because our children must be heard, and when it comes to the work of safety, it must be approachable and child-friendly. They must know who they can tell, and they must be believed, and they must know where they can go.

All Australian governments are now working together to establish a national database, to ensure higher standards for working with children and that data about people's ability to work with children is shared nationally.

And our work does not stop at our borders.

We are ensuring children across the world are protected by stopping child sex offenders from travelling overseas without permission, which will disrupt, prevent and investigate the abuse of children globally.

And we recognise that as survivors age, those who were abused in or by an institution, have real fears about entering into aged care facilities.

It's an understandable fear given what happened during childhood, and we will work with survivor groups about what we can do to alleviate those fears and indeed the work of the royal commission into aged care will be able to address this as well.

And to assist with lasting change we recognise that there are many more survivors who were abused in other settings such as their own homes and in their communities, who will not be covered by this redress scheme.

These survivors also need to be heard, and believed, and responded to with services to address their needs. So today, I commit to fund the establishment of a national center of excellence, and I call on the states and territories to work as partners in this venture. This centre will be the place to raise awareness and understanding of the impacts of child sexual abuse, to deal with the stigma, to support help seeking and guide best practice for training and other services.

All of this is just the start.

The Australian government has not rejected a single recommendation of the royal commission.

We are now actively working on one hundred and four of the one hundred and twenty-two recommendations that were addressed to the commonwealth. The eighteen remaining are being closely examined, in consultation with states and territories.

We will shine a spotlight on all parts of government to ensure we are held accountable.

Today we commit that from December this year, we will report back to the Australian people, through the parliament, to be held accountable each year, on the progress we are making on the recommendations over the next five years and then beyond.

We will shine a spotlight on all parts of government to ensure we are held accountable.

And the institutions which perpetrated this abuse, covered it up and refused to be held accountable, must be kept on the hook.

Already, many of those organizations have made their own apologies and have signed up to be a part of the National Redress Scheme, as they should.

But there are others yet to join, and today I simply say that justice, decency and the beliefs and values we share as Australians, insists that they sign on.

Today I also commit to establishing a national museum, a place of truth and commemoration, to raise awareness and understanding of the impacts of child sexual abuse.

We will work with survivor groups, to ensure your stories are recorded, that your truth is told, that our nation does not turn from our shame, and that our nation will never forget the untold horrors you experienced.

Through this we will endeavour to bring some healing to our nation and to learn from our past horrors.

The national child abuse apology shows that institutions can heal, as well as harm.

In The Shadows of The Honey Trees

We can never promise a world where there are no abusers. But we can promise a country where we commit to hear and believe our children.

To work together to keep children safe, to trust them and most of all respect their innocence.

Mr Speaker, I present the formal apology to be tabled in this parliament today, which will be handed to those in the Great Hall shortly. It reflects all of the sentiments that I have expressed on behalf of the Australian people, this parliament and our government.

And as I table that and, as I do, I simply say: I believe you. We believe you. Your country believes you."

§

I didn't hear this. I read it. It was visceral. My first thought was: "Too little too late!" Forgiveness was exactly what should have been begged from the outset so survivors could move forward with the rest of the words which lost their meaning without the 'asking' of forgiveness. Surely someone with such close Christian values, as this leader professes, must grasp the need for forgiveness to be asked for? Forgiveness comes when the other party can learn to put themselves in the survivor/victim's shoes and recognizes verbally the harm done and expresses remorse for it. It is not rocket science! Morrison's words seemed to have been insidiously scrubbed of meaning from his first feeble uttering.

I googled the school. Case after case of damaging incidents brought by individuals spread over half a century popped up. You could have knocked me over with a feather.

Platypus Flats

The knowing stabbed cleanly, a double-edged blade, slicing open a memory contained in an old bag hung at the farthest corner of some far ago long away place for forgetting ...left there to rot like the poisonous skeletons that swung high in the rafters above the shearing board at *Platypus Flats*, hiding silently above the cacophony of sweaty-shearer-swearing, sheep bleating, dogs yipping, heat rising, stinky diesel engine spinning, long endless leather belts slapping out the magic rhythm that caused the billowing mass of frothy, warm, silk-soft fleeces to fall away from the backs of the scrawny animals whose toothpick legs flailed haplessly in the air as they were ravaged of their fleece by the smooth, sweeping caresses of the half-naked men whose backs arched in long rippling seas of sinew under the luminous light that cascaded into the otherwise dark shed from the high skylights like a beam of religious illumination in a landscape by Caravaggio. Such had been my life. The crimes of institutional neglect seemed lost in the din of the Prime Minister's oratory!

I suffered an explosion of insight a lifetime fermenting. The *Gods of Guilt* had spoken. A boulder of responsibility crushed me in that instant.

Overcome with the moral injury of my long silence (which, in the depths of my denial, had permitted evil to flourish) I wept. They were tears of long, long away and far, far ago ...tears from another lifetime in which the grey thrush had spread its wings and soared out through the chip in the skylight of the shearing shed at *Platypus Flats*, the chip put there by a long-ago-far-away stone thrown by my father, then a boy. The bird had flown into the blue cathedral sky and flitted away over field and stream and had all but forgotten the beautiful blue eggs it had failed to hatch. It now returned to find them fetid and poisoned, like the carrion in which they were cradled.

I read on. There were others. This I knew but the investigation into institutionalized abuse of the vulnerable revealed tens of thousands of cases from institutions throughout Australia. I was swallowed by an unimaginable sadness. I had only tried to forget and to put as much distance as I could between myself and that place, I had escaped. Now I had to acknowledge its poisonous presence and come to the realization that it was a part of me which would never go away. Even in my wish to forget I realized that it was with me when I fell asleep and when I awoke. I trusted when I should have feared and then feared those I should have trusted. This is part of the price of admission to this unsavory club.

I saw clearly the internal conflict reflected in the woes of others who had come after me. I had failed them. I felt remorse for having buried my denial so deeply; for having stilled my young voice out of fear for my life; for the shame and coercive scars I had hidden even from myself.

The more light I shone on it the more confusing were the shadows it cast. After such a Prime Ministerial performance of 'how not to apologize' I never expected the silence that followed. In response to this formal speech to the invisible crowd of the abused their collective silence was deafening. Search after search unearthed no published response. Simple, absolute ... *"SILENCE!"*

I felt a responsibility to reply in order to lift the boulder of guilt off my chest:

CHAPTER 17

A Letter to The People of Australia

"The future depends on what we do in the present."
—Mahatma Gandhi

I addressed 'the country' in this missive so 'privilege' could not be claimed. I stuffed it in a large brown Manilla envelope and put it in the post.

Dear Prime Minister

Today I have read your pseudo apology to the victims of institutional abuse who were children in the care of various Australian institutions from orphanages to foster care to expensive boarding schools and many official institutions including aged and handicap care centres some dating back more than eighty years. Abuse in all its many forms continued unchecked and unreported for many decades long after the arrival of the telephone. Your apology is not much but I suppose it is more than I ever expected. It was a moment for a demonstration of exemplary civic courage. I appreciate how painful and uncomfortable this speech must have been for you, but it falls far short of being inclusive.

In The Shadows of The Honey Trees

I feel you were saying "Sorry" to the whole nation, including the abusers. It didn't seem directed inclusively to the survivors of abuse (and those who didn't survive). Sorry!

Words have consequences. Had you read the "Definition of Terms" in the opening pages of your Royal Commission into institutional Responses to Sexual Abuse Investigation your speech might not be so bereft of understanding. I assume the details left you speechless. I am certain you only glimpsed the tip of the iceberg. Sorry!

My copy of your speech specifically mentions only sexual abuse although the press generously framed it more inclusively. That was really your job. Trust me, there are many more forms of abuse all equally or more harrowing and uglier for an innocent child. Excluding other forms of atrocities from your official acknowledgement is the abuse of "exclusion". Sorry!

I have been victim to many forms of insidious physical, psychological and sexual institutionalized abuse so feel I can call on my hands-on expertise to call you out. By your calloused omission of all the forms of abuse you failed to embrace us while you held sway on the national stage.

My abuse started when I was barely eleven years old when I was afforded what my parents thought was the best opportunity, they could give me by sending me to XXXXXX where I boarded for four years. I was under the care of the N.S.W. Department of Education. Coming from a remote sheep and cattle property (almost everyone there did though many were also from remote Pacific Islands) established by my great-grandfather in 1892, I had few social skills. My parents thought a good education here was their best effort for me. It cost them and I dearly. I do not draw lines between the different forms of abuse I suffered there. Which were sexual abuses, and which were simply torture? You acknowledged only part of our suffering. You omitted to make mention of the rampant tyranny and human rights violations ..."atrocities" would be a more accurate description than that soft, sweet and short easy-on-the-lips five letter word "abuse". Could you not bring yourself to say that word? Sorry!

The abuses of fresh-faced youngsters in a strange place started almost immediately upon our arrival. I was not the first. I was not alone. Certain people were picked on and brutally bullied by seniors while some received more favourable attention creating schisms among the ranks of minors. I am sure many of the abusers had themselves been abused when they were the youngest. You can choose many shadowy terms for it ...assault, sexual assault, humiliation, abuse, bullying, harassment or hazing. Whatever it is called, it was cruel.

"At first the evil impulse is as fragile as the thread of a spider, but eventually it becomes as tough as cart ropes"
- Babylonian Talmud

In The Shadows of The Honey Trees

That is an evil side effect of abuse. It normalizes it and too often becomes learned behaviour projected and passed on by those knowing nothing else. It becomes embedded in the psyche of an institution, seeping under a door which nobody ever opens because their soul recoils in horror, in fear of what might be seen. The collision of childhood into adulthood can be a tremulous voyage under the best of circumstances. Are there better ways for the human soul to make the journey? Always. Abuse cannot be stamped out with rubber stamps, Prime Minister. Sorry! Like the abolition of alcohol, you won't stop people abusing others, you simply drive it deeper underground where it is most comfortable. Sorry!

Some of the abused develop anxiety disorders or have a hyper-responsive amygdala where the fight-or-flight response is bloated and exaggerated out of sensible proportion and into the realm of the ridiculous and unfeasible simply because it had no avenue of escape under the forced circumstances. Watch the movie 'Sophie's Choice' if you still don't grasp the subject. I was deprived of control over who touched my body and how, and my human dignity and autonomy were criminally violated on an almost daily basis …for years. I suppose "abuse" is a neat five letter word for the horror-stricken, a neat package they can easily digest. Sorry!

For most it results not only in the development of deep psychological (and often physical) scars but often a deep empathy for the suffering in the world around them. What happened to me was more than half a century ago, yet I still cannot witness violence against another in movies or on television without feeling a searing pain in my own soul as if it is I who has been struck. "Sorry" doesn't help that. Sorry!!

To separate out the scars of one form of abuse from another is to also exclude those who might not have admitted to their innocent selves that their abuse might well have been "sexual", or has "sexual" has been added just to give ourselves a stroke of subliminal salve whenever we mouth the word? At the age we were abused we did not necessarily understand the word "sexual" let alone all its adult connotations. Your seemingly couched narrow embrace and shallow appreciation of what transpired, even after years of investigation, troubles me deeply. It is telling that you set your sights so low. If your speech writers have trouble with the sincerity of your speeches, I offer my assistance in matters of such national importance if it would help. I suspect your scribes knew exactly what they were doing. Your words were so obviously individually prepared and wrapped in self-serving legal bubbles. What were you hiding?

I am more deeply troubled when a young boy aged six asks me what to do if someone keeps hitting him and I tell him to tell an adult and he said:" I've done that, lots, but they don't do anything." How far we have NOT come.

Prime Ministers come and go but the effects of abuse last forever. If we need a self-serving excuse, we

In The Shadows of The Honey Trees

could label it a horrific legacy of our brutal convict colonialism. If not now when shall the country tear the scab off the wound that it might truly heal Prime Minister? Sorry!

Let us call it what it is that our words might give form to this evil that casts its long, cold lifelong shadow over our most vulnerable; that we might see it for what it is; that we might learn the words to talk about it and always be on watch for it. It should always (at the very least) be suspect in institutions involving minors.

Let us hear the words: Meanness, sordidness, evil, wickedness, iniquity, immorality, sinful, wrong, unscrupulousness, unseemly, unsavory, shoddy, vile, foul, tawdry, low-minded, debase, degenerate, depraved, corrupt, dishonest, disreputable, contemptuous, ignominious, wretched or turpitude - all the baseness of which humankind is capable. You could have chosen any one of these words or more) with the warning to "Watch for it. It is coming soon to a dark corner near you." That would be calling a spade a spade Prime Minister!

To my credit I was strong. After about three years things gradually improved as I "aged out" as I believe it is called in abuse circles today. Really it means" became too large and able to be easily physically intimidated." I suffered a fractured wrist while being beaten with a broom stick for failing to produce a cigarette as demanded by a senior nicotine addict in withdrawal when I was fifteen years old. Humiliation was also a heavy rod to bear ...worse by far than any physical insult. I could not wait to walk out the gates of that place and put it behind me. I got up, brushed myself off, and kept going and made a life for myself, far from "friends" and family to whom I became estranged, rather than spend my life "bumping into" people who had abused me or who knew of my abuse on the streets of Australia. I left ...the school ...my family ...even the country itself. All are poorer for it. Sorry!

I still find it hard to form words to describe what happened. It was ongoing, relentless and brutal. I had no need to take notes. It was a form of slavery where anything I had, including my self-worth and dignity, were not just taken away but insulted regularly. Anything I had could be taken away including "free" time outside of school hours and my personal belongings. Flagellating minors amused these abusers, seniors and teachers alike. I think of what might have been had my early life been different ...had I really received the education my parents paid for ...had I resided in a place where my physical and emotional integrity was respected and protected ...had I felt safe ...had there been someone to turn to. I don't need a museum!

I have learned there are different levels of having nothing. There is the physical reality of having nothing other than the cloth in which you stand then there is wanting 'nothing' of remembering. The brutality of a flagitious experience is that it leaves very deep indentations on the formative soul. The trauma is everlasting. We cannot unsee the devil. It's a difficult concept I concede, but I assure you it is real. The numbers are staggering. I am sorry you are now being subjected to another round of abuse "exposure" from your Seniors and Disabled Caregivers enquiry. Truly, Prime Minister, when will Australia confront itself about behaviour so entrenched and widespread that it conjures up the brutal imagery of our shackled convict history and projects it forward two hundred years with invisible brutality on an IMAX screen of life! Also the ink is hardly dry on the enquiry into the grievances of the country's indigenous nations. Perhaps it could all be rolled into one and remembered as the Sorry Century and we can all celebrate our sorrows together on the same day so you can sincerely beg institutional forgiveness and we can then all move on together. You should be incredulous. If not now, Prime Minister, when? Sorry!

Despite my love of this sunburnt land I gave up my birthright and sought refuge in other lands where I have felt truly comfortable among strangers. Sorry if you felt abandoned! I went on to be proclaimed valedictorian (with a GPA of 98.5) of a university with more than thirty-five thousand students proving to myself that the Australia's worst crimes against me could not pull me down (and that your school's Maths Master might have been wrong when took regular delight in humiliating me in class and calling me 'stupid'). I must be humble …it is only a very good example of what happens in a society where people lift each other up rather than trying to chop each other down. Sorry Australia!! There is so much room for improvement.

Trust is the most valuable of universal currencies. It is also the most difficult to build. It is damaged every single time it is abused until it reaches its limits. Then it breaks down ...always.

Neglect is on the same line as evil. It is a crime of omission for the care promised or purchased but not provided - fraud of the worst possible kind and evil by any other name! And not just any old business fraud but fraud by a government of the people for services for children in their care bought and paid for but not provided.

Extenuating factors in cases of abuse include the length of time the emotional/ physical/psychological/sexual abuse went on (in my case years) and what relief was provided (in my case none). 'Sorry' falls far short of the mark. That is what you say when you accidentally tread on someone's toes in a supermarket queue. We are speaking of sinful, wicked, pernicious atrocities. Call it out clearly with a loud voice Prime Minister. Be brave. Rise above your crocodile tears. Don't do a legal feint to avoid begging for our forgiveness. It is only the brave and the truly remorseful who beg for forgiveness. You are our Prime Minister, not a pampered pet! This heavy lifting was assigned to you.

When abuse is suffered continually for long periods major crimes have been committed. Heads should roll. If such crimes were tried against adults it would result in years of incarceration for the perpetrators. These were grievous, very serious offenses and there were significant aggravating factors that made it even more cruel. We were isolated and vulnerable, and it was egregious and a gross neglect and abuse of institutional trust not to provide us that level of safe care. The harm done to many was no doubt substantial. Sadly, even if they had the language to express what the problem was, there are many still too shocked half a century later to speak the words.

I should have stood up to those bully prefects wielding their cat-o-nine tails of knotted electrical wire which they did not spare to use full force across our thinly-pyjamaed buttocks. I should have called them out ...reported them ...but to whom? The violence was dealt from all fronts all with a liberal helping of humiliation to undermine whatever feeble hope of escape we might have dared to imagine.

I was alone and afraid of incurring their wrath. They were big and armed. I had nowhere to run. I was eleven years old. I was separated from my loving family whose voices crackled for a few minutes once a week over the distance on the single pay phone serving two hundred and fifty students. I call it out now Prime Minister from where it hides among the petticoats of Right Honourability in your very house. I am no longer small. I am no longer alone. I am no longer afraid of bullies twice my size. The Pope must have felt like this when his institutional abuse scandal first landed on his desk. A single strand of a web becomes a torrent. A single lie tarnishes the biggest truth.

Platypus Flats

The journey of a thousand kilometres, Prime Minister, begins with the first step. You have yet to take it. Your tearful words were eloquent evasive exclusions. The tears were not enough to salve the wounds. It felt a little like a sales pitch for a used car. It felt like a hug where you don't actually touch the other person, the kind of hug without kisses on either cheek or the warmth of friend or family pressed close. It felt a little like you were talking to yourself in what must have seemed like a bad dream, the kind I sometimes have. It reminded me of a scene from 'Hamlet'. It was the kind of soliloquy I associate with the flag of moral high ground being waved while doing an absolute minimum to affect my suffrage.

Those who neglected their obligations should not be spared exposure even if they cannot defend themselves from beyond the grave. There is no defense for those employed as civil servants who were responsible for our safe care not to have provided it. I suspect we were also overcrowded as well as some cots always spilled out onto glassed-in verandas. There was no heat of any kind. Winter tempraturess fell regularly to minus 5. The polished cement floors were freezing in winter. Someone had to know. I'll await their identification. Sorry!

Perfectly ordinary people commit evil acts, Prime Minister. Those capable of evil move amongst us, unknown and unremarkable in their appearance. The wicked, the bad, the immoral, the sinful, the ungodly, the unholy, the foul, the vile, the ignoble,

In The Shadows of The Honey Trees

the dishonourable, the corrupt, the iniquitous, the depraved, the degenerate, the villainous, the nefarious, the sinister, the vicious, the malicious, the malevolent, the demonic, the devilish, the diabolical, the fiendish, the black-hearted, the monstrous, the shocking, the despicable, the atrocious, the heinous, the odious, the contemptible, the horrible, the execrable; the shady, the warped, the dastardly, the egregious, the peccable - they all walk invisibly among us in numbers far greater than most care to acknowledge. On the other hand we have the 'good'!

Humans have known this fact for millennia yet use their blind eye when they see things they don't want to see. Edmund Burke, the 18th century Irish statesman, author, orator, political theorist and philosopher thought this:

"The only thing necessary for the triumph of evil is that good men do nothing." (sic)

You had the opportunity of a lifetime to do something all-inclusive, Prime Minister. You could have drawn the sword of righteousness and smote the beast! You did not! You paused too long!

Martin Niemöller believed that many Germans were complicit with the Nazi through their silence. It gave birth to his famous exaltation:

"When they came for the socialists, I wasn't a socialist and I was silent! When they came Jews, I wasn't

a Jew, and I did nothing.... etc." in variations on the theme that he used to call out the complicit element in human nature.

When they came for me, Prime Minister, there was no one there to defend me. I can no longer remain silent nor complicit. You speak of apology, but not once did you truly apologize in an inclusive fashion. You pointedly did not ask for forgiveness for the betrayal by the government and other institutions of their responsibilities? To quote you Prime Minister: "A sorry that dare not ask for forgiveness."

This purposeful omission of 'beseechment' is completely unforgivable. Was that too great a burden for you to grasp? Is the moral pond your mind wades in that shallow? Is it too much to ask a grown man and the leader of a country, to put his shoulder to the load and do a bit of heavy lifting? Your tears and your mouth were oddly out of sync. Too staged, too eloquent, too rehearsed with an evasive quest to miss the point ...too bereft of the clear ring of sincerity, an inflection even abused schoolboys learn to master young to cover their transgressions.

Forgiveness is a large part of moving past the event for the wronged. In some ancient cultures the criminal convicted of a serious wrong is bound and thrown into a lake while the wronged look on. If none among them is moved to forgiveness and leaps in to save them the perpetrator drowns. Sorry Prime Minister! You obviously realize forgiveness is a heavy lift but grovelling a little and begging for it may have shown some form of institutional regret if only to foster a wish to relieve the burden on those innocents on which it had been heaped. I know you are a busy man Prime Minister. You could freely supply the words that would enable the country to heal and move on.

It could have been a defining moment in your legacy to the nation. Instead it was a speech that, on the face of it, was self-serving. You begged that we simply accept your "Sorry". You refused to beg for institutional forgiveness. We are not talking about inadvertently bumping into someone in the crowd. You obviously failed to grasp what a sincere and deeply felt apology should sound like and the role 'beseeched forgiveness' plays in that. It was your opportunity to be bigger than this horror. You mumbled the ball, Prime Minister. Sorry!

The sheer numbers of complainants revealed by the Federal inquiry is staggering. Tens to hundreds of thousands stood up or remained silent, too bruised to walk that dark passage of their life again. However, inquiries tend to cost a lot of money and lead to a lot of group hand wringing, a report that gathers dust on a forgotten shelf ...a few evasive apologies and not much else. It would seem it is over already before the ink is dry.

It is now too little too late. You have paused too long again! Do not think pearly words cast from a lofty perch can eradicate evil. You have, by way of this investigation, shone a bright light in a very dark place for me and thousands of others. We did not expect it would prove so devastating in the breadth of its revelations. We did not ask for it. We are in shock. In my response I shine a bright light back on your darkness. Forgive me for having the gall to call out your institution. Your government is just beginning the journey through the torturous annals of the institutional abuses of your seniors and disabled care residents. Tears will again be shed; hands will again be rung; and heart-rending stories sobbed once more. I hope you have the institutional intestinal fortitude to stand and ask for forgiveness of all those persons wronged in institutional care rather than quickly skipping the denial of apology before waxing lyrical like a thespian stealing center stage making it about "you". Categorizing us by which parts of us were abused is not helpful to the individual. Or do you use the strategy "divide and conquer"? To ignore this critical point in healing displays a willingness to seek to cover your institutional tracks now so clearly revealed by the froth of your speech. How are we all to move on without the language to address these abuses being made available to everyone? It starts with you dear leader! You must be bigger!

As you do, please remember that lax government oversight and lethargy created these environments in which the most vile and violent behaviour has long festered and perpetrated on the innocent and most vulnerable. When will it end, Prime Minister? Is it such a deep societal canker it takes someone far removed from your inner court, someone outside the circle but with insider information, to point out that the emperor has no clothes! Ink on paper will not solve this nor will a million "sorrys". You may find it a tad overwhelming to have these chickens come home to roost on your watch. I appreciate that you might wish the timing had been different. It requires strong leadership to fess up to the government's historic failures (or is someone threatening to politically assault you behind a locked Parliamentary "washroom door" if you "own" too much of this shameful history? You can tell me, Prime Minister. I know how to keep a secret.)

How do we, the survivors and victims, move forward in reconciliation if you cannot demonstrate for the institution and for all Australians that you know how to sincerely express extreme sorrow and remorse and how to inclusively embrace all abused people regardless of age and gender and race and creed or abuse by type? Any judge has stern words for parties found guilty on clear evidence who express no remorse. In law it is generally considered "telling" in its absence and worthy of extra penalty.

This enquiry began when then Prime Minister Julia Gillard bravely recommended a nationally representative study to understand the true extent of the abuse problem; to establish a baseline to measure the effectiveness of child protection policies; and to better understand Australia's future progress in protecting people from sexual abuse and other forms of maltreatment in institutional contexts.

Platypus Flats

While not the primary focus of the enquiry those parameters challenge the narrow grasp of "sexual abuse" and while these matters were reported on as being common adjuncts to "defined sexual abuse" you skipped that part completely.

The person standing beside you might well be capable of doing evil things. "Good" people do evil things. Evil dives deep at the same time holding aloft a banner of invented morality claiming the moral high ground as a distraction much like your tears and your "sorry" speech, bemoaning one form of abuser while ignoring others and giving them a free pass; even inadvertently continuing the abuse by frank omissions; claiming the moral high ground while ignoring that which you find convenient to ignore? When the vice-principal punched me in the face when I was fourteen, I already knew there was no use trying to squeeze out words I didn't have to seek redress with those "in authority". I am sure he thought he was a "good" man. I am sure you do too, Prime Minister. Sorry!

We were beaten across the palms of our hands by teachers with canes so cruelly at times that I often had trouble holding my pen because the blood blisters on my fingers were so large. I don't recall the offenses. I'm sure the teachers felt no guilt. They must have thought it was best for me. They had "right" on their side. The Nazi came to power clutching to that same straw of belief. Sorry!

In The Shadows of The Honey Trees

Bravery is a mixture of power and strength inspired by a confident anger telling you that no matter what happens you must cling to what is right. It is better to die fighting for your freedom than to live under tyranny. Whether we die old or young the only thing we take with us is our integrity.

The institution in which I was incarcerated was hardly a winning learning environment when coupled with constant abuse of one sort or another from staff and senior students. Sorry! Sometimes I feared for my life. Sorry! I was alone. Sorry! I was isolated with nowhere to reach other than deep into my psyche to find my own resistance. Sorry! Ad Aspera Virtus: "In Adversity Strength". What cruel irony to foist on an eleven-year-old. Sorry!

I was under the care of the N.S.W. Department of Education, although some of the abuse I suffered was inflicted at Maitland Army Base where we were sent on "army cadet camp", so I was doubly betrayed by two government departments. So So Sorry!

Let's call it what it was/is? It was/is systemic institutional physically brutal lawlessness. Sorry! Still evident to me when I visit Australia is a less than subtle harshness in the way some people hold clear dismissive biases proudly and loudly and I rarely walk a block without seeing or hearing something troubling. Sorry Australia! It has improved but you have a very long road ahead. You must learn how to hold each other accountable and call out callousness and cowardice without fear when it shows itself. Thousands of innocents paid dearly for the country's systemic silence. The government of the people by the people for the people failed us miserably. We, the people, wait silently to be taken into the fold inclusively ...not just the sexually abused parts of us. Only then might forgiveness happen. It is a road you cannot simply pave with "sorry!"

In isolation the word "sorry" has no meaning. It is an adjective ...hardly so much as a pebble on the path of speech. As a singular part it has rhetorical value only when eating humble pie. Sorry!

Yet it was used repeatedly in isolation in your apology, almost pointedly. You did not embrace the whole spectrum of abuse when you had the opportunity. The media was kind enough to generously frame "abuse" more widely for you. Sorry!

A true apology qualifies the matter:" I am sorry ...you were abandoned; I am sorry...you were hurt; I am sorry...you were aggrieved; I am sorry...you were isolated; I am sorry...you were alone; I am sorry... you were brutalized; I am sorry...you were assaulted; I am sorry... you were humiliated; I am sorry....you were neglected; I am sorry...you were ignored; I am sorry...you were fearful; I am sorry...you had nowhere to turn;...I am sorry...you were abused; I'm sorry a government institution was irresponsible for your safekeeping; ...I'm sorry we failed you! The list goes on ...and on ...and on. "Sorry" by itself means nothing...

In The Shadows of The Honey Trees

It is a lame duck without qualifiers and quantifiers. Sorry! I would have found your statement more sincere if you had shed some greater shade on it ...expressed regret, remorse, contrition, repentance; been rueful, penitent, conscience-stricken, guilt-ridden, self-reproachful, ashamed. Were the words too hard to say? Sorry!

There is a subtle difference between saying "I'm sorry" and "I apologize". An apology is a formal admission of wrongdoing. That you would not "beg" for apology translates to: "I won't admit to institutional wrongdoing". Nothing more. Nothing less. An apology may or may not be heartfelt. A person may apologize without feeling remorseful. On the other hand, saying "I am sorry for ..." is usually seen as being a truer admission of regret. When the sentence isn't completed, it lacks sincerity. Sorry!

One of my abusers was an ambitious sociopath who went on to become a Federal Member of Parliament and sat for many years within the chamber from which your apology echoes. A search of the internet reveals he has been publicly called out for his abuses by others (who also attended that school) when he was in office but he took shelter behind the petticoats of parliament and, from that safe "Right Honourable" position, called his victims liars thereby inflicting the very same abuse all over again while tarnishing the very chamber where the country's Prime Minister made his pathetic attempt at redress for past institutional abuses.

Platypus Flats

In his contempt the abuser held parliament a hostage yet walks proud and free! His slanders of his victims are but a reflection of his still dark heart.

Sorry to be the one to point out how deep Australia's form of institutional blindness to injustice is. This abuser continues to 'tweet' as if he is some figure to be adulated when he is simply evil hiding in plain sight.

In his case an honourable man would have owned the actions of his younger self and apologized and perhaps held out a few feeble self-serving excuses for his violence and begged for forgiveness of his victims. That didn't happen. You Prime Minister chose a similar path in "not begging for forgiveness". This seems to be a common theme in this house. Your speech falls short ...far short. Perhaps you felt better afterward but reconciliation cannot even pretend to occur under such circumstances. Sorry!

Instead, with contempt, from the highest office of the land, this abuser perpetrated the abuse by denying it. This permitted him to be in the room again. That is the nature of the beast. Sorry! I can hold no hope that your official Prime Ministerial apology will change anything if you cannot purge your own house of evil Prime Minister. Sorry!

Can you really think your words will make a difference when your own house is complicit? You promised action. Start there! This abuser now enjoys the fruits of his ambitious evil by way of parliamentary pension.

In The Shadows of The Honey Trees

There is no mechanism in the Australian Parliament to challenge abusive behaviour by a federal parliamentarian. There is no ethics commissioner to oversee the parliament to ensure there is no abuse of power by those "Right Honourables" in power. Despite your words and crocodile tears Prime Minister your house still sanctions the abuse of victims by allowing our abuser to hide behind the petticoats of power. Sorry!

Australians can only complain about abuse if it falls under a government department but not when it falls from the seat of power itself. Sorry! Your second act should be to create an office of Parliamentary Ethics Commissioner to independently oversee the actions of elected federal officials to ensure such mendacious behaviour does not happen again. Shame me once Prime Minister, shame on you ...shame me twice, shame on me! So I call you out. You have failed us. Sorry!

I recall an expression about people who live in glass houses not throwing stones. You have shone a light on my own private hell. I ask that you start by clearing abuse and any future potential for it from your own house Prime Minister. Sorry!

After learning of your apology I called the local Australian Consulate to seek out your promised avenue of redress, but they were unaware you had even spoken. I sense you wanted to play those cards of embarrassment close to your chest not out in the world where victims might have found refuge. I was referred to a Canberra number but that proved ineffective. Sorry! They could not help me. Sorry! It was not their department. I am sorry to report how ineffectual all this wallowing in pain and self-pity has been at affecting change! It seems you are new to this "abuse" game. Sorry!

The apology may have been spoken by your lips but from where I stand your words are empty of substance. After promising compassion and relief you are effectively continuing the abuse by not paving the Road of Sorrow. (No, wait, that was the name given aboriginal abuses, wasn't it?) You have so much to be sorry for. It might lead somewhere if you can but master the sincerity it requires to steer it in the right direction. You hold out a bouquet of hope but then leave the way unfinished without clear signposts for those who need it most, something everyone could all easily follow. I am not interested in children enduring that type of treatment ever again ...Sorry! Nothing has changed for me. I continue to be met with jittery stonewalling from government officers unsure of how to disengage from me as quickly as possible when I state my mission in a clear strong voice. Sorry!

In my attempts to lodge a complaint about this now-former parliamentarian's re-abuse I tracked my way long distance through the parliamentary maze all the way to the Sergeant-at-Arms who declared (rather impatiently) there was no oversight of unethical behaviours by Australian Parliamentarians (the impertinent implication being "they" are above that?) You have

In The Shadows of The Honey Trees

*rats in your own attic, Prime Minister. Evict them.
It tarnishes your attempt to paint over the cultural
malaise you pretend to seek to redress. Paint, however
pretty and sincere, simply flakes off when applied to a
corrupted surface. That is simply a fact. Sorry!*

*From my view I am still receiving the same old punch
in the face...the same old "ignore it and it will go away
business as usual" governmental ineptitude that causes
us to meet this way in the first place. The road to Hell,
Prime Minister, is paved with good intentions. Sorry!*

*Your embrace was too narrow, your sincerity lacking
substance; your words too carefully couched not to
raise the suspicion of one used to sifting through careful
words to make sure nothing sticks to you. Strong people
stand up for themselves. Brave people stand up for
others. I challenge you to pick a side. Your speech did
not reflect which you were on? Perhaps you are neither
because you are aware that Parliament is guilty of
having been an "enabler"...and recently. Sorry!*

*I did not leave high school with a cohort of friends and
family to start off life with. I avoided them. They knew
too much. I can run but I cannot hide. I go to sleep with
the memories, and I wake up with them. I must sleep
with the enemy every night of my life. Agents of the
government are responsible. You rush to the convenient
side of refugees tortured by their respective governments
while denying the injustice of your own. Why?
I would appreciate names of who oversaw my care
and safety from 1964 to 1968 that the shame might be*

placed where it is due …and that I might know which shadowy bureaucrats failed to keep me safe from their lofty, salaried perch in the rafters of power. As the commission recommended, I am due appropriate support and properly holding to account those who committed, facilitated or concealed my abuse. Only time will tell. Sorry!

The government of the day was complicit. It seems nothing has changed. Sorry! It may not have been your fault personally, but you have inherited the burden of that responsibility. I am sure you have moved on since your speech of contrition. I appreciate you are a busy man Prime Minister. Sorry!

The government had a duty, and it did not just stop with simply ensuring children were not sexually abused. There are many insidious forms of abuse equally if not more damning. To not address all forms of child abuse raises the scepter of abuse-isim. Which part of my abuse is it you wish to separate out to be apologized for? Like all "isims" you either are or you aren't Prime Minister. Sorry!

I made a successful career as a wordsmith including N.S.W. Prodi and Australian Walkley awards to my credit. I found my vocation. Still it took me fifty-five years to find the voice to tell my own story. Sorry!

Regardless, I still have trouble forming the words to describe the unspeakable and see no benefit in reliving it in print. I don't have your luxury of a quick wallow in self-pity before moving on. Sorry!

On the count that these horrors leave us speechless, you are right. I feel for the people who came forward to tell their stories to the national enquiry ...for what end? Such is merely a reliving of the horrors, refreshing the indelible toxic chemical scar that was left across our young, impressionable hippocampi. Nothing can erase that ...not even wishing. The days when wishing worked are past. Sorry!

Talking does not make it go away. We cannot change what happened to us ...only how we perceive what happened to us. Your blithe lack of genuine understanding of the wide spectrum of abuse brings me no solace for the children of tomorrow. Sorry! Perhaps fifty-five years too late, I lay my insights on your table. Sorry!

You reached out, I reached back. Your arms seem very short. I have lived long enough not to expect inclusive reactions when I step forward to authority and call a spade a spade. I understand that human frailty. Sorry!

I have had my trust in "government" deeply abused. Forgive me if I regard your promises of a professed embrace with callused skepticism. Sorry!

I know I am not the only abused person who left Australia's shores to seek inclusion elsewhere in kinder, safer, unknown, caring places. Sorry!

What I want to see is not some central museum where politicians bask in the glow of cutting ribbons of self-aggrandizement with golden scissors, a place the children of tomorrow will be able to rarely access. No, it must be some measure that speaks to the children in their special places …simple bronze plaques on memorials in playgrounds and school yards where children will see them every day with numbers they can contact if they need help, and with a rider attached to any media coverage (much as Australia does with stories of suicide) after stories of child abuse. If we do not know what our rights are how can we know when they are being abused?

E.g. If you need information or support relating to child physical, emotional or sexual abuse call national information and support line toll free on 1800 xxx xxxx, Kids Help Line on 1800 xxx xxxx or Lifeline on 1234 etc. In an emergency always call ….?

I only hope those who need it are old enough to read it. I hereby place the ball squarely in your court and bravely wait to see what bureaucratic maze you will direct me to for standing up from afar and declaring: "Me too!" We must do better! We are not there yet. The smallest coffins are always the heaviest Prime Minister. It seems "Australia" still hasn't developed any institutional insight into what "abuse" is. You came to mourn but the coffin you have brought doesn't fit. So sorry Prime Minister! I do not ask for forgiveness for I did nothing to forgive! That was your first error. It derailed the rest of your long diatribe.

I am sure a man of your perceived stature is familiar with Luke 12.1:

"Be on guard against the yeast of the Pharisees — I mean their hypocrisy. Whatever is covered up will be uncovered and every secret will be made known. So then, whatever you have said in the dark will be heard in the broad daylight."

Most respectfully,

Neville West

My fears of continuing wilful institutional blindness were confirmed. I am not a religious person but by any measure a single lie destroys a whole reputation of integrity and tarnishes a thousand truths. The greatest crimes are hidden in the smallest details.

I was, again, a lone voice in the wilderness and, as per my expectation, my response was totally ignored! I was not shown even a sprinkle of *'right'*. The silence continued to be deafening but now was not the time to quail.

CHAPTER 18

Ad Aspera Virtus

It takes courage to forgive someone who has wronged you.
—Mahatma Gandhi

An autobiography is not a scripted story with glorious heroes and happy endings. One must tell their story but end somewhere and I certainly had no idea when I began (lying as I was in a hospital bed after having my spine reconstructed after a car accident) that it would be such an emotional marathon as this. A writer must draw a line in the sand …or sometimes life draws it for you.

I was sitting in that cafe, where the news of the Royal Commission into Institutional Abuse found me during my daily ambulations, mulling over my manuscript and wondering why I had such a hard time acknowledging to myself the horrors of my teenage years.

It wasn't that I couldn't remember. Just the opposite. The abuses were so horrific I couldn't forget. Forgetting is not an option for those violently brutalized. The fear fades, even if I can still taste it at the back of my throat. Fear can be a fleeting emotion …but the shame remains, always a fresh anxiety just below the surface. Like a rare vessel shattered to pieces, inner security can never be made whole again … no matter how hard one wishes or tries. Survivors learn to live with being condemned to sit beside the slovenly drunk of memory, invisible to others, and forced to endure their sour miasma forever.

Daily I remind myself to replace any sign of remembering with something positive right in front of me ...something "right now". When times are hard, we must seek out the hidden calm in our world. With 20/20 hindsight I can now look over my old shoulder and watch myself stumbling through life. It is never easy to forget our embarrassments and move forward. They remain with us as 'learning moments' but with abuse just what is the lesson? The inability to forget is the greatest loss to those whose basic human rights have been savaged, who have been wronged, oppressed, hurt and used and ...well, there are not enough words to explain the extent of degree of every degradation.

Nothing could have prepared me for what happened next in that cafe. First one, then many more cases popped onto my screen. Former children suing the New South Wales Department of Education, and other institutions, for *failing to provide a safe environment* and being acknowledged by the courts of justice.

It was a moment of catharsis. In the instant I saw clearly to a great depth with a dry eye ...the eye of the outsider who was once victimized as an insider. I realized I had taken my survivor's crown and my inner kingdom and retreated in exile to the most compassionate realm in the world of victims ...denial.

The thunderheads of internalized grief, which had been brewing just beyond the horizon of my psyche for more than half a century, now rumbled into view. The sunny sky I always maintained overhead went suddenly dark again in a horrible way. An earth-shattering thunderclap reverberated through my soul and shook me to my core. Lightning sparked across my brain's synapses and then torrents of tears, pent up for more than five decades, guttered spontaneously down my face like muddy water in a flooded creek as I sat there in the cafe and sobbed uncontrollably. It was a moment of spontaneous internal combustion!

Huracan, the Mayan god of fire and wind and storms and renewal sent a muddy rush of tears of hidden turmoil, tearing loose the stunted vegetation that hid old fissures of eroded emotions. This moral flash flood was the accumulation of the uncried tears since I had wept in the school telephone box, as a terrified child sobbing uncontrollably into the empty line with my frantic mother at the other end unable to comprehend my evisceration. I couldn't speak of my abuses. The knowledge of the *Ioa* has no words. I am still rendered mute. A part of me will always be a silent serpent. It is a raw, unpleasant part of my internal geography that I choose not to revisit. I cannot show it to you. I can only reveal it by illustrating the spaces around it with this tale.

To give form to the horrors eludes me like a lurking swampster. I have seen it. I know what it looks like. It is so perverse it can't be spoken lest it might somehow be reconjured. The face of evil is a desolate abomination. It is a *djinn* which cannot be put back in the bottle. Standing in that long-away-far-ago red telephone box I could only sob and pee myself as Mum tried to convince herself I was feeling homesick, and it would "get better".

The story of my abuser turned parliamentarian was most perverse. Fifty years on he had forged ahead to become a member of Australia's federal parliament. Here he had stuffed his face and his pockets at the public purse (and probably does so still on his parliamentary pension) yet he had the gall to deny his abuses from behind the cloak of Right Honourability. I had been a survivor for decades. Then, with his public denials, I was suddenly a victim again. This fresh shame to an old injury was different. It rose up and morphed into a *tiger*, no longer afraid of the enemy.

The stories unearthed by a simple Google search in that café revealed that several of his victims had come forward to confront him. He had called them all down as "gutter journalism." If truth be in the gutter let courage be to the journalists who recognizes it for what it is and pick it up and expose it! My abuser's slanders reflected his own dark heart.

The instant you take a position into the public arena, your facts will be rightfully contested. When you suggest others should also believe they will be challenged. When you ask that the taxes of your fellow citizens support you in that stand you will be resisted. This is how an open society operates.

When the Parliament of a nation fails to create an oversight office, independent of the powers that be, where ambiguous moral behaviour by *any* of its public officers can be challenged, the state is guilty of 'neglect' ...and is complicit ...by omission. Oddly, N.S.W. and other Australian states (and most western democracies) all have such ethical political oversight, but it is oddly lacking in Federal politics in Australia.

The examination of the ethical behaviours of those who bask in the glory of Right Honourability is imperative or its citizens are denied a fair and open society. Otherwise society permits the perversion of political power, granting haven to ambitious sociopaths who can sully the cape of honourability they have wrested control of for the purpose of cloaking dishonourable deeds. Does a wrong of half a century ago have any less value that a wrong of today?

One's deeds are not immune to criticism just because one expresses them loudly and with sincerity or from a high place. The rule of law must apply to all. A lie is a lie is a lie whether it passes from the lips of a monarch or a monkey and it will never morph into a 'truth' no matter how often it is repeated..

To grant honour to an abuser who perpetrates their abuses on their victims by accusing them, from a high social position, of lying under the rule of "anything goes" perverts the purpose of the basic principles of democracy. Ethical oversight must exist to validate the success of any nation on its journey to nationhood.

Platitudes which outright refuse to ask for forgiveness deny the abused the very balm required to soothe their wounded souls.

An authentic apology can be an exquisite tool. Earnestly crafted, it can sooth the wronged and assuage the guilty; it can dissipate resentment and heal bruised souls. It is the key to allowing mercy to fall freely. There's a certain magic in the words *"I'm sorry you were ...."* but it only works if you say it while looking the wronged party in the eyes with sincerity. It can be as exquisite as it is painful for both parties. But when perpetrators, or their representatives in the case of institutions, do not make the apology clear and sincere, rather than protectively self-serving, it cannot dispel the pain. Equally the words *"I forgive you"* carry tremendous force but cannot be uttered without the abuser first asking for it. William Shakespeare reminded us that mercy should fall 'unstrained'…like rain, to be of mutual benefit to both giver and receiver.

Rational probes into the world, when they function, place us all on solid intellectual ground. When we fail to provide for the possibility that power can be perverted, it becomes an "elephant in the room". Everyone knows it is there, but no one wants to address it in case it dirties their hands. It creates insular, silent bubbles of knowledge beyond reproach. People of honour should have no qualms in putting such a stamp of authenticity on their authority. The Australian Parliament has discussed at length establishing a watchdog with ethical oversight of federal politicians. It simply never has, making it complicit in perpetuating the institutional abuse by a Prime Minister's own open admission he would 'not beg forgiveness'. That no one noticed this sleight of political hand, or said anything, left me shocked.

We need to re-fashion our thinking to consider more deeply how our parliament and other institutions succeed or fail and how that trickles down to the population.

Parliament must consider the ramifications and consequences of what it says by its actions or inactions regarding the people it serves, past, present and future. There can be no place for those who subvert the truth to serve their own selfish purposes by hearing only what they want to hear and disregarding the rest. I do not refer to the political practice of whitewashing something less than 'the truth, the whole truth and nothing but the truth' but instead refer to the crime of perpetuating an earlier abuse by slinging mud at victims of one's former misdeeds by denial from the privileged position of The House.

How can government hope to convince its population that it has eradicated a cruel system of abuse of children at the grassroots level when an abuser hides behind its highest office? Words matter. The dignity of the victims of institutional abuse are failed by this. We are all sacred.

We must challenge our reasonings. We can and must do

better. We must learn to step out of our safety bubble more often or it becomes monastic.

It is easy to make arguments when abuses are brought forward: …'it is better to forget' …'it was such a long time ago'…

A wrong of half a century ago is no less wrong than one committed yesterday. Is freedom lost then less valued than freedom lost today? Is emotion born of memory any less valued than it was in the moment? Rights abused are still rights. We have a right to reclaim our justice, and with it, our peace. There can be no statute of limitations on something that can never be forgotten nor restored. We cannot tell our children about our history if we remain ignorant or mute, nor render unto them that which is theirs!

We must all do more than feel like we are making a difference – we *must* make a difference. It is perverse to simply bark up the dark tree of history while continuing to permit the same wrongs to be re-committed over and over (especially by the public denial of an abuser occupying a high perch), particularly if we are to avoid a silent, septic, cultural lividity polluting our world.

I too was the survivor of abuse by this parliamentary fraud while a student at XXXXXX. I stand with others who have confronted him. I join them in calling him out! I left XXXXXX as fast as I could. Then, at the earliest opportunity, I left the country, where he and my many other abusers still lurk, thanks to Sir William Walkley, who personally gave me the vote of confidence I so needed in 1972 (and a reminder that there might be more to a country than its acres, its ores and its gases). I hope he would approve of this end result of his patronage.

The pain of more than half a century ago has not abated. It was only by chance that I happened from afar on the scandal which broke in the early 2000s with the case of a fellow survivor who had the courage to stand and to shine light in dark places in the courts.

In truth, things were much worse than has ever been revealed to date. So few public cases from so many victims of this institution can only indicate that they are paid to go away. A few fellow survivors of this rouge parliamentarian's insidious physical assaults came forward. He eventually lost his comfortable seat. It takes the courage to want to heal, to step up to the plate alone and reveal your deepest vulnerabilities unbridged and unvarnished when confronting abusers.

At this stage the man in question had the opportunity to show that he had, in the interceding half century, developed the moral worth to come clean, hang his head in shame and say: *"Yes, these things happened. Forgive me for I have sinned. I was but a child myself acting on my own painful circumstances. Please forgive me for my trespasses."* He simply chose not to!

Instead, this common thief of human dignity wrapped himself in the cloak of "Right Honourability" and derided his accusers as liars, flinging the muck of distraction while clutching at legal straws with which to make bricks to throw at his victims. Some role model he proved to be.

To quote Shakespeare again: He *"doth protest too much"!* The abuser knows his guilt and convicts himself by his adult actions as nothing more than an ambitious sociopath. He was drummed from the house by the electorate only after many years, but that does not mitigate the crimes he re-perpetrated on his victims.

What happened at XXXXXX is nothing short of a crime against humanity in which the government of the day and its agents ignored abuse that could only have been missed by the wilfully blind. Had these things happened at the hands of an invading army the country responsible would have been judged at The Hague! That the victims, including myself, were rendered mute by the horror of their experiences does not diminish the crime. Quite the opposite. It seems the NSW Department of Education has sought to quench the fire in the belly of public discontent by joining the circus of hand-wringing that has become another federal Royal Commission - outrageously expensive events that produce thick volumes of verbiage now left on shelves to gather dust. The findings frequently translate to deafening silence.

I do not believe the systemic abuse we were victims of has been eradicated by this official 'ignoring'. The crimes I survived require something more significant than a quick disinfecting with political hand sanitizer. If I and other victims are to lay our ghosts to rest, we deserve to see the silent witnesses, the walls that hid our victimization, razed and a monument erected from the rubble warning its future residents and visitors: *"Never Again!"* It would be such a simple step to take. That building must be old and rotten now.

The corruption which has continued to contaminate the system for more than half a century must surely be a residue from the penal colony nature of the country's history. Australia's governance morphed out of a military system of justice, not a social one.

In a just world there should be parliamentary oversight to strip this former M.P. of his disguise and the riches extracted from citizens instead of forcing them to continue to pay the abuser, thus perpetuating the abuse. Those who shield abusers join in the abuse.

Still, sadly, perpetrators find safety in outdated, inconsistent legislation which both protects them while their victims' peace is denied. Good faith requires positive action. Deceptive silence is a common form of misrepresentation.

We receive peace when we correct the false narrative and take control back from abusers who seek refuge in our systems and institutions which, by their nature, have no soul and often shield abusers, not just from the full extent of their moral crimes, but by hiding the truth that their crimes against humanity happened at all.

Public trust in our institutions cannot be restored by quietly sweeping the fallout under the parliamentary carpet just because the perpetrator has chosen to drop from public view, his tail between his cowardly legs, abusing his victims again as his parting salvo. Peace, order and good governance requires positive action based simpy in truth, integrity and good faith.

Evil does not dwell in the light but under a cloak of darkness when good people remain silent. I suspect this evil has dropped deeper underground, beyond where 'good people' think to look.

In life there are only two positions to take: The glass is either half full or half empty. We can be a part of the problem or part of the solution. If these revelations have left you unsettled it is an opportunity to decide what kind of person you are; what kind of world you want to live in; and not to be afraid to show your true colours and to face difficult truths when confronted by them.

I don't profess to wear the white flower of a blameless life. My tale is not told with any sense of intellectual arrogance nor to burnish celebrity. Instead, I hope to demonstrate how to find your voice; to get up; to brush yourself off, speak the truth, and keep going, lest we forget to live in the moment while remembering the past. In telling my story I am fulfilling my *duty* to the future.

I have turned a complex wilderness Eden survival story into a tale of good and evil. I don't feel a burden to hold onto this grab bag of abject emotions but 'unseeing' is impossible. The uninvited house guest of a memory has squatted and cannot be evicted. We must all stand against such dark visitations, precisely because they last for eternity.

Learning of the string of abuse cases and the negligence of so many institutions so many years later was hard. That is called moral injury …the guilt of not having found my voice sooner in a way that might have spared others. Hardest of all was the blatant denial the abuse by a Member of Federal Parliament.

In Australia you can complain to someone about almost everything except an ambitious sociopath who has weaseled his way into the sheltered fold of Federal Parliament, where the citizens have erroneously given their elected officials complete immunity from oversight. This, I can only imagine, was, without foresight that a member of parliament would abuse this shield by issuing statements that revictimized their earlier secret child victims. Was this beyond the comprehension of the founding fathers? I am now glad I chose a country that, while not blameless, is not afraid of pointing out the error of its collective past ways and demonstrates the daring to take new steps toward being better. It is The Land of *"We"* rather than the divisive *"Them"* versus *"Us"* of many political landscapes. Almost every second Canadian citizen was born abroad and at least a hundred and fifty languages are spoken in its homes. Almost everyone is multi-lingual, radically changing the texture of our shared culture. Refugees are welcomed with deep compassion and although many return to their roots eventually the kindness they were shown in their hour of need is never forgotten. It is a country comprised of many nations. It is a Roman form of empire rather than an isolationist one. Australia and Canada may speak a common tongue and share a British colonial heritage, but they seem to have very different values when it comes to the full spectrum of Human Rights and Freedoms.

Underlying Canada's mandate of 'peace, order and good government' (and its Peace and Reconciliation efforts for its first nations) is a simple piece of legislation that specifically permits individuals to apologize for institutionalized wrongs without it being construed as a legal admission of wrongdoing or having to be documented or ruled on by a court of law. It is only with this protected apology that victims of crime in Canada are offered the earliest opportunity to forgive, which is a fundamental step in moving on with their healing journey. It legislates away a heavy obstacle for victims and survivors. It is evident in the careful choreography of official apologies that this 'protection of apology' is lacking in Australia. Why else would a Prime Minister rush to skirt that very issue in his opening words before forcing the waiting survivors to listen to pages of rehearsed platitudes unless in the hope the tens of thousands of waiting victims would forget his early distinct withholding of the very tool that might assuage their suffering, withholding that which should be freely given. It was a blatant sleight of political/legal hand that Mr. Morrison pulled on the more than eighty thousand victims of institutional abuse who waited, expecting to drink at the well of forgiveness, which would have been real compassion. The inhumanity of it left me staggered.

My day of reckoning arrived. I had waited almost six decades, sheltering my terrified younger self in this shell

I inhabit. Unlike hermit crabs I am cursed to continue my whole life in its confines having to grow in ways I might never have chosen under less constricting circumstances.

In anticipation of receiving an official verbal apology (three months after long negotiations concluded) I spent a week making points I needed to cover. I would only get one shot at this if I was to truly effect inner change. I knew when the call came, I would have to fly by the seat of my pants to try to deliver my young soul from the evil of the wanton neglect of care and duty of some long-ago petty functionary.

I accept I cannot change what happened to me, but I must try change what I cannot accept. My lofty ambition, with my unique hindsight, was to point out the rotten cornerstone that supported this lauded government institution and that there could be no more meaningful ambition for the NSW Dept. of Education than embracing a vision for the future firmly grounded in human rights and restorative, timely justice.

Coercive control is power wrought without the slightest trace of compassion and if anything is true of coercive control it is that absolute power corrupts absolutely. Manipulation is performed for power or some other kind of reward for the manipulator. Compliance arises from fear or to obtain safety or protection. While the NSW Dept. of Education processed my complaints, they proceeded by using the same coercive control I had been subjected to in my childhood under their care. They withheld a verbal apology for another three months after settlement was agreed on and six months later, I was still waiting for the written apology. It only came after I pointed out it was long overdue. Such behaviour is akin to withholding water from the thirsty. It demonstrates a profound disregard for the orderly administration of justice.

In The Shadows of The Honey Trees

When the written apology finally arrived it expressly forbade any sharing of it. Secrets and coverups are the signs of abuse.

The personal humanitarian need for apologies for institutional failures must be put ahead of drawn-out liability trials to hold those accountable for their neglect of duty.

There is no relief, let alone joy, when genuine apologies are withheld from victims of institutional neglect. Mercy should fall freely …like rain. That can only come with forgiveness when the weight of institutional neglect is clearly acknowledged. To withhold this simple moral gesture is to add insult to injury. My *'feathered thing'* was left to tremble thirstily at the well of forgiveness, unable to drink the fabled water without the needed acknowledgements by the guilty party.

Eventually an emissary was sent to make a personal apology. They began: "We are sorry…." I stopped them there.

"Sorry is something you say when you accidentally step on someone's toe in the line-up at a store check-out. Please do not sully what happened to me with such a trifling discourse."

Perhaps I was too blunt. The conversation moved on but it took half an hour before they finally stated unequivocally: "We failed you!" I said I accepted that, even if it took a lot of questioning to get to that salient point. The institution had not only failed me, but it had failed my parents, my family and the country, since one of its best and brightest turned their back on a place I loved and found peace in another realm.

Australia likes to promote itself as the land of *'fair go'*. Statistics say otherwise. The phrase is repeated so often without any justification that, when spoken, should raise suspicions that it might be masking something else. It can be hard to enjoy perspective when you stand too close to something for too long repeating maxims that do not reflect the truth.

In the case of the Royal Commission into Institutional Abuse it swept onto the headlines professing rainbows and unicorns but behind it stood a dark vacuum now conveniently gathering dust on a government shelf. The moment to heal was shunned. Morrison made that painfully evident in his quickness to *"not beg forgiveness"*...

Even as I sought justice, I had to fight with one hand bound behind my back. Even as the government professed to seek my emancipation it remained institutionally blind to its lack of compassion. Institutions must be represented by someone with soul.

Australia claims to be egalitarian, yet it hobbles social justice with antiquated legislation. While I do not doubt the desire of individual representatives to make whole again the institutional trespass against me, and so many others, there is an obvious hole in the bottom of the institutional bucket of compassion which renders it compromised! Only *'the power of apology'* enshrined in legislation can bring that water to the parched souls of victims in a timely way. Sadly, there will be others.

On the journey to maturity every nation must learn to accommodate the collective humility of the people …all the people …to make the necessary changes to acknowledge *all*. The shocking treatment of refugees by Australia in recent decades raised eyebrows around the democratic world. Canada took in some Australian asylum seekers, not because their human rights had been abused in their homelands but because of what had happened to them at Australia's hands.

Australia has demonstrated in the recent pandemic that it doesn't hesitate to shut its people in but also to shut them out. That again shocked the world. In contrast, Canada chartered flights to bring their people home. Tribalism is an isolationist tactic justified by using fear. It is the tool of tyrants. In hindsight, it is now no surprise I became alienated and rootless. Enlightenment and clear dry eyes are the curse of the expatriate.

Coercive control seems built into the Australia's institutions. A nation must ensure that Charter Rights are in place to ensure justice, accountability and above all, humanity. When rights and freedoms are not trumpeted, they are apt to be trampled by the ego of politics. If we do not know what our rights and freedoms are they can quickly be eroded.

A Charter of Human Rights and Freedoms ensures the decisions and actions of all levels of government are guided by the values of freedom, equality, compassion, dignity and justice, things no law can take away. While Australia has signed many such international agreements, it seems to neglect that it is needed most at home. It seems to suffer from its penal colony collective psyche and in this way differs markedly from Canada, which had no such basis.

It is far better when people celebrate each other's success and hold up other's achievements; when people don't invoke their ego or try to tear others down rather than enjoying mutual respect; and when people are generous in their applications of apology and mercy, those things which can be so freely given.

Justice should be tempered with mercy but that implies forgiveness. If one is apologizing without understanding and reflecting what they are apologizing for, then the apology is worthless, and forgiveness is impossible.

*

Destiny is thrust on us. It is our destiny to change destiny. As life unfolds, we react in the moment and do our best to make the right decisions to meet our immediate ends. A response takes thinking about it for a moment before reacting. Yet despite our best insight our destiny is often obscured from our view - far off over a distant horizon.

Looking back brought me face to face with some shocking events in my teenage years, events so terrible they had been masked by complete denial for decades. As an articulate adult I re-navigated the treacherous evils of my youth and realized that some greater force than I had guided my life on a trajectory I could never have seen leading to this moment of inner confrontation …but it also equipped me with the confidence and skills to not only liberate myself from this state of denial but allowed me to share my soul, my journey to access my inner bliss. If it paves the way for a single other soul to process their own emotional wasteland it will have been worth my time and effort.

We cannot change what happened, but we can change how we see it and use language to calmly confront the failures from our now adult-centric world to make it a safer place for our most vulnerable. I remained in denial believing such bad things only happened to me, even though I knew there were many silent others. The really damaging part was learning that bad things continued to happen to others for decades after. Had my denial not been so deep and complete I might have spoken sooner and saved others from these abusive, cruel circumstances. Now I must do everything in my power to effect change with every sharp edge of my quill to cut through the darkness and shine a bright light on the failures of society to protect the innocent. I could not have seen this coming. It has been like running full speed into a brick wall on a moonless night ...again. That's destiny for you!

§

Of late I returned to my country, to that to which I was born. *Ra* still rained a fearsome terror down and scorched the land. As I stood in the shadows of the same great Honey Trees where I had stood as a child, I was again shrouded in their still-gentle glory ...the heavenly scent of their crown of feathery blooms ...the hypnotic symphony of busy bees swarming above ...and the realization, in that moment, that I belonged to this land, not it to me.

More than half a century had passed. I had wandered out an open door into the greater world and found its song so enchanting that I had wandered thus a lifetime ...in the blinking of an eye ...witnessing all ...the good, the bad and the ugly. When I finally returned everyone was gone and a charred ruin stood in its place.

The water in the creeks where the platypuses had played was gone, sucked dry by *Ra's* wrath for the first time in eternity. It was confronting, a heavy blow ...I was looking extinction in the face.

The same birds that sang overhead there for a million years still sing overhead in my mind, their songs lovelier than any I can remember. Silently their chorus overflows my ears ...as it has been since time began ...with no beginning ...nor end ...a *dreaming* where my soul sings *'the tune without the words and never ends at all.'*

Sad? Yes, for I so loved the land of Oz. Dutiful parents gave me confidence to leave and see the world. What I find in Canada that I do not find in Australia is *"not something I can show you. You must look and see it for yourself."* It is the curse of the expatriate to see with a clear, dry eye the weak points in a system they left because they did not remain immersed in it. The traveller returns home changed in ways that those who never left have not. I wish I could say I don't see this, but it has been up close and personal. Protecting financial interests should not trump humanity but it is clear Australian institutions are not well equipped to deliver redemption.

Violence is a human failing. In Australia it forms part of a consistent pattern, a known culture of cruel and barbaric abuse of the helpless, the isolated and the defenseless. Its many Royal Commissions have established this. The rogue former parliamentarian I mentioned should be convicted of abuse, not so much for the actions of his youth but for his denial of it as an adult who crawled his way to the top of the societal pile only to pollute it with the manure of his denials …and for what? …to protect his precious government pension? For shame!

History is replete with stories of ignoble deeds done out of fear, cowardice, confusion, or for ambition, lust, power or for apparent honour …but simply for money? Only one such sinner stands out in all of history …*Judas*. It is doing something cruel for money that should offend everyone.

The role of the NSW Dept. of Education, in withholding apologies until litigation is complete, is not dissimilar to the coercive abuse I suffered under its care as a child. It requires a survivor to go back into battle for their justice with one hand bound behind their back, while the institution withholds what could be freely given. Human acknowledgement is a necessary ingredient for forgiveness to then fall freely. It is the very definition of coercive control at the institutional level.

I apologize for dragging you through the suffering and discomfort of this necessary part of my story. To whom much is given much will be asked. To rise above a wrong we must acknowledge it. Eradication is only possible if we recognize all parts of the cancer.

Cognitive dissonance is the most obvious path to the mental shelter of denial when we need to rationalize reality when what we had believed to be true turns out to be not only *'Not So'* but the completely ugly warts-and-all *opposite*!

What defines a *'free'* country? There must be Rights and Freedoms that 'spring from' the land itself, not just a birthright but equally applied to all who stand on it ...Rights and Freedoms which trump the reach of any law and prevent divisive *'othering'*.

Without such inalienable Rights and Freedoms any nation will always remain subjugated by laws concocted by self-serving political minds ...often long ago. We nourish the future through the influence we have on those who follow us. Change can happen in many ways. But first a nation must collectively want to change!

CHAPTER 19

The Homunculus

*"No one can take away our self-respect
if we do not give it to them."*
—Mahatma Gandhi

It was late in the day, and it had been a hot and dusty way. Long shadows were being cast. I had no need to peer out the celestial windows of my utilitarian vehicle to realize I was at a crossroads. The dust stirred up by the tramping of a thousand feet hung in the air like a golden curtain refusing to settle or drift away as if waiting to cushion the setting sun. Here there was a certain human thrum to the shuffle of the sweaty masses of humanity grinding away at their toils, all going their different directions, treading their mountains of loneliness, swimming their rivers of tears, crossing their plains of despair and reaching for the stars in their fragile pursuit of the ever-elusive butterfly of *'joy'*.

Of all the many to-ings and fro-ings in such a place there is the usual conundrum of good manners in the throng. Is it polite to pass an elephant on the left or on the right? Do donkey carts trump camels? Do the blind have the right of way over the downtrodden? I have seen some crucifying human sights along my *Appian Way*. I cringe remembering a life so littered at times by such bottomless human despair.

Among the many souls toiling at this crossroad one stood alone by the verge, a mere shadow …a young lad of barely eleven years. His obviously once-fine robes were dirty and threadbare, and scratches and abrasions were evident where his skin was exposed. His clothes seemed held together mainly by stains and his pernicious wounds looked old and scabbed over. Without doubt he had crossed many plains of despair and swum many rivers of sorrow.

In a moment of epiphany my inner elf recognized the homunculus I had left weeping and wounded in that telephone box in that long-away-far-ago prison. He had obviously stood there fearfully facing down his evil for so long his tears had dried on his face and were now outlined with the dust of the way. I looked down perplexed for a moment. What of this vehicle I had been driving around in for the last sixty years without thought nor favour? How could we have possibly become separated? It was like finding a limb I hadn't realized I'd lost or perhaps, like Señor Perez, I had simply soldered on regardless in denial.

This urchin standing by the way was my own homunculus, long ago abandoned to the silent sufferings of his physical confinements while I, the being, had fled the scene and never went back for him. The *Gods of Guilt* demanded repayment for that neglect now. We know not what we are made of until we are broken. The body may be frail, but the spirit possesses an extraordinary strength that defies our mortal powers.

I leapt out and pushed boldly through the crowd of ghostly shadows. The boy failed at first to recognize me and drew back, afraid as if his fear of more than half a century had failed to pass, as fear is supposed to pass, giving way to relief and optimism.

"It is me! It is me!" I exclaimed as I burst into tears and clasped him to my heart. It was obvious there could be no forgetting for either of us. He too began to weep and together we sobbed by the side of the way like the long lost, oblivious to all. It seemed so long since we had parted that it was almost beyond our memory ...yet neither of us could ever forget.

We had both endured the cruelty; the physical pains which were healed and passed and the scars where injury ran invisible but deep. I had healed through the humanity of little old ladies with marmalade cats; the religious rapture of an old woman in black; a tow-haired Mayan maiden speaking the balm of simple truths directly from the heart; and the kindness of strangers at critical low points in my life. No fame nor fortune led to my enlightenment.

It had taken strange angels in black limousines and blind lepers and downtrodden people who begged piteously of my grace at my passing; also total strangers who stepped forth onto the stage of my life uninvited and unknowingly lifted me up and gave me the salve of humility to heal my own torn soul.

As we sat there on the dusty grass of the verge we spoke a jerky, sobbing, aching tongue. Neither had to speak for both knew the terrors inflicted on the other. It morphed into a series of heaving, happy sobs that communicated in a cosmic way like elephants' inner rumblings rolling across a dark unknown savannah; not the weeping of the desperate or the bereaved; our heavy breaths a sighing swan song that only we could hear or understand; a tongue so rarely spoken it takes a lifetime of apartness to learn to comprehend it; an innate language of human experience for which there are no words. It is by our tears we are defined. It is our *'feathered thing'* speaking.

For more than half a century I had pursued my peregrinations while this sad boy wept dusty tears to himself by that fateful red telephone box whose paint had blistered and peeled under *Ra's* assault, as his soul had blistered and peeled under the weight of his terrifying ordeals. I felt ashamed I had not searched for him sooner.

I had abandoned him to his brutalities and separated my spirituality from his physical abuse and had lived my life as an observer, a detached cosmic cloud that floated around in its vehicle without giving much thought to what was under the hood. You don't see much unless you get out of the car.

The tighter I clutched him the more we sobbed. The watershed of tears dissolved the strands of the evil spell which had long ago befallen us. Simultaneously the strands of a new spell began to form until it seemed we softened like gum-chewed-too-long and soon our being-human began to stick us together again like wetted clay simply by the strength of our embrace ...merging until we were again whole. It was only by finding the missing piece of a complex puzzle laid out over half a century ago that I could now see a key piece had been missing.

Unbeknownst to both of us his long-ago tears had fallen on *The Plain of Misery* and the unseen Goddess of Mercy *Quan Yin* had reached across the choppy sea of life to the dark, dank puddle where we were cast in our circumstance by institutional neglect.

The *"Hearer-of-Cries"* had caressed that bud so covered in the slime of evil. She had blessed my being with compassion and washed me with *'the tears of humanity'*. She had cleansed me, and I had burst from the swamp like the fragrant lilac lotus in those long-away childhood billabongs ...blossoming toward the sun...never looking back to its murky past

...following the light ...leaving my homunculus behind mired there in the weeds. Words had freed me; made me weightless; able to travel at will; riding my carpet of magical thinking; dying it in the myth and legend of my life until now it disintegrated into dusty tears.

Freed from the mire I had left my poor homunculus behind. Now with joy I glowed as I welcomed him back - my angel, my all, my other self - pushing back the darkness, paying tribute to the power of joy, of finding someone lost and found again most unexpectedly ...of being filled with the knowledge and grace of inner bliss.

With compassion and unconditional love I welcomed him in and washed the dust of the road from his face and his feet with my tears, such were they shed. We both '*knew*' without saying a word.

As I arose from yonder murk *Tara* had gifted me a fetish of words; the knowledge that unwritten words in a pen were the knots of a fine fabric, capable of tracing the elaborate contours of the landscapes of a human life; its contrasting colors, scraped from experience, cast in seemingly easy random; chaotic shades of hope and hues of optimism; all washed with the salt of tears making the colours bleed; caressing the whole with a phantasmagorical patina any genie might envy ...all in the hope of creating a whole far greater than the sum of its parts.

That I once walked through a curse which turned my sunshine black, I cannot deny but somehow, I did not let it bleed me. There could be anger there, burning a hole in the bottom of the pocket of memory, but there is not. The macabre and gory often ignite a morbid voyeuristic fascination but, for those on the receiving end, violent realities are no picnic. I tell this tale not for morbid attention but because

I have something to say. These were staggering abuses of which there can be no "unknowing". It speaks to a larger depravity in all cultures which should leave us to wonder why, with insight, it is so difficult to address. You can put lipstick on a pig, but it remains a pig. Humankind seems forever innately caught in a *Sisyphean* struggle between justice and injustice - humanity versus inhumanity. Is it a value we wish to perpetuate? A victim rolls the rock of one truth to the summit only to have it roll back down and morph into another injustice to be laboured again over and over. We must learn to find fulfillment in the inner journey, not look for it at the source nor the destination.

Tears are their own special language. There is a point on the "unspeakable" scale where words fail us and we automatically revert to tears and soulful, wrenching sobs, the words caught unsaid in our throats.

I weave these simple words one letter at a time ...*Tara's* rug. I roll it out as a homage to *Pandora's* 'Hope' that it might age well and be of service, a window, however bruised, into another's world as seen with a clear dry eye and the almost unbearable burden of 20/20 hindsight.

There is no doubt I have walked a long and dusty road and now my shadow falls long in the failing light of a long life. Along the way I have been humbled by the majesty of nature and by small giants with grey hair and orange cats; by dead ancestors; and by a fragile ball of wet feathers with a heavenly voice. I often stumbled ...sometimes fell ...perhaps was even pushed. I always got back up, brushed off my knees, and kept going, accepting that the sometimes terrible/sometimes fulfilling responsibility of living my life as it unfolded was mine and mine alone. I kept moving toward the light, however faint. *"This too shall pass"* motivated my many footfalls forward, even through my darkest hours.

In the telling of my story I have tried to paint with words something that is invisible. Do not look for it. Our life is an illusion no one else can see. I cannot touch it, yet it still touches me ...a kingdom of the mind. Remembered fragments, synthesized places and generalized relationships intermingle here so many diverse memories can be woven into a common thread without sacrificing the telling of the tale to plodding facts. I have tried to avoid creating a self-referential piece of throw-away nothing while still telling my truth. It is a tapestry of time, no one knot more important than another but the whole represents an eternity ...today is yesterday but also tomorrow ...a *dreaming*. To make sense of it I have had to reach beyond myself using plain *w*ords found in any dictionary. When they failed me, I invented others.

I tend my words, my garden ...plucking weedy split-verbs here, planting little thoughts there and seasoning it all with punctuation. I do this to create a garden for my *'feathered thing'*.

I tried not to leave unsaid that which I ought to have said, as in living I have tried not to leave undone the things that I ought to have done. It is better to regret some things done than to rue squandered opportunities. I have tried to refrain from saying anything ugly for it serves no purpose to wallow in gore. I confess to taking artistic liberties with the feather of truth in the service of this saga, for I had to lose myself in the narration that I might render my experience tenable.

How does one measure the sum of a life? Joy and sorrow are drawn from the same well. Without one can we truly know the other? If we know great joy when the well is full, we will also know great sorrow when we find it empty.

When the ancient Egyptians came to the entrance of their afterlife they had to answer two questions. The first was:
"Have you found joy in living?" The second was:
"Have you brought joy to others?"
Your heart was then weighed against the *Feather of Truth* and only then could your eternal enlightenment be apportioned.

Truth? The only truth is that no one gets out of here alive! When we go, we can take with us the only thing that was ever worth anything ...our integrity; nothing more ...nothing less ...ashes to ashes ...dust to dust ...mud to mud.

Thoth, the ancient Egyptian God of Reckoning, of learning, the inventor of writing; the creator of languages; the scribe, interpreter and adviser of the gods, has guided my hand through the dust and flies and swelter of this voyage, which was thrust on me by *Fate*, with the challenge to bring yesterday into the light of today in the hope it will not be repeated tomorrow. This story has been woven with *Thoth's* invisible ink and strung together using his enchanted golden quill.

The sun warm on my shoulders, the breeze caressing my hair, the rain wet upon my skin ...these are the silent whispers of *Platypus Flats* ...yet my eyes have seen the world and can't forget. We all tread our time upon this planet, a mere mote of dust floating in the sunbeam of the universe, where I appeared out of nothing and was so enchanted by the nightingale of life that I failed to realize just how late I had wandered before telling my tale. Now it all seems to have passed in the blinking of an eye.

Those who suffer any kind or degree of abuse can become alienated from parts of their inner self. It is often a lifelong sentence. Recovering from those deep, moral wounds has been this road I write, word upon word, like bricks, cobbled as artfully as I am able. We must all walk our own life and bear our own burdens, crossing seas of despair and deserts of anguish. On the surface the victims and survivors of abuse look quite normal but within their breached security important personal foundations are corroded.

If we want a magical life, we must weave it with the allotted yarn. *Klotho*, the ancient Greek goddess, is said to spin the thread of our life from the moment of conception. Her second sister, the one-eyed *Lachesis*, weaves it as best she can with her affliction (making occasional blunders), and the youngest, the blind sister, *Atrophied*, cheekily severs the thread when she believes the cloth complete. We cannot change what happened as our life's yarn was spun. We can only change how we perceive how it was woven from the current end point of our life's web of choices and circumstances, appreciating our finest feathers plucked from our greatest accomplishments and finding silver linings within any dark clouds which darkened our past. Eventually, everyone dies. Some sooner than others. Without tears to water them dreams can quickly turn to dust. We don't cry because we are weak. That is our healing power speaking. Sometimes my tears and my silence were all I could count on.

I have here harvested my orchard of friendships planted through my life. Its fruitfulness is the wonderful touch of those great and small who graced my life and cast their bright spells upon me, freeing me from curses which had, at times, left dark shadows in my life's thread. In the weaving of this cloak I have taken artistic licence to make it fit the page. Once silenced by denial a dormant part of me has been parolled. In writing this I leave something of myself behind. My voice, now found, has spoken. I have finally learned this is part of learning to forget.

In The Shadows of The Honey Trees

I leave you with the reminder that smiles are contagious, and kindness is free and the two words which carry the most currency in any language ..."*thank you*"...for your company on this journey. I must now take the last few steps to bring my awkward corroboree to a close for the memories of this life have here seeped from my soul. I need to find that blind sister with the scissors so I may retire from this elucidation.
Yours autobiographically,
Neville West

> "The Moving Finger writes; and, having writ,
> Moves on: nor all thy Piety nor Wit
> Shall lure it back to cancel half a Line,
> Nor all thy Tears wash out a Word of it."
>
> —Omar Khayyám

EPILOGUE

"It is unwise to be too sure of one's own wisdom. It is healthy to be reminded that the strongest might weaken and the wisest might err."

—Mahatma Gandhi

A negotiated settlement was reached between the author and the N.S.W. Department of Education in 2021. That outcome is subject to a non-disclosure agreement. However, further prompts were necessary before in-person and a single written apology for the neglect of duty were received. No indication was ever forthcoming that the school in question was advised of the many crimes against humanity committed within its walls. While I have no desire to do its current form harm, I find this kind of *'secrecy'* unacceptable. How can I know the appropriate people are aware of the breadth of such institutional neglect if they do not directly acknowledge it when I bring it to the attention of the institution's overlords? Secrecy is the main ingredient of much abuse.

Of most concern to me is that a state which fails to rejoice in justice is doomed to fail again. This is what happens when the state withholds things which rightly belong to others! Such behaviours are exploitative and lacking empathy and compassion, especially unacceptable when the injury was due to institutional neglect and abuse; more especially so when the institutional behaviour is still entrenched after years of moral hand-wringing and harrowing stories presented to repeated Royal Commissions into institutional abuse; and when resolve could be freely given but is denied.

I have learned to recognize arrogance, disdain and contempt in their many disguises and in many confected circumstances. I have also learned to recognize truth in all its beauty and ugliness. If this story results in any small measure of institutional insight and brings even a sprinkle of justice to the vulnerable of the world it will be a small step forward toward the light. Justice delayed is justice denied.

Again, for the wilfully hard of hearing, an apology should first seek the forgiveness of the person wronged. It is a critical component. Someone seeking forgiveness for institutional neglect should first reflect how the victim 'must have felt' due to the institutional failing. This is not about you, the apologist. The focus should then be one hundred percent on the offended and delivered in a timely way.

A pernicious evil cast me forth as the bearer of this message. I did not volunteer to be pushed to the front of this bus. A culture of imperialism, penal colony savagery and brutal power just might have developed, with time, some built-in fractures now revealed as human expectations change and are ultimately "voiced" and finally, dare to be spoken in a clear, calm voice. I have searched to find the bright lining in that dark cloud in the telling of this tale.

Institutional leaders should minimally google what a genuine apology looks like before taking center stage, where they risk adding insult to injury without genuine, respectful reflection of the survivor's reality, especially 'post' any settlement agreements when there is nothing left for an institution to lose. This can't be done until those in authority are willing and able to deeply comprehend what it was like for the victim. To do less is stingy.

Reasonable expectations of the survivor cannot be met in the absence of a human face which can reflect the necessary understanding to provide the key to the survivor's door to peace. This is not to be found with a counsellor but from the representatives of the institution whose neglect of duty led to the abuses. Institutions have a moral responsibility to the humans they profess to serve. It is reflected by the action of its leaders, especially so after expecting their victims to stand naked before them.

It was my *Fate*, it seems, to be sent as a witness to grave institutional failings. I did not choose this. It was forced on me. I never dreamed my life of letters was destined to make this simple failing clear.

I have done my duty to shine a light in the dark places and point out the error of abusive institutional failings. As the human representative of heartless institutions, those in charge must be able to shoulder the human burden assigned to them to assuage their victims in a compassionate, timely way. I can't compromise on justice and truth but even speaking the words of the crimes commits moral harm to others. Causes are furthered by brave people who are not afraid to point out the failings they witness to those who cannot or do not want to see. It is easy to stand in a crowd. Not so much when we take a stand alone.

We don't like to admit our mistakes because we may think that making mistakes reflects badly on our character. In truth not apologizing, or making a feeble non-apology, only adds insult to injury. The shame rightly belongs to the institution which permitted it to flourish. It should be openly acknowledged, or the secrecy continues, and the dust of truth is swept under the mat.

When you put an apology in writing, you have the luxury of polishing and editing the thoughts so that they say precisely what you mean to convey. When that is not done it is painfully evident.

Regret and sincerity can warm a cold heart that resulted from any institution's sad neglect. Human Rights include the right to life and liberty, freedom from slavery and torture, freedom of opinion and expression, the right to work and education, and many more, without discrimination. Unfortunately, without expressing regret about the deprivation of any of these rights as a result of institutional neglect, it makes it difficult for victims and survivors to forgive and move on. Freedom is eroded one pebble at a time.

Unless the matrix of an apology is sound the response comes across as intellectually and emotionally 'full of emptiness'. As someone who 'fell through the cracks' more than half a century ago it now seems the beam of institutional integrity is rotten to the core, even to the withholding of the water of compassion when it could be freely given. For me this was never about the *lucre*.

For the cost of a few magic words institutions can unlock the door to peace for victims of abuse. An attempt to slap a coat of new paint on an old house that is rotten does nothing to correct the corrupt foundation. I was assured reforms have been initiated within 'all Australian institutions'. This as I was left waiting long months for my ounce of justice from the responsible institution. Victims deserve to see positive action, not more wilful blindness.

Mnemosyne the mother of all the muses, is essentially our sense of self. It collects our salient sensory impressions and sews them together into the fabric of our life. Without it there can be no sense of identity, no consciousness of being, no past, no future, no books, no poetry, no relationships. We would be just a blank page. Without it we would quickly starve to death. An apology is the only chance to write magic words recognizing institutional responsibility on the torn, neglected page of a victim/survivor's life at little cost, which makes the withholding of it even more stingy.

In Greek myth dead souls drank from the *River of Lethe* so they would not remember their past lives when reincarnated. In *Orphism*, the initiated were taught instead to drink from the *River of Mnemosyne*, the water of memory, which stops forgetting and the transmigration of the soul. I cannot 'unsee' the past any more than I can 'unlearn' how to read a book.

The central focus of *Orphism* is the suffering and death of the infant god *Dionysus* at the hands of the *Titans*. *Dionysus* is killed, torn apart, and consumed by the *Titans* (the institutionalized abuse of victims). In retribution, *Zeus* strikes the *Titans* with a thunderbolt, turning them to ash (figuratively the function of victim/survivor settlement meetings). From these ashes, humanity is supposed to be reborn, like a *phoenix*, in all its loveliness. This is the theory, but memory of brutal abuse does not brush off like ash. Institutions need to know that their officers can take human responsibility for their failures before appointing them to the task and provide support for them when they are injured by the heavy lifting.

I am not one to waste my valuable life shouting into empty rooms so, with the blessings of *Thoth*, I here simply shred my words into the winds of time, shrug and walk away, comfortable knowing I tried my best to make the invisible bunyip of institutional abuse visible to others by illustrating, in detail, the space around it.

Neville West

Printed in the USA
CPSIA information can be obtained
at www.ICGtesting.com
JSHW021753240524
63318JS00003B/116